T0278476

Leonid Hurwicz: Intelligent Designer

How War and the Great Depression Inspired a Nobel Economist

Jews of Poland

Series Editor
Antony Polonsky (Brandeis University, Waltham, Massachusetts)

Other Titles in this Series

A Man of Success in the Land of Success: The Biography of Marcel Goldman,
a Kracovian in Tel Aviv
By Łukasz Tomasz Sroka

Polish Jews in the Soviet Union (1939–1959): History and Memory of
Deportation, Exile, and Survival
Edited by Katharina Friedla and Markus Nesselrodt

Bolesław Prus and the Jews
Agnieszka Friedrich
Translated by Ben Koschalka

Palestine for the Third Time
Ksawery Pruszyński
Translated and with an introduction by Wiesiek Powaga

Blooming Spaces:
The Collected Poetry, Prose, Critical Writing, and Letters of Debora Vogel
Debora Vogel
Edited by Anastasiya Lyubas

Macht Arbeit Frei?: German Economic Policy and Forced Labor of Jews
in the General Government, 1939–1943
Witold W. Medykowski

New Directions in the History of the Jews in the Polish Lands
Edited by Antony Polonsky, Hanna Węgrzynek and Andrzej Żbikowski

Warsaw is My Country: The Story of Krystyna Bierzynska, 1928–1945
Beth Holmgren

For the Good of the Nation: Institutions for Jewish Children in Interwar Poland.
A Documentary History
Edited and Translated by Sean Martin

Shadows of Survival: A Child's Memoir of the Warsaw Ghetto
Kristine Keese

Leonid Hurwicz: Intelligent Designer

How War and
the Great Depression
Inspired a Nobel
Economist

Michael Hurwicz

BOSTON
2023

LCCN: 2022059204

ISBN 9798887191331 (hardback)
ISBN 9798887191348 (paperback)
ISBN 9798887191355 (adobe PDF)
ISBN 9798887191362 (ePub)

Cover design by Ivan Grave
Book design by PHi Business Solutions

Published by Academic Studies Press.
1577 Beacon Street
Brookline, MA 02446, USA

press@academicstudiespress.com
www.academicstudiespress.com

Contents

Acknowledgments

First of all, I would like to thank my partner, Sharon Abreu, who read, supported, encouraged, copy edited, and reminded me to eat. Thanks, too, to the many members of my immediate and extended family who helped me retrieve, revive and refine so much of the material in this book. You were an absolutely invaluable resource and support while I was researching and writing.

I am very grateful to Eric Maskin, co-recipient with my father and Roger Myerson of the 2007 Nobel Memorial Prize in Economic Sciences, and to economic historian Roger Backhouse, Professor of the History and Philosophy of Economics at the University of Birmingham, for valuable suggestions, critiques and warnings. I really feel very privileged to have had so much expertise and concern focused on steering me away from potential errors, both in facts and in the expression of those facts.

I am also extremely grateful to Sylvia Nasar, author of *A Beautiful Mind*, who provided feedback and advice, and even detailed suggestions for edits and major revisions. Many thanks, too, to Robert Blobaum, Eberly Professor of History at West Virginia University, who went through an early draft of the "Born a Refugee" chapter with his expert red iPencil. Both of these individuals went far above and beyond what I could have hoped for, much less expected. The same is true of my friend, screenwriter/director James C. Wolf, who read a draft and gave me the benefit of his wisdom and well-honed instincts.

Special thanks to my cousin Ari Kolbar and my friend Anna Frampton, both of whom provided generous help with translations of documents in Polish. Thanks also to Zina Santing (a first cousin of Ari's on his father's side) who, at Ari's request, was kind enough to translate Adek's Russian-language postcard, referenced in "Born a Refugee."

Many thanks to USC Shoah Foundation Institute for permission to quote from the testimony of my father's younger brother, Henry.[1] Much of the information in the chapter, "Blood, Fire, Smoke, Exile and Human Kindness" is based on Henry's testimony.

I am also indebted to the extraordinarily helpful people at the David M. Rubenstein Rare Book & Manuscript Library at Duke University—and in

---

1   https://collections.ushmm.org/search/catalog/vha47655

particular to Elizabeth Dunn—who helped me retrieve many interesting and illuminating documents from their archive of my father's papers. Graduate student Amanda Lazarus also went out of her way in her efforts to help me.

Wendy Williamson, Graduate Program Coordinator in the Department of Economics at the University of Minnesota, was unfailingly responsive to my requests, and provided a number of very helpful documents and videos, for which I am extremely grateful.

At the London School of Economics, a number of people went well beyond responding to my inquiries in directing me towards resources I did not know enough to ask for, and even searching through resources such as photograph collections, on my behalf. These include Jim Thomas, Research Associate, STICERD; Angele David-Guillou, Library Assistant, Reader Services, LSE Library; and MacGregor Knox, Stevenson Professor of International History emeritus.

Thanks to Romain Simona, Carine Leu-Bonvin, Yves Corpataux, and particularly Isabelle Cramer, all of the Graduate Institute of International and Development Studies (formerly the Graduate Institute of International Studies) in Geneva, for their kind assistance in retrieving documents relating to my father's time at that institution.

Patricia Barnett, Executive Vice President of the Mises Institute, was also very helpful in providing information about the courses that Ludwig von Mises taught in Geneva during my father's time there.

I would also like to express my gratitude to Dennis R. Starleaf, Emeritus Professor, Department of Economics, Iowa State University, who shared material with me from my father's personnel file at Iowa State, and also went beyond that to provide comments and guidance which helped me interpret that material.

I am very grateful to Peter Gatrell, Professor of Economic History at the University of Manchester, who provided comments and suggested reading that helped me understand the history of population displacement in modern times.

Amy Majczyk, Supervisor, Customer Service, at the RAND Corporation, provided me with complimentary copies of a number of my father's articles, for which I am very grateful.

For assisting me in obtaining information pertaining to the activities of my father and mother at the University of Chicago, I would like to thank the Office of the University Registrar, Campus and Student Life, at the University of Chicago. Both Hugo Vasquez (Project Assistant II) and John J. W. Plampin (Assistant University Registrar for Convocation and Academic Affairs) took time to respond to my requests, and the information they provided was very helpful.

Although I never knew her personally, I would like to thank Klara Samuels for writing her memoir, *God Does Play Dice*,[2] which contains some very interesting information about my family. Reading this book cleared up some mysteries for me that might never have been solved otherwise.

My sincere thanks to author Ann Bauer for her generous permission to quote freely from her excellent article, "Leonid Hurwicz's Game," published in *Twin Cities Business* magazine, March 1, 2008.[3] Many thanks also to Gene Rebeck, editor and correspondent at TCB, for his help in getting the article onto leonidhurwicz.org.

Thanks to Cambridge University Press for permission to quote from *Designing Economic Mechanisms*,[4] the book in which Leo, ". . . the founder of the theory of mechanism design, and Stanley Reiter, a leading pioneer in the field, consolidate their long-standing collaboration on how to design mechanisms[5] . . ."

I would also like to thank Professor Philip Mirowski, Koch Professor, University of Notre Dame, for sharing notes from his research in the Duke University Archives, and for his efforts in helping me find material I was looking for in those archives.

My thanks also to the late Olav Bjerkholt, Professor of Economics, Department of Economics, University of Oslo, for his quick and positive response to my query about using material from his Memorandum 26, "Trygve Haavelmo at the Cowles Commission" and for other thoughts and insights he shared.

Many thanks to Piotr Koryś PhD, Adjunct, Faculty of Economic Sciences, University of Warsaw, who shared his enlightening work on the interwar period in Poland. I am very grateful to Professor Tomasz Zylicz, Economics Department, University of Warsaw, for looking over several chapters, confirming information I had originally gained from his writing, correcting my Polish spelling, and sharing a memory of my father. Waldemar Piasecki, author of "Jan Karski, One

2   Klara Samuels, *God Does Play Dice: The Autobiography of a Holocaust Survivor*, BainBridgeBooks, 1999.
3   "Leonid Hurwicz's Game," by Ann Bauer, *Twin Cities Business* magazine, March 1, 2008. Reproduced with permission from the author and *Twin Cities Business* magazine at https://www.leonidhurwicz.org/tcb/ and quoted here with similar permission. Adapted at https://www.nobelprize.org/prizes/economic-sciences/2007/hurwicz/biographical/ It is also at https://www.coroflot.com/ambauer/Articles, as of 12-16-19
4   Leonid Hurwicz and Stanley Reiter, *Designing Economic Mechanisms*, Cambridge University Press, 2006.
5   Eric Maskin, review on https://www.amazon.com/Designing-Economic-Mechanisms-Leonid-Hurwicz/dp/0521724104

Life,[6]" wrote a wonderful article[7] about my father and was extremely helpful to me in understanding the "ghetto bench" period of my father's life.

Meghan Baxter, Communications Associate, Guggenheim Foundation, was unfailingly helpful in unearthing details of my father's 1945 Guggenheim grant.

Finally, to the many others who, over the years, have shared their memories of my father with me and with the world at large: I thank you for keeping his memory alive, both as a good economist and as a good human being. This book has benefitted from your efforts.

Of course, any remaining errors of omission or commission are entirely my responsibility!

Professor Hurwicz says that he is simply a product of his history.

"I cannot tell you my life story and what I did without telling you about politics as well."

—*Leo's Nobel biography*

6 Waldemar Piasecki, *Jan Karski Jedno życie*, Insignis Media, 2015. http://www.insignis.pl/jankarski/

7 Waldemar Piasecki, "Noblista z. . . getta ławkowego," Tygodnik Przegląd, November 11, 2007. https://www.tygodnikprzeglad.pl/noblista-getta-lawkowego/

Prologue

———————

"Learning was everything to Leo."
Friend and colleague Marcel "Ket" Richter[1]

My father, Leonid Hurwicz ("Leo" from here on out), didn't focus fanatically on one great achievement to the exclusion of everything else. He didn't consort with movie stars or seek power and glory. Not many people recognize his name. Fewer still can correctly pronounce it (HER-wich) and spell it.

He was married only once, from the age of twenty-seven until he died; he and Evelyn had four children and a stable, normally chaotic and typically overwhelming family life, with work, friends, colleagues, travel, pets, politics and chicken pox. When asked what he wanted for his birthday, he would invariably say, "Twelve hours of uninterrupted sleep." (Dream on, Leo.) Instead, he developed the ability to lose consciousness over a book or newspaper at any convenient time, in an easy chair or on a couch.

He was an excellent pianist and played Beethoven, Schumann, Mozart and Chopin with great verve and precision. In addition, gathered around the piano in the evening, he would accompany as the family sang "Oh Susannah," "The Wraggle Taggle Gypsy," "Clementine" and "Hallelujah I'm a Bum" from the *Fireside Book of Folk Songs*. All his children developed a lifelong love of music. How much might those times of family closeness and warmth have contributed to that?

At bedtime, however, he was at his creative best, improvising stories for his attentive children: marvelous adventures in far-off lands, peril and escape, vast journeys across land and ocean, tales for which they never questioned the inspiration. At other times, he shared the classics: *The Adventures of Peter Rabbit, The Wind in the Willows, Winnie the Pooh, Alice in Wonderland*. Each one he recounted in a rich, resonant voice, full of conviction, as if—as my sister Ruth noted—he himself had fallen down the rabbit hole and landed in a strange new world.

There were also more obscure tales. Ruth particularly remembered the "Yes and No Stories," by George and Helen Papashvily—folk tales from what is now the Republic of Georgia. Each story begins, "There was, there was, and yet

———————

[1] The sources for all the quotes in this prologue will be found in Appendices A and B.

there was not, there was once..." In the first story, "The Tale of the Tales," a boy sits at the campfire night after night, listening to stories from the elders of his village. Then one night, the eldest of the elders turns to him and tells him that it's his turn. The boy insists that he doesn't know enough, that he prefers to just listen. But the elder insists: if he wants to keep coming to the campfire, he must take his turn. No one gets it all right, he assures him. If he leaves something out, someone else will fix it. But it's vital that we all pass on what we've learned to others. And so the boy hesitantly begins, "There was, there was, and yet there was not..."

Learning was important to Leo; so was teaching, even if you didn't have all the answers. When appropriate, he might reply, "That's a very good question. It's a very interesting question. But it's not my question. It's your question."

Leo attended the symphony, danced to New Orleans jazz, owned classical and Broadway musical albums, as well as those of singer-satirist-mathematician-crazy person Tom Lehrer ("Poisoning Pigeons in the Park") and lefty folk favorites Harry Belafonte and The Weavers. He relished sauerkraut and dark chocolate, had equal energy for exploring cities and camping out in national parks, where he seemed to be able to identify every tree, shrub and flower. He delved deeply into archaeology, history and current events.

Active participation in politics—local, national and at the university where he worked—was a mixture of a pastime he enjoyed and a duty he would not shirk. In 1968, at the Democratic National Convention, he was a delegate for presidential candidate Eugene McCarthy, who was running on an anti–Vietnam War platform and challenging incumbent Lyndon B. Johnson. Evelyn shared his dedication to activism; they attended their last Democratic caucus together the year he died.

His motivation for these activities was reflected in a paper he worked on from the mid-90s until 2007, "But Who Will Guard the Guardians?" The article suggested that economic measures may be enforceable due to the presence of *intervenors*: "guardians" (people or organizations) that had both the power and, because of their ethics or beliefs, the willingness to enforce the rules.

Ruth said, "As long as my dad was living, I felt that someone wise and good was watching out for all of us. Dad tracked world events as one who understood that they are happening to us, not 'them.' He valued an active citizenry, and took his role as guardian to heart, doing his part to help steer the world in good directions."

His native language was Polish; he spoke his adopted language, English, with a mild Polish accent and grammar superior to that of his American-born children; he achieved fluency in French and German, could read Russian with some difficulty, and had a smattering of Latin, Greek and Hebrew. Late in life he took up Chinese. On his office shelves were yards of dictionaries.

As a Fulbright Scholar teaching in Bangalore, India, in 1965–66, Leo became particularly interested in Anglo-Indian locutions. His colleague and friend Ket Richter remembered questioning the existence of an exotic word used by economist Arijit Mukherji in the course of a dinner at Leo and Evelyn's. Mukherji insisted that, in his home city of Calcutta, this word was commonly used, adding that if they had a Hobson-Jobson, they could settle the issue. Leo, at the other end of the table, heard "Hobson-Jobson," disappeared and came back with the very thing: "A Glossary of Colloquial Anglo-Indian Words and Phrases, and of Kindred Terms, Etymological, Historical, Geographical and Discursive," which no doubt did settle the issue. (What the word was is lost to history. Ket thought it was "prequel," which is neither Anglo-Indian nor in Hobson-Jobson. Feel free to imagine "pish-pash," "poggle," "pootly" or "pucka," all of which are.)

Leo's fascination with language extended to the meanings, origins, and geographical and temporal travels of personal names. A student seeking guidance on a dissertation would wait hours outside Leo's office (due evidently to Leo's in-depth interaction with another student), finally gain admission to the inner sanctum, and then spend the next hour learning all about the name they had been carrying around for the past few decades but, as it turned out, knew less about than their thesis advisor.

What the impatient student might not realize is that earlier that day, Leo had taught a class that ran over either because, as Evelyn once noted, the students "wouldn't stop listening" or because Leo had to go through the article he was reviewing with them, perhaps one article for the whole semester, as Richter said, "line by line, definition by definition, theorem by theorem, proof by proof, until at the end, every student in the class knew exactly what was true and what was not true." In Leo's classes, students not only learned, but learned to learn.

He might that same day have attended an ancient studies group tracing the migrations of Proto-Indo-European language speakers into Greece at the end of the Neolithic—a study group spontaneously formed and initially consisting of Leo and a few classicists and graduate students; Leo's enthusiastic urgings eventually brought in scholars from a variety of other disciplines, including geography, linguistics, zoology, botany and archaeology.

He might have spoken on the floor of the faculty senate, for example, in defense of colleague Jacob Schmookler, who was under attack in the state legislature for, as Ket explained, "foisting a communist, subversive, radical textbook on the students." *Economics: An Introductory Analysis*, by Paul Samuelson, would go on to become a worldwide standard, the best-selling economics textbook of all time.

Though no one would say Leo had a flamboyant personality, in a social setting he could be lively, fun and interesting—often in an educational way. University of Chicago professor Roger Myerson recalled making an obscure comment at an academic cocktail party about the divide between the Mississippi and Great Lakes drainage systems—"the kind of remark that normally kills the conversation. But not when Leo was there. Then my remark could stimulate a 30-minute discourse on great dams of the Midwest."

A frequent comment about Leo was that he seemed to know everything. The more cautious would say "almost everything." A close friend, Nina Reiter, was rapturous when she correctly contradicted Leo about a tree he had misidentified on the Reiters' farm: "It was an amazing triumph, one not duplicated very often."

With all this, he had time, when the occasion demanded, to lend a sympathetic ear to a friend's personal troubles. He was sensitive to the moods of those around him, though he would seldom intrude by mentioning it. He might observe, for example, that his secretary at the economics department seemed depressed, though she hadn't said anything about it.

Ruth remembered talking with him about various problems and situations, and benefitting from his "wise and sensitive counsel in matters of diplomacy, relationships, strategies and ethics."

As with students, he seemed to have all the time in the world for his kids. Sometimes, as with the students, this could be frustrating: you didn't want to ask him for help with your algebra, or your history or social studies lesson, if all you wanted was to get through it as quickly as possible. On the other hand, were you perhaps open to going down a path you could never have thought of, to an intriguing destination that might have nothing to do with your grade in social studies that week? Willing to risk starting out for the north side of town and ending up traveling on foot to the North Pole and back with a guide who knew every inch of territory? Interested in stopping along the way to examine maps showing political boundaries, natural features, geology, weather patterns and human migrations, including some ancient maps that were actually inaccurate but of significant historical value? Leo was your guy.

With all this, he managed to continue to turn out groundbreaking original research. This could also turn out to be quite a painstaking endeavor.

Harvard professor Eric Maskin remembered a "summer camp" for economic theorists at Stanford during which a colleague, Andy Postlewaite, discovered a puzzling phenomenon: it appeared that, in a competitive economic "game" in which players might behave "strategically" (for instance, by not communicating privately held information honestly), an outcome that was technically feasible might not be implementable in "Nash equilibrium"—that is, in such a way that no one would want to unilaterally change their strategy even if they knew all the other players' strategies.

"Well, Leo, Andy and I thought about that for a while and soon got to the bottom of it. And we wrote up a short manuscript of eight pages or so, suitable for publication as a note, say, in the *Journal of Economic Theory*."

But did Leo want to submit the paper for publication?

Actually, Leo asked, wouldn't they like to know what happens if agents can destroy their endowments? And of course they did want to know that. So, about a year later, they had answered that question and had a manuscript of thirty pages, suitable for an article in *Econometrica*. But was Leo now ready to send it in?

Actually, he thought before publishing the paper, it would be very interesting to find out what happened if production could occur. And it was very interesting to find this out. So, six years later, when they had actually done the finding out, they had a gargantuan manuscript of eighty pages, too long for any journal. So they thought they should turn it into a monograph.

Was Leo prepared to do this?

Actually, Leo thought the proofs and exposition still needed some refinement. So, over the next eleven years or so, Andy and Eric would at erratic intervals receive from Leo updated versions of the manuscript, in which a proof or a definition would be improved. And naturally the paper only got longer.

This would have continued indefinitely, Maskin was sure, if their colleague Stan Reiter "had not been gracious enough to reach an age where it was appropriate to present him with a Festschrift." The piece was finally published in that collection of papers honoring Stan, twenty years after they had started work on it.

Even after that, from time to time, Maskin would get phone calls or notes from Leo, suggesting for example that they really should think more about the case in which agents could hide their endowments. "Relentless curiosity" was Maskin's term for it.

Leo was philosophically opposed to "elegance"—brevity for its own sake—in proofs, and frequently quoted Austrian physicist Ludwig Boltzmann's famous condescension: "Elegance is for tailors."

Colleague Jim Jordan remembered going over with Leo a paper Leo had written. Jordan found himself merely confirming the correctness of everything Leo had done, a situation which engendered in Jordan a feeling of intellectual insecurity "verging on panic." Luckily, the phone rang mid-session. It must have been Evelyn, because Leo picked it up. Desperately trying to think of something useful he could contribute, Jordan suddenly remembered seeing a result similar to Leo's in a book, which he now ran back to his office to consult.

"I found the result I was looking for, which stated in a very compact way, and using much more abstract mathematics, exactly what Leo was verifying by brute force using the necessarily more cumbersome calculations of elementary calculus. So I felt very much better about myself then, because although this was hardly a creative observation, at least I would have the pleasure of saving one of the world's great theorists several hours of calculus homework."

Leo finished the call. Jordan showed him the elegant statement that would replace all of his calculations.

"Yes," said Leo, "That's right. Now, where were we before the phone rang?"

"I guess," Jordan said later, "I should feel grateful that he had the kindness not to tell me that my comment was purely sartorial."

Part of the problem, no doubt, was that Leo loved his work and tended to be blind to the tedium in it. He often told us that he would have done what he did for free.

It all might never have happened if it hadn't been for Hitler, Stalin and Franco.

[*All quotes in this prologue, both direct and indirect, are from Appendices A and B—M. H.*]

CHAPTER 1

1939, sierpień/août/August

Le pacte germano-soviétique!

The news ran like a contagion through the streets: Hitler and Stalin, suddenly the best of friends—or at least promising not to fight each other for the next ten years. Hitler, who had persecuted Marxists even before Jews. And Stalin, who had decried fascists as the armed wing of the bourgeoisie. Now safe from one another, the two dictators were free to point their guns elsewhere. For the French, it meant that Hitler could now concentrate his forces in their direction. It meant war.

Leo had only a transit visa for France. His only officially permitted final destination was Poland. However, he had been "transiting" as slowly as possible—staying put in Paris, to be precise—since it would have been entirely irrational to place oneself between the claws of the Russian bear and the talons of the German eagle at this moment in history. Now, the German-Russian pact made France just as vulnerable as Poland.

How many others like him were getting up from little round cafe tables, or from green wooden benches in parks, or by the Seine, clutching that morning's *Gringoire* or *New York Herald Tribune*, and hurrying off to make preparations to be as far away as possible as quickly as they could?

The pact was signed on a Wednesday, August 23—just two days after Leo's twenty-second birthday. The following Friday[1] found him striding, suitcase in hand, toward the railway station. He had no money to spare for the Métro, and that was fine. His younger days hiking the Carpathians served him well now. He often reached his Paris destinations faster than he would have on the underground.

---

1   Date based on a form later provided to the American Consulate in Zurich.
Leonid Hurwicz Papers, David M. Rubenstein Rare Book & Manuscript Library, Duke University, Box 23, File: Correspondence 1938 Nov 21–10 Sept 1940 1.
https://www.leonidhurwicz.org/american-consulate-zurich/

Today was more tiring than usual, since his suitcase contained all his worldly belongings, including the weight of his thesis papers: "Currency Devaluation with special reference to the experience of the Gold Bloc Countries." Increasingly historical, academic, pointless. The gold bloc countries, the last stubborn adherents to the gold standard, had abandoned their project years earlier. Meanwhile, there were questions of economic organization that desperately needed to be addressed. Or perhaps just one fundamental question: how could modern nations design and implement economic systems that maximize the welfare of their people, peacefully—without the waste and destruction of war? He had, however, spent years on the gold bloc thesis, and hopefully it would still serve to help him get his PhD.

In the massive central hall of the Gare de Lyon, he found his way through a sea of muffled conversation, echoing off the high glass-and-cast-iron ceiling. Where were all these people going? It was not clear that any country in Europe would be safe from the super-predators. Especially for a Polish Jew who was, for all intents and purposes, homeless, stateless, a refugee with no refuge.

It felt somehow genetically familiar, like a hereditary condition.

CHAPTER 2

Born a Refugee

———

Moscow. August 21, 1917. Near the end of a long, violent summer, a baby boy is born to a Polish Jewish couple, Zina and Adek Hurwicz. She is 24 years old, he is 27. Leonid—Leo, or affectionately *Loluś* (Lóloosh)—is their first child.

Adek's father, Max, saw something special in his grandson. Before little Leonid was a year and a half old, Max would pronounce him a "chochem": Yiddish/Hebrew for a genius, or at least a wise man. Though Max may have been a good judge of character, his comment also reflected his values: wisdom above cuteness.

The world was much in need of that wisdom: governments were struggling to fight an all-out war without losing political support or upending their economies. Meanwhile, revolutionaries debated how best to tear down old political and economic systems and design new ones that would allow ordinary working people and peasants to live decent, secure lives.

Baby Leo is a refugee at birth: his parents fled Warsaw not long after they got married, near the beginning of the Great War, as Russian and German bayonets, sabres, bombs and artillery ripped into Poland. The couple made a long stopover (perhaps as much as a year or two) in Ostrów-Mazowiecka, a largely Jewish city about 100 km northeast of Warsaw, where an aunt, Helen Kotzin, had settled back in 1913[1] while her husband Morris was in Canada establishing himself enough so that he could bring Helen and their four boys over. (Morris was the brother of Max, Adek's father.) In Ostrów-Mazowiecka, Adek taught history at the secondary level, while Zina was most likely an elementary teacher.

However, they eventually joined Adek's parents, Max and Sara Lea, in Moscow. Here they were far to the east of the German armies spreading carnage and chaos in Poland, Romania and Hungary. Even farther away, of course, were

---

1   Katarzyna Kasia Kacprzak, "Kotzin Genealogy," https://www.leonidhurwicz.org/wp-content/uploads/2020/08/Kocyn_research_report_2018_07_10.pdf

the rain-and-blood-soaked trenches of Belgium, France and Switzerland, and German bombers reducing whole sections of London to rubble.

Even in Moscow, the Hurwicz family did have problems: food, for instance. For years now, with Russia embroiled in the Great War, trains and supplies had often been diverted to the front lines, interrupting the transport of grains and other food to areas like Moscow, where there were many mouths to feed and little food production. Muscovites experienced shortages and skyrocketing prices for basics like bread, milk, meat and sugar. People—mostly women and children—stood in lines stretching down the sidewalk, in all kinds of weather, complaining, gossiping, speculating, hoping to buy meat or a loaf of bread. If they did not start near the front of the line, often little or nothing was left when their turn finally came.

Adek and Zina could perhaps get by on less than most: he was only five feet tall, and she half a head shorter.

If dinner was not all that might be desired, the Hurwicz family fed on news, rumors and hope. Hopeful news about government attempts to fix prices for grain at the national level. Discouraging news about producers and middle-men hoarding their supplies, hoping that prices would rise. Good news about attempts by Moscow and Petrograd to regulate the price of meat on a local level. Bad news about "meat wars," with wholesalers taking their meat to the highest bidder, leaving the other city meatless.

Then, in March of 1917, the announcement—wonderful and amazing to Polish-Jewish ears—that Tsar Nicholas II had abdicated under duress. The ancient, outmoded autocracy that had crushed Polish hopes for autonomy and Jewish hopes for equality: gone, collapsed, never to return. True, the collapse came only at the price of political, economic and military disarray. So many deaths at the front lines. Privation, suffering, hunger. Still, if that's what was required to wake people up, they were roused now: hunger-maddened rioters and striking workers in the Russian capital of Petrograd, soldiers defecting *en masse* to support them, even the elites losing faith in the tsarist government's ability to govern.

True, Nicholas had not been all bad: he had expanded civil liberties and sponsored literacy programs. But ultimately he stood in the way of real democracy, refusing to relinquish his autocratic powers. Adek, even as a teenager during the Polish Revolution of 1905–1907, had participated in student strikes and demonstrations, making "revolutionary" demands like classes conducted in Polish. He was arrested and even spent a day or two in a crowded Warsaw jail cell, where a doctor taught him how, if necessary, he could fake a heart condition to get early release or less harsh treatment in prison.

Adek's "crimes"—striking and demonstrating—reveal his activist nature. His socialist sympathies would also have brought him into contact with groups that organized such protests, like the Polish Socialist Party (*Polska Partia Socjalistyczna*, PPS) and the secular Jewish socialist party, the Bund (*Der Allgemeiner Yiddisher Arbeiter Bund*, "The General Jewish Labor Union"). Adek was active in both.[2]

Many schools in Warsaw were shut down for long periods in this era. Polish families with college-age children often sent them to study outside of Russian-controlled Poland, either in Galicia (Austrian-controlled and more accepting of Polish culture) or in Western Europe. As one indicator, at the University of Warsaw, the proportion of Polish students fell from 60–70 percent before 1905 to less than 10 percent afterwards.[3] When it came time for Adek to start university, his parents sent him to Paris, to get a law degree from the Sorbonne.

Adek returned to Poland/Russia in 1911,[4] after three years in France, going first to Ukraine for "nostrification" (getting his foreign degree recognized in Russia/Poland), then returning to Warsaw, where he married Zina.

In 1917, the collapse of the tsarist monarchy opened up new horizons for Russia and Poland. Would leadership be found to bring the various factions together as peacefully as possible, to construct a new, fairer economy and society? Adek was active with the Menshevik party, which he thought was the best hope for accomplishing the needed makeover with a minimum of conflict and suffering.

Adek saw good leaders coming to the fore: the spiky-haired 36-year-old revolutionary attorney, Alexander Kerensky, had distinguished himself by his ferocious oratory against the tsarist monarchy and his equally fierce legal defense of political prisoners. He was a friend of the Jews, too: in 1913, when the ridiculous charge of ritual murder of a Christian boy was leveled against Mendel Beiliss,

---

2   Henry Hurwicz, testimony for the USC Shoah Foundation Institute: https://collections. ushmm.org/search/catalog/vha47655

3   "W 1905 r., pod hasłem walki o polski uniwersytet, został ogłoszony bojkot rosyjskiej uczelni. Udział Polaków wśród studiujących w Warszawie spadł poniżej 10%, a większość dotychczasowych studentów wyjechała do innych uniwersytetów."

    [In 1905, under the slogan of fighting for a Polish university, a boycott of the Russian university was announced. The share of Poles among students in Warsaw fell below 10%, and most of the current students went to other universities.] https://www.uw.edu.pl/uniwersytet/ historia-uw/ Accessed October 15, 2022. See also: https://www.communications-unlimited. nl/the-university-of-warsaw-one-of-the-worlds-top-400-celebrates-its-200th-anniversary/ Accessed October 13, 2022.

4   "Adek," https://leonidhurwicz.org/adek/

a Jew, Kerensky had championed a resolution of the St. Petersburg bar that denounced the trial as "a slanderous attack on the Jewish people."

At 5'10" when the average Russian male was 5'8," with an upright bearing and intense gaze, Kerensky was a commanding figure, as well as an inspiring orator. He put his gifts to good use: as early as the spring of 1915, as a member of the Russian parliament, the Duma, Kerensky appealed to the tsar to proclaim, among other things, a general amnesty for political prisoners, autonomy for Poland, freedom from harassment for legal trade unions, an end to all forms of religious intolerance, including restrictions on Jews, and cultural autonomy for all national minorities, among which Jews were also included—were, in fact, the largest group.

When revolutionaries wrested power from the tsarist government and founded the Russian Provisional Government in March 1917, Kerensky emerged as a passionate proponent of western-style democracy for Russia via an elected Constituent Assembly—a program fully approved by Adek. Adek was a Menshevik, Kerensky a Trudovik, but the two parties were closely allied. In the Duma, both parties were in the Progressive Block. In addition to agreeing on high ideals such as democracy and an open, tolerant society, the Mensheviks and Trudoviks often joined forces strategically and tactically. They also shared the belief that all sectors of society, even including capitalists and aristocrats, needed to play a role in the transition to socialism. They both favored a transformation by peaceful and legal means, such as union activity, demonstrations and political organizing. These, they believed, would bring more stable and lasting progress than a violent revolution.

Leaders like Kerensky brought hope that the baby Zina was carrying might be able to pursue education, career and prosperity as an equal and in safety—something Hurwicz ancestors had been striving for, usually with only short-lived success, for hundreds of years.

Then, in April 1917, a train entered Russia carrying what would prove to be a deadly threat to Hurwicz family hopes. The Bolshevik leader, Vladimir Ilyich Ulyanov, known as Lenin, exiled for sowing seeds of revolution in Russia, had spent years in Siberia, England and Switzerland. Now, with those seeds sprouting, he returned from Zurich, by way of Germany, Sweden and Finland.

Arriving at Petrograd's Finland Station, Lenin climbed to the roof of an armored train car and proclaimed to thousands of assembled followers: "The people need peace; the people need bread; the people need land. And they give you war, hunger, no bread. . . . We must fight for the socialist revolution, fight to the end, until the complete victory of the proletariat."

The "they" in this speech was the Provisional Government, with which the Mensheviks were allied. Thus, though Lenin ostensibly sought the same goal as Adek—a democratic socialist state—in his first speech on returning to Russia, he cast all those in the current government as enemies. This did not bode well for groups like the Mensheviks who were attempting to work with the government. In fact, it was not long before Lenin condemned the Mensheviks as "traitors to socialism" and urged total rejection of the Provisional Government. As time passed, the Bolshevik ranks swelled. In May, another Bolshevik leader, Lev Bronstein, known as Trotsky, returned from a decade and a half of wandering the world, having escaped from Siberian exile hidden in a hay wagon in 1902.

In July, as Zina was contending with the final stages of her pregnancy, an early spontaneous attempt at revolution—the July Days—wreaked havoc on major Russian cities, especially Petrograd. Military discipline broke down as rebellious soldiers, machine guns and rifles in hand, were joined in the streets by sailors and factory workers. They demanded "All Power to the Soviets"—referring to workers' councils which had come to be Bolshevik-dominated. In Moscow, demonstrations were smaller, unarmed, and likely to be countered by groups of mocking citizens.

Petrograd, however, was the seat of power, and the actions there were a serious threat to the Provisional Government, which now used police and remaining loyal military to try to quell the disturbance. But chaos reigned. Shots were fired, including loyal army units firing on protesters, turning demonstrations into riots. Accusing the Bolsheviks of fomenting violence, the Provisional Government seized the Bolshevik headquarters in Petrograd and arrested hundreds of people, including Trotsky and other Bolshevik leaders. Lenin fled the country again, finding refuge in Finland.

Kerensky was perhaps the only prominent politician with broad support in the government and among the revolutionaries; many looked to him to unite the country and prevent civil war. Prince Georgy Lvov, an aristocrat with no allegiance to any particular party but also with no particularly inspiring message or vision, had become prime minister of the Provisional Government in March. He had now resigned.

Kerensky became prime minister in early July—a hopeful development for the Hurwicz family. However, the Bolsheviks opposed Kerensky from the start. In late July, urged on by the Bolsheviks, around 400,000 workers went on strike in Moscow.

Once Kerensky took office, his approach to unifying the nation became increasingly heavy-handed: he imposed severe restrictions on public gatherings and, trying to restore military discipline, brought back the death penalty at the front lines. Kerensky's biggest mistake was insisting on pursuing the war with Germany, a war no longer supported by rank-and-file military or by workers who were much more responsive to Lenin's promise of peace, bread and land.

In the first few weeks of Leo's life, the commander-in-chief of the Provisional Government's armed forces, Lavr Kornilov, ordered an assault on the Petrograd Soviet and the Provisional Government, perhaps because he blamed the Petrograd Soviet for the breakdown in military discipline and felt the Provisional Government was unable to take charge effectively. The attack failed, and Kornilov was arrested. The result of "the Kornilov Affair" was loss of confidence in the Provisional Government and a corresponding resurgence of support for the Bolsheviks. Working people and the military lost faith in the idea that the revolutionary soviets could form a coalition with the Provisional Government, with its large component of aristocrats and capitalists. Kerensky's attempts to distance himself from the episode were not entirely successful, and his popularity was shaken.

As October approached, total rejection of the Provisional Government became Bolshevik policy. This created a dangerous climate for people like Adek who had advocated a more moderate, coalition-building approach: the Bolshevik party officially considered them enemies of the revolution.

The battle cruiser *Aurora*, anchored in Petrograd harbor, was emblematic of the many mutinies, revolts and uprisings touched off across the length and breadth of the Russian Empire. Already in February, she had been taken over by Bolshevik seamen, her captain shot dead when he tried to suppress their revolutionary organizing. By October, though theoretically positioned where she could fire on the Peter and Paul Fortress in Petrograd, her guns were loaded with blanks: it had become clear that the fortress would be taken without much of a fight. On October 25, the *Aurora* fired the blank shot that signaled the start of the revolution and the occupation of the Winter Palace, formerly the home of emperors, now the seat of the Provisional Government. It was one of the few shots fired as the Bolsheviks took over the seat of the national government in Petrograd. Kerensky beat a hasty retreat in a car provided by the American Embassy, managing to get through all the checkpoints because of the American flag on the vehicle.

These events were naturally more strongly felt in Petrograd, where they took place, than hundreds of miles away in Moscow. The engaged population in Petrograd became massively, solidly Bolshevik: the Petrograd Soviet was approaching 90% Bolshevik. Moscow was much more evenly divided: the Bolsheviks occupied perhaps 60% of the seats in the Moscow Soviet, with the rest to some degree loyal to the Provisional Government.

Accordingly, the Bolsheviks had a much tougher fight in Moscow, with armed battles continuing for almost a week, from around October 25 to October 31, killing hundreds of people. For the first few days, it seemed that the Provisional Government might maintain control of the city. Ultimately, though, the Bolsheviks did triumph, even in Moscow.

Lenin pledged to hold the scheduled November elections, with Bolshevik rule remaining provisional until confirmed by the elected Constituent Assembly. The vote was not without its chaotic elements, with both voting and tallying of votes interrupted in various places. In fact, there was never a complete and authoritative count. It was clear, though, that the Socialist Revolutionary (SR) party came out the winner, with around twice as many votes as the Bolsheviks. (By Lenin's own account, it was 58% to 25% of the vote.)

There were factions and splits on all sides, however, and the political machinery was not able to adjust quickly enough to allow for the rapid shifts in allegiances: between the distribution of candidate lists and the election, the SRs split into Left-SRs and Right-SRs, with the Left-SRs increasingly aligning with the Bolsheviks. The Bolsheviks themselves split over the question of accepting the Constituent Assembly, with Lenin against it but the Bolshevik Central Committee in favor. The Mensheviks by this time had lost most of their constituency because of their support for the Provisional Government and the war. Though they represented only around 2% or 3% of the vote, the Mensheviks nevertheless managed to split, with the Menshevik-Internationalists opposing their party's pro-war stance; in August, 1917, many of the Menshevik-Internationalists broke off and joined the consistently anti-war Bolsheviks.

With all the fracturing and realignment, the Bolsheviks were able to reasonably argue that the votes as tallied no longer represented the will of the people. Accordingly, they dissolved the Assembly after its first meeting in January 1918. Over the next year, as Leo was absorbing his first words of Polish at home, much of the talk was of civil war, counter-revolution, independence movements, opposing socialist factions trying to reverse the Bolshevik takeover, and how a more fair and just economy and political system could be built.

When Leo was around a year old, the Bolsheviks launched the Red Terror. Tens of thousands of "traitors" (people who didn't agree with Lenin) ended up in gulags, on gallows or in front of a firing squad.

Adek could not avoid the conclusion that he was now in very serious danger.

CHAPTER 3

Now or Never

On November 11, 1918, combatants in the Great War laid down their arms and began negotiating the terms under which they would coexist in peace. The end of hostilities made a potential trip back home to Warsaw much less dangerous for the Hurwicz family.

They would have a stopping point about two-thirds of the way, in Vilnius, Lithuania. The family went back a couple of generations in that country, where Adek's father Max and paternal grandfather Tevye had both been born. Vilnius itself was a major center of Jewish population—"the Jerusalem of Lithuania." It might be a place where the Hurwicz family could stay for a time if travel onward to Warsaw seemed risky.

Now there were excited discussions around the Hurwicz dinner table about Poland's resurrection as an independent, sovereign state—a constitutional democracy with Józef Piłsudski as Chief of State and military commander-in-chief. Piłsudski was supported mainly by leftists and centrists—a point in his favor from the Hurwicz perspective. During the Polish Revolution of 1905, Piłsudski had in fact led the most militant and nationalist wing of the Polish Socialist Party, with which Adek had also been connected.

In addition, Piłsudski was regarded as a friend by the Jews. He would be encouraged in that direction by statements from powerful leaders like Woodrow Wilson, who had said that, as part of the peace agreements, Poland should promise to respect the rights of minorities.

There were, however, serious impediments to making the journey as well.

First of all, available transportation could hardly have been worse. There were no trains running westward from Moscow: the only real option would be to hire a horse-drawn wagon. However, horses—used for cavalry, transport, reconnaissance and message carrying—had been killed or wounded by the millions in the war. They had dropped from exhaustion, been killed by various diseases, and starved to death for lack of fodder. Most of the decent horses that survived were "requisitioned" by the various militaries.

It was a 900-mile trip: 600 miles from Moscow to Vilnius, and another 300 to Warsaw. The first leg in the wagon would be by far the hardest, and could easily take three weeks, depending on road conditions and possible detours or delays due to the civil war or weather. With December approaching, they were coming into the coldest months of the year, with lows in the teens, and highs seldom out of the 20s °F. Zina, nervous by nature, was terribly concerned for little Leo, now just over a year old. If they could wait even until mid-March, things would become a bit less frigid.

Most worrisome of all for the Hurwicz family was the likelihood of being attacked while on the road. Although the Great War was ending, the Russian civil war was escalating rapidly, with multiple armies and militias, frequently hungry, sick, ill-clothed and mutinous ("marauding Bolsheviks and soldiers of various kinds"),[1] likely to commit all sorts of mayhem, including robbery, rape and murder. Jews were always favored targets.

The possibility of attacks on women was one of the reasons why Max decided that he, Sara Lea and Adek's four sisters would remain in Moscow. In addition, it may have been that he believed—Wilson and Piłsudski notwithstanding—that Poland would be more antisemitic than Russia.

Adek and Zina didn't relish the idea of putting themselves and their child in danger, only to reach uncertain situations in Vilnius and Warsaw. Ultimately, however, they were more afraid of the Bolsheviks than all the hazards and uncertainties of flight.

They couldn't wait forever. The civil war could end any time. Then the winning faction would no doubt secure the borders, and it might be impossible to get out. Accordingly, they made their plans, and in the winter of 1919—in February, the coldest month of the year—they loaded their baggage into a wagon drawn by "some lame horse" and bumped and bounced their way along the long, frozen, war-torn road from Moscow to Vilnius.

Lithuania, however, turned out to be overrun with troops: Russian, German and Lithuanian armies competing for control. The Hurwiczes quickly caught a train for Warsaw.

---

1   All quotes in this chapter are from an interview with Leo in 2007. Appendix E, and https://leonidhurwicz.org/interview/

CHAPTER 4

Home Safe?

———————

Finally back home, after nearly five years away! Here, at least for the moment, bloodthirsty Bolsheviks held no sway. The German army had gone home, its puppet government dissolved. Everywhere, there was a feeling of excitement and passion for the newly resurrected homeland. Polish language, culture and education would flourish once again.

With the yoke of monarchy removed, Poland had a unique opportunity to sky-rocket into modernity, to create a free, democratic and just society, with equal rights—and at least a minimal standard of education, housing, nutrition and sanitation—for everyone. Protected by international agreements and championed by Józef Piłsudski, the Jews would be part of it. Adek and Zina would be part of it—and in years to come, hopefully, their children and grandchildren.

Everything wasn't wonderful, of course. Already in the winter of 1918, the Russians had begun trying to take back much of eastern Poland. Border conflicts were intensifying. A Bolshevik triumph could pose a threat to the Hurwicz family. But Poland was raising a large and dedicated army, while one might hope that Russian soldiers had lost much of their fighting spirit. One thing was certain: if Adek was called up to fight for Poland, he wouldn't hesitate; preventing the Bolsheviks from taking over was as much in his own personal interest as in the interest of his country.

Poland had been ravaged by the Great War. No one knew how many Polish citizens had died, probably over a million between military and civilians—well over three percent of the population. (By contrast, the Americans had suffered "only" around 117,000 casualties—about 0.13% of their population.)

Polish lives that weren't lost were often upended. The occupying Germans had conscripted 300,000 Poles for forced labor. The Russians and Austrians had forcibly resettled 1.6 to 1.8 million Poles from the war zone. "Scorched-earth" retreats devastated agriculture, water supplies, transportation, communications and industry.

All this would make life difficult for some time. But not forever.

Money was tight. Although Zina had previously been a teacher, now she was staying home with Leo. Adek had his law degree but could not practice law independently until he completed his bar training (*aplikacja*), which included two years clerking for a judge and three years interning with a lawyer, and examinations after each phase. While he was completing this training, he supported the family by teaching history and/or Hebrew at *Chinuch*, a Jewish boys' school.

The most directly troubling aspect of life in Warsaw was the persistence of a strong conservative element in society that saw Polish identity as being defined by Roman Catholicism and a narrowly defined Polish ethnicity—one that did not include Jews. If such people came to dominate the government, the universities . . .

Thankfully, left-wingers, with Piłsudski as their leader, were in the ascendancy, embracing Poland's multi-cultural, multi-ethnic, multi-religious character. Adek would join them. The flow of history was on their side.

The Hurwiczes eventually settled at number 10 *ulica Graniczna* ("Border Street"), Apartment 5. One of the busiest streets in central Warsaw, Graniczna had acquired its name some 150 years earlier because it defined the border between the jurisdictions of Wielopole and Grzybów. It now defined a different boundary: modern and Polish to the east, traditional and Jewish to the west.

A five-minute walk to the east, Marszałkowska Street offered cinemas, elegant shops and cafes. One saw gents in suits who would not have looked out of place in the London of that era, and ladies dressed according to the latest styles from Paris. One heard mostly Polish spoken.

In the same area, the Hurwicz family could enjoy the public 38-acre Saxon Garden with its beautiful foliage, large trees, ornate fountains, ponds, colorful patterned flower beds, formal Versailles-like vistas, and grand, historic buildings and monuments. A five-minute walk east of the park was the Presidential Palace, which had become the central governmental building for the Second Polish Republic. North of the park was *plac Teatralny* (Theater Square), home to theaters, including the fashionable *Teatr Wielki* (Grand Theater) with its opera and ballet performances. Nearby were more cafes, bars and cabarets for the after-theater crowds. Just beyond that were the boulevards along the Vistula River, not far from the market square where the *Syrenka Warszawska*, the Mermaid of Warsaw, had stood for more than half a century with sword raised, guarding the city from attackers.

All this, within a half-hour walk of their apartment, was a world the Hurwicz family relished.

To the west of ulica Graniczna, while there were certainly also people who would blend in just fine on Marszałkowska, what really struck one's eye were the many traditional Jews: women in dark dresses reaching nearly to the ankle, wearing *babushkas* (head scarves); men with long beards, dangling sidelocks (*peyos*), ankle-length black robes, and pillbox-like *kashket* caps or round fur hats; and strolling street vendors with household goods or mousetraps dangling around their necks, hawking homemade candles and candies, or pushing handcarts among the crowds, operatically proclaiming, in Yiddish, the merits of today's pickled herring or bagels.

Hurwicz ancestors had been moving farther and farther away from this traditional Jewish world for at least the past 100 years, and the Hurwicz family now felt almost no connection with it. The Hurwiczes were Jewish by birth, of course, and would admit to some pride in the great thinkers, artists and leaders their culture had produced. They did celebrate Passover, though in the homes of relatives. A niece, Klara (daughter of Zina's brother Moses), in her book *God Does Play Dice*, describes a charming scene in her family's apartment, where Zina drank too much mead at Passover "and the heavy wine went to her feet instead of her head. She sounded perfectly rational, if overly loud and rambunctious, but was unable to stand up."[1]

Family oral history claimed fourteen rabbis in the lineage: so Leo was the product of a long line of readers, arguers, and seekers after deep truth and proper rules of conduct. Adek had attended Jewish schools, where Hebrew was a required subject, and even taught Hebrew at *Chinuch*. He had been bar-mitzvahed and, at a seder, could rattle off the Hebrew prayers as well as anyone.

Their friends and family, however, were assimilated Jews like themselves, with eyes turned toward the future, not the past. There were, of course, shades of gray within the assimilated community. For instance, Zina and her brother Moses had been brought up in an Orthodox home. Moses would have continued at least somewhat in that vein, but his wife Roza was raised in an assimilated home and wanted to continue moving in that direction. The compromise was to go to synagogue a couple of times a year. In other words, assimilation mostly won out over observance.

Adek's views were clearly more the determining factor in the Hurwicz home. Adek and Zina did not intend to bar-mitzvah Leo. They never went to synagogue or prayed at home. They dressed like any other middle-class citizens of the modern western world, whether Polish, American, English or French. They were certainly interested in Jewish culture and history, but they ignored Jewish law, even working on the High Holy Days, Yom Kippur and Rosh Hashanah.

---

1   Klara Samuels, *God Does Play Dice*, p. 30.

At a time when Yiddish was the first language of 80 percent of Jews in Poland, the Hurwicz family spoke Polish with one another, even at home, with only the occasional Yiddishism thrown in—along with the occasional phrase in Russian, French, English, German or Latin. Adek was more fluent in Russian, French and German than Yiddish.

And these old stories of angels and miracles and so on . . . Well, it was a rich heritage—a fascinating work of semi-historical fiction, with two unauthorized sequels, runaway hits titled "Christianity" and "Islam."

The family lived side-by-side with non-Jews on ulica Graniczna, on the line between Jews and Poles in Warsaw. Physically, one could move easily between the two parts of town, on foot, in electric trams or—for the more upper-crust— in horse-drawn taxis. Social mobility, however, was a different matter: the Hurwicz social circle, for example, included virtually no non-Jewish Poles. In some ways, the Hurwiczes and their assimilated Jewish social circle were a part of both the traditional Jewish and the non-Jewish worlds. More deeply, they were part of neither.

But perhaps that was changing. Perhaps little Leo could grow up in a country where people were judged by their loyalty and service to their homeland, and by the contribution they made to the future of their society, rather than by some religious or racial label inherited from the past.

CHAPTER 5

Get an Education!

———

Loluś lived up to his grandfather's admiring assessment, even in these earliest years: for example, it is said that before he could read, with the aid of a set of dominos, Leo independently discovered a method for adding up long strings of numbers that math prodigy Carl Friedrich Gauss didn't come up with until the advanced age of eight.

Zina and Adek had both been teachers and were well qualified to educate their little *chochem* and to inculcate in him the importance of learning. In any case, this was a family tradition. Over the centuries, education had functioned as a uniquely portable form of wealth—one of the few valuables you could always take with you when you had to flee, the one thing no one could take away from you.

Family stories illustrated the point.

According to family oral history, even as early as the sixteenth century, the Italian version of the Spanish Inquisition inspired a Hurwicz ancestor who had obtained a medical degree from the University of Padua to cross the Alps and head a thousand or so miles north to set up practice in Lithuania. He carried his wealth with him in the form of his education, attested to by his colorfully illustrated parchment medical diploma. Although his name was lost, his story was not.

The Hurwiczes owed their last name to the good doctor's migration, because Max had borrowed the name "Hurwicz" from a neighbor in Lithuania. "Max Hurwicz" was actually born "Max Kocyn" (pronounced, and later in Canada and America spelled, "Kotzin"). How did he acquire the name "Hurwicz"? The story had to do with the tsar's army in the nineteenth century, when Lithuania was part of the Russian Empire. The army was a terrible place for Jews. They rarely became officers, and there was a tradition of forced baptism of young Jewish men. Methods of persuasion included beatings and starvation. Once drafted, it was a 10- to 15-year commitment.

Max's parents, Tevye and Elka Kocyn, had two sons, both born in Lithuania: Max (born in 1862) and Morris (born in 1869). Normally, if a family had two sons, one could be drafted into the tsar's army. An only son was exempted.

Morris, as might be expected, was registered as Morris *Kocyn*. But his older brother somehow was registered as Max *Hurwicz*—probably the last name of a neighbor who had no sons. So, instead of the unfortunate situation of one family having two sons and the other having none, each family much more conveniently had only one son, at least as far as official records were concerned.

Max was also the subject of a story of education and relocation—and assassination. When he was around nineteen, Max was being tutored and wanted to attend college, something several previous generations had been unable to do. However, in March of 1881, an assassin threw a bomb under Tsar Alexander II's carriage, leading to the tsar's death and (among other repressive actions) a series of anti-Jewish pogroms and antisemitic legislation ("the May Laws"). One of those laws made it difficult for Jews to attend college. (This despite the fact that none of the assassins were Jewish, and the revolutionary organization they belonged to, *Narodnaya Volya*—"People's Freedom" or "People's Will"—was only around 15% Jewish.) Max's tutor was arrested. Max fled for fear he might be next.

Fear-of-tsar was, of course, also the reason that Adek's law diploma was in French rather than Polish.

Thus, little Leo absorbed a simple survival strategy:

If the Italian inquisition is after you, get an education.

If it's illegal to get an education, get an education.

If Germans are closing in on you from one side, and Russians are harassing you from the other, GET AN EDUCATION.

CHAPTER 6

The Miracle

In August 1920, just as Leo was turning three, the Bolshevik threat suddenly appeared once again too close for comfort. Poland had sent troops into Ukraine, hoping to help Ukrainian rebels free their country from Russian domination. The plan was that, once liberated, the Ukrainians would ally themselves with Poland, thus creating a buffer for the Poles against Russia.

Lenin objected, and after some initially successful campaigns by combined Ukrainian/Polish forces, the Russians came back with a vengeance. On August 14, the town of Radzymin, less than 15 miles east of Warsaw, fell to the Red Army, while a scattered Polish army beat a ragged retreat westward.

Lenin saw the Polish collapse as an opportunity to carry the revolution to the west. He ordered his troops to pursue. Visions of the Polish working class rising up to welcome their liberators danced in his head. Whether that happened or not, it was widely believed that the Russians would easily roll over any Polish resistance.

Once again, it seemed that the Hurwiczes might have to pack their education and head . . . Where? For the Bolsheviks, Poland was only a stepping stone to Germany: Trotsky, who was the Russian Commissar of Military and Naval Affairs, and at the head of troops attacking Poland, had bragged that they would "give water to red horses out of the *Wisła* (Vistula) and Rhine." And after the Rhine, why not the Seine? It really seemed there might be nowhere to run, at least nowhere in Europe that they could conveniently get to that would let them in.

Perhaps, like Morris and Helen Kocyn and their boys, they could find their way to Belgium and board a ship for Canada from Antwerp? Until recently, they would have felt sure that the Kocyns would help them get settled in Canada. Now, that was not certain. Bad blood had developed between the brothers, Max and Morris, and to some extent at least it seemed it was extended it to other members of the family. Morris had even forbidden Helen to communicate with her sister Sara Lea. Thousands of miles across the ocean, it would not be hard for the Kocyn family to cut themselves off if they chose to do so.

The problem had developed because Morris had asked Max for financial help in getting his family over to Canada. When Morris had gone over alone in 1912, Max had helped him. Morris emigrated initially to Edmonton, Alberta. While trying to learn English, he became a peddler, loading a backpack with clothing and other items and hawking them throughout western Canada.

By 1920, Morris had established a store. (There's a photograph of him leaning in the doorway of a typical "Old West" type general store, with foot-high lettering on a squarish false facade proclaiming M. KOTZIN, GENERAL MERCHANT.)[1] At this point, he returned to Poland to get his family. He once again asked Max (who was now in Moscow) for financial assistance for the trip back to Canada. But when Morris came back asking for money again, Max concluded that Morris had not really made a success of things in Canada, as had been expected. Apparently, he felt "enough is enough." He refused any further financial help.

Ultimately, of course, Morris did return to Canada even without Max's help, but it stretched him to the limit financially. Morris was very angry and vowed to cut off contact with Max—and Max's family.

Still, the Hurwiczes could be hopeful, since they knew both Morris and Helen to be extraordinarily kind and generous people. For instance, in Ostrów-Mazowiecka, where Helen ran a boarding house for students attending the local *gymnasium* (secondary school), it was said that she fed them so generously that "what she lost on each customer, she made up in volume."

Morris' generous spirit was revealed, for example, when he was leaving Edmonton for Poland to collect his family, and a neighbor asked if he would bring his two nieces back as well; Morris readily agreed, and did exactly that. Again, in Poland, on the train as Morris was going to join his family, a young man from Warsaw asked Morris to fill out papers claiming him as a nephew so that he could emigrate with the Kocyns. Morris consented, and the young man ended up living with them in Canada.[2]

These were good people, and a terrible loss to the family if they were alienated. But one could never know; sometimes one felt more kindly toward strangers than one's closest relations.

Luckily, the Poles turned out to be less than enthusiastic about "freedom" brought to them on the bayonet points of the Red Army. There was no proletarian

---

1   https://www.leonidhurwicz.org/moritz-kotzin/
2   Sol Kotzin, "Fragments from a Life," pp 4–5. https://leonidhurwicz.org/sol-kotzin/

uprising in Poland. Instead, the Polish population rose up to defend their homeland, and the Polish Army launched a valiant—some said foolhardy—counterattack on August 16, following a strategy laid out by Józef Piłsudski. Over the next nine days, the defenders of Poland achieved a decisive victory, which became known as "The Miracle of the Vistula."

Exactly how and why this occurred is a matter of debate among historians. Some in the Hurwicz/Kotzin clan attributed it to Russian antisemitism, believing that the Russians hated Trotsky because he was a Jew, and therefore didn't allow him to invade Warsaw, thus allowing the Poles to win the day.[3]

Though this explanation may not be found in many history textbooks, there is at least one possible piece of supporting evidence: when the Russians were attacking Poland, Stalin, who was commanding troops in Ukraine, never joined the forces closing in on Warsaw—though some believed he had been ordered to do so. Stalin was known both for disobeying orders and for being antisemitic. Did the fact that Trotsky, a Jew, was high commander of troops attacking Warsaw influence Stalin's decision? How much did the absence of Stalin's troops contribute to Russia's defeat?

This was obviously an explanation that would appeal to Jews: the great Russian Goliath, by setting itself against little David, had brought about its own downfall. In any case, the Hurwicz family was once again, it seemed, safe for the moment.

---

3   Ibid., p. 5

CHAPTER 7

Hurwicz Home School

_____

Leo's brother Henry was born in November 1922. One might expect that when Leo turned seven in 1924, Zina would have been glad to enroll him in primary school. In fact, however, she continued home schooling Leo while caring for toddler Henry at the same time.

The Hurwicz home was a good school, for several reasons:

- Zina was a warm, loving, nervous (i.e., diligent) parent/teacher.
- Adek was a strict, demanding parent/teacher, and an omnivorous intellect.
- Poland, and Warsaw in particular, provided a rich cultural environment.
- Problems were many.
- Hopes were high.
- Fear was intense.

Zina

Zina was a primary school teacher by training and profession, well-prepared to provide Leo with a good education. In fact, her training and experience may account for the fact that the Hurwiczes were allowed to home school Leo despite a compulsory education statute which required school attendance for all children from ages 7 to 14. ("Concerning School Obligation"—_O obowiązku szkolnym_ was one of the first legislative achievements of the new Polish state in 1919.)

In addition, Zina was a warm and nurturing mother. Slightly plump, cuddly, watchful and nervous, Zina provided Leo with all the love and attention he could want, and perhaps a bit more. For example, Zina thought Leo was too thin and urged on him milkshake-like concoctions to try to address his (probably-perceived-only-by-Zina) malnourished condition. Leo came to dislike anything that resembled a milkshake.

Zina also served as an intermediary between the children and their father, who was in many ways an opposite personality to Zina.

Adek

Adek was very much the ultimate authority, not only in his immediate family but even in the extended family. This is illustrated by an incident from Ostrów-Mazowiecka, where Helen Kotzin operated the residence for students. This was probably around 1915–1917, so Adek was only in his late twenties. On Shabbat, some friends of the Kotzin family were visiting, and they had kids about the same age as Morris' son, Sol, perhaps ten years old. The children were eating cake, and the owner of the house came over with his big dog, which started begging for a piece of cake. These kids were not used to dealing with dogs, and they started teasing the animal. The dog lunged for the cake and ended up biting off a piece of Sol's cheek.

When the doctor was stitching up the wound, Sol took the whole thing stoically, not crying at all, despite admitting that it hurt a lot. When asked why he wasn't crying, he replied that Adek had told him not to cry. As far as Sol was concerned, Adek's word was law.[1]

Adek was well-respected, energetic and motivated: once he completed bar training, he quickly established a solid law practice, with his own interns and law clerks, all of whom worked out of Adek's home office. Klara, who visited the Hurwicz apartment frequently confirmed Adek's dominant role in the family:

> Adek was a difficult man, loved but also feared in his home. He was a successful lawyer, a marvelous raconteur—an art almost lost today—who, when so inclined, could also cut you down with just a few sarcastic words if you did anything to displease him. He was an absolute tyrant in his home and office. The latter was located in the apartment, so I had an opportunity to see how he treated his subordinates when he was angry.[2]

In many of the cases he handled, Adek could not lose. He specialized in civil as opposed to criminal cases, and particularly in business law. But he did not spend a lot of time in court, because most of his clients were Jews; as such, they could

---

1   Ibid., p. 4.
2   Klara Samuels, *God Does Play Dice*, p. 31.

not count on being treated fairly by the legal system and were strongly inclined to settle out of court. Thus, Adek was often essentially an arbitrator. With his strong, authoritative personality, he was well-suited to the role.

In response to Adek's commanding presence, Leo adopted an understated manner, in which probing questions took the place of direct opposition. He also attempted to approach his studies and other duties in a way that was beyond reproach.

Adek was well-informed on a wide variety of topics, expressed his opinions with great force and clarity, and engaged intellectually with the children in his life. Klara, for instance, described how, when she and her mother visited the Hurwicz home, Adek would invite her to go for a "promenade" with him, preferring her company to the "women's chatter." They would pace the length of the living room and the long, dark hallway, often for half an hour or more.

Adek, whom Klara described as "by far the best-informed man I knew," was an educator at heart. He would ask her what she had learned in school and use that as a jumping off point for discursions into everything from the inadequacies of the Roman numeral system to the legislative mess during the French Revolution.

Nourished by a similar flood of information, and following Adek's example, Leo developed an omnivorous intellectual appetite. Growing up, both Leo and Henry were acutely aware of current events, both economic and political, and their historical background. They understood political factions—left wing, right wing, socialist. Much of that was thanks to Adek. Of course, much also came from reading: given the dramatic, even life-threatening impacts of current events on their lives, it is not surprising that the Hurwicz family avidly consumed newspapers, books and radio news.

Cultural Renaissance

With the rebirth of the Polish nation came a renaissance of Polish culture in music, art, literature and theater, all of which had been suppressed—though never extinguished!—for more than a hundred years. Intellectual and scientific life also blossomed in areas from anthropology and linguistics to logic, mathematics and economics.

Warsaw was known as *Paryż Północy*—the "Paris of the North"—a busy, modernizing city celebrated for its institutions of learning, elegant architecture, beautiful gardens, luxury hotels, shopping, movie theaters, cabarets and cafés.

The location of the Hurwicz family apartment in central Warsaw allowed them to enjoy all of this.

The cultural renaissance in Warsaw was not purely Polish: American culture was in ascendancy throughout the western world, in the form of automobiles, telephones, fashions, films, radio, and electrical appliances, and Poland was no exception. In Warsaw, the majority of the movies shown were American. Amerykański jazz and swing were also popular. Varsovians loved the music of Duke Ellington and Louis Armstrong, Irving Berlin and Cole Porter. The Charleston, the Shimmy and the Black Bottom doodle-hopped the Atlantic, it seemed, almost overnight. Polish flappers with bobbed hair, close-fitting cloche hats, and "short" skirts (shockingly exposing a bit of knee) paraded boldly down the streets of the Hurwicz neighborhood.

The spirit of the Roaring Twenties was alive in Poland, and the Hurwiczes embraced the novelty, the modernity, the break with tradition. Through new technologies like the radio and movies, they kept up with events and popular culture worldwide, from New York to London to Berlin—and especially Paris, which was having its own *années folles*.

Life was rich, exciting and full. Leo, even as a relatively young child, took all this in, walking freely and without fear through the bustling streets of this city of more than a million people. For example, at the age of eight, he walked on a regular basis to the Vistula River, where there were small fields where students learned agricultural skills by maintaining gardens; it was around a half hour walk each way from their apartment on ulica Graniczna.

Many Problems

Dinner table conversation included the damaged country, an economy hampered by hyperinflation and Germany's excessive influence, prejudice and discrimination (especially towards Jews), a myriad of political parties that could seemingly agree on nothing, gerrymandering aimed at reducing minority representation, and attempts to reintegrate the Russian-Prussian-Austrian zones that had been kept forcibly apart during partition.

Runaway inflation was making both public and private life very difficult. The country's currency, the mark, went from 1,000 per dollar in the summer of 1921 to over 6.4 million per dollar by December 1923. In 1924, in an attempt to re-establish monetary sanity, the złoty was re-introduced to replace the mark. (The złoty had been the Polish currency from the middle of the fourteenth century to the middle of the eighteenth century.) However, bad crops in 1924, a tariff war with Germany and a run on the banks in 1925 left the Bank of Poland with almost no foreign exchange. From 1924 to the spring of 1926, Polish currency lost almost half its value, depreciating from 5.18 to 10 złoty to the dollar.

Things were tough economically, especially for Jews. Although many European economies had post-war economic problems, Warsaw was worse off—in terms of overcrowded apartments, for instance—than many other European capitals.

A dominant question now was whether the nation could survive, given hostile Russians and Germans, as well as a challenging economic environment. Within that context, a major issue was whether minorities, and particularly Jews, could or would contribute to national unity and survival.

High Hopes

After decades of struggle, Poland had been reborn as a democratic republic. Piłsudski had triumphed, even though his powers as chief of state had been greatly curtailed by the passage of the March Constitution of 1921, through the machinations of the National Democrats (or "Endeks" a term derived from the initials ND), a nationalist, right-wing, antisemitic political party. Nevertheless, in repudiation of the Endeks' antisemitic program, in November 1922, a follower of Piłsudski's ideas, Gabriel Narutowicz, had been elected as the first president of independent Poland. A professor of engineering and a prominent left-wing member of the lower house of the Polish parliament, the *Sejm*, Narutowicz had won with the help of Jewish political parties, a great symbolic victory, even though the president was basically a figurehead, the real power resting with the *Sejm* and the prime minister.

Anything seemed possible now: Poland could find strength in its diverse, multicultural character. Three million Jews could be accepted as an important and constructive element in Polish society. Warsaw, this wonderful, vibrant city, by definitively choosing to be tolerant and cosmopolitan, could really take its place among the very greatest cities of the world, a blessing both for the Hurwiczes and for the nation as a whole.

To hasten this evolution, Adek got involved with the party that most strongly supported equal rights for minorities: the PPS. Of course, the most important point of the party platform was preserving an independent, democratic Republic of Poland. As a necessary underpinning, PPS advocated for freedom of press, speech and assembly. The platform also included "radical" economic proposals like progressive taxation, an eight-hour workday, equal wages for men and women, compensation for injury in the workplace, free public education, and banning child labor up to age 14.

As assimilated, non-religious, non-Zionist Jews, the Hurwicz family particularly appreciated the socialists' support for political, educational and social equity and inclusion for minorities. They also respected the courage it took to advance this policy; it was in fact the most contentious policy promoted by PPS.

Fear

The dark side of these high hopes was the ever-present possibility that threatening neighbors would prevail; that the idea that being Polish meant being Catholic would win the day; or that economic instability would bring the country to its knees, quite probably taking democracy and tolerance down with it.

After Narutowicz's election, there were mass demonstrations on the streets of Warsaw, largely organized by the Endeks. Their slogans: "Down with Narutowicz!" and "the Jewish choice."

All this lent a sense of urgency to the task of building a strong, tolerant, independent, united and prosperous Poland. From a young age, Leo absorbed that urgency on a cellular level.

CHAPTER 8

Crisis, Coup, Catastrophe

In December 1922, Gabriel Narutowicz was assassinated after only five days as president. Despite the fact that the president had little real power, the assassin claimed the deed was necessary to prevent Poland from falling under Jewish domination.

Those who were officially in power also had trouble enacting their legislative agendas due to constantly fluctuating coalitions within the parliament: during the five years (1921–1926) that the March Constitution was in effect, there were nine governments formed; the prime minister position passed among seven different political parties. Polish democracy was dysfunctional and often nearly paralyzed at a time when it needed to be nimble for the sake of defense, social progress and economic recovery.

Meanwhile, the external threat increased. In October 1925, France and Germany concluded a treaty fixing their borders but leaving the borders between Germany and Poland "open to revision." A non-aggression pact between Russia and Germany, signed in April of 1926, was also interpreted as freeing Germany to attack Poland at some point in the future. Significantly, Polish representatives were not invited to either of these meetings.

Even if the Hurwiczes had wanted to shelter young Leo from these anxious realities, ultimately that was not possible. The most dramatic example of this came on May 12, 1926, when eight-year-old Leo was in the student gardens by the Vistula. Gunfire erupted close at hand, and not just a few shots: an ongoing battle.

Zina, hearing the same sounds, waited anxiously for Leo to come running in the door. When he didn't, she went out into the street and hailed a taxi, which took her as far as the driver was willing to go towards the Vistula. When she arrived, on foot and breathless, at the gardens, Leo was nowhere to be seen.

Then it occurred to her: Adek's brother Stefan lived nearby. Rather than going home, Leo might have run to Stefan's apartment, which was closer. She rushed to Stefan's—and found Leo there. But the apartment hardly seemed a safe refuge.

There were piles of shiny glass fragments on the floor, and jagged fragments of glass hanging in the window frames: Stefan's windows had been shot out. Stefan was taping something over them and emphatically forbidding his little nephew to look outside.

Over the next few days, it emerged that an attempted coup d'état was in progress. In early May, Piłsudski had become convinced that the chaos of "sejmocracy" threatened the survival of the Republic, especially with the French-German and Russian-German treaties making it imperative to be ready to respond to aggression at a moment's notice.

A large contingent of the Polish military had more faith in Piłsudski as a leader than in the current system. He had gathered these troops and marched on Warsaw. He believed the government, not wanting to get into a violent confrontation with massive numbers of its own troops, would step down peacefully.

He was wrong.

After a couple of false starts, Piłsudski's troops crossed the Vistula on the Kierbedź Bridge (now replaced by the Śląsko-Dąbrowski Bridge) not half an hour's walk from the Hurwicz apartment, and quite close to the children's gardens. Piłsudski's contingent was fired on by troops loyal to the government. It was the ensuing battle that interrupted Leo's agricultural pursuits.

The fighting lasted several days, killing 215 soldiers and 164 civilians and wounding perhaps 900. In the end, the government, fearing a nationwide civil war, did step down.

Despite maintaining some of the superficial trappings of democracy, Piłsudski became for all intents and purposes a benevolent dictator. Just as he had hoped, his regime solved—at least temporarily—Poland's most difficult challenge: economic instability. The three years from 1927 through 1929 were relatively good years economically.

Beginning in the Fall of 1925, at the age of eight, Leo was enrolled in a progressive private school referred to as "Buki" after its founder, Felicja Buki. He remained there through the 1925/26 and 1926/27 school years.[1] It was co-educational, a rarity in Poland at the time. In addition, though attended and staffed mostly by Jews, it offered no Hebrew language or religious instruction: classes were conducted entirely in Polish. There were three instructors devoted to Polish, two to German, one to French, and another divided between French and philosophy. The school's main focus, however, was mathematics and natural sciences: there were three instructors in mathematics, and four in physics—more

[1]   Based on Leo's Admission Application to the LSE, September 8, 1938, in Leo's Postgraduate File at the LSE.

than any other discipline.[2] It also had an impressive faculty-to-student ratio: one teacher for every nine students in 1926.

For the academic year 1927, Leo moved to a private boys *liceum* (high school), Spójnia,[3] where he excelled in academics. When Henry started at Spójnia a few years later, he complained about having to try to live up to Leo's reputation. Though attended and staffed mostly by Jews, Spójnia conducted classes exclusively in Polish and was more assimilated, more "humanistic" and less focused on Jewish topics or culture than the Chinuch where Adek taught.[4] For instance, while Adek was listed as teaching Hebrew at Chinuch in 1926,[5] Spójnia had classes in German, French and Latin, but none in Hebrew. Where Chinuch taught Judaic studies specifically, Spójnia simply had a "religion" class. Spójnia also inculcated patriotism: at age ten, Leo's stellar performance in a patriotic play at school got his picture in a Warsaw newspaper.

At both Buki and Spójnia, staff and students also signed, in 1926, a Declaration of Admiration and Friendship for the United States, commemorating the 150th anniversary of the signing of the U.S. Declaration of Independence. This was not unusual: about five and a half million Poles—almost one sixth of the population—signed similar declarations at the time, expressing deepest admiration for American institutions, where "Liberty, Equality and Justice have found their highest expression and have become the guiding stars for all modern democracies."[6] Poles, who had regained their independence only a few years earlier, naturally felt a kinship with the Americans and their story of liberation from foreign oppression.

All this reflected the Hurwicz family hope that they, as proud Polish citizens of Jewish extraction, could help foster the rebirth of liberty, equality and justice in their home country.

Then came the great crash of 1929. Poland's economy, to an even greater extent than many others, was shaken by the catastrophe. Among twenty-two European nations, Poland was second only to Austria in the percentage of GDP lost in the early years of the depression: more than twenty percent from 1930–1933.

---

2   "Buki," https://www.leonidhurwicz.org/buki/
3   "Spójnia," https://www.leonidhurwicz.org/spojnia/
4   Henry Hurwicz, testimony for the USC Shoah Foundation Institute: https://collections. ushmm.org/search/catalog/vha47655
5   "Chinuch," https://www.leonidhurwicz.org/chinuch/
6   "Polish Declarations of Admiration and Friendship for the United States, 1926," https:// www.loc.gov/collections/polish-declarations/about-this-collection/

The Hurwicz family was comfortable financially. This was reflected, for example, in their ability to send Leo and Henry to private schools, which entailed significant fees. Nevertheless, like millions of others around the world, Leo came to think of himself as a child of the Great Depression, deeply affected by his awareness of the economic woes of his childhood and the political events they triggered.

CHAPTER 9

Astrophysics,
Chopin and Jazz

In June 1934, Leo graduated from Spójnia with *bardzo dobrze* ("very good") in every subject. He could have been accepted at any number of universities. At Adek's urging, in October, at age 17, alongside a throng of returning students, he walked through the ornate Grecian portals of the University of Warsaw, enrolled as a law student.

Leo was not all that interested in a career in law, but was drawn to the science of physics. In the interwar years, under the guidance of then-rector of UW Stefan Pieńkowski, the Physics department at the University of Warsaw also constructed world-class experimental physics laboratories for researchers, lecturers and students, particularly devoted to atomic and molecular optics and X-ray physics. Foreign scientists came to the university to investigate the phenomenon of photoluminescence under Pieńkowski, and the first international congress devoted to photoluminescence was held in Warsaw in 1936.[1] In courses at the Institute of Experimental Physics, Leo acquired a grasp not only of some advanced physics and mathematics, but also of the fundamental tools of statistical inference that made it possible to extract useful information from observed data and test theories by comparing predictions with new observations.

He also took an interest in astrophysics.[2] These were heady times in the universe: Einstein's general relativity was shaking the foundations of physics, with implications like the curvature of spacetime, dark matter, and the bending of light by gravity. It took inspired mathematical modeling and inference to plumb the depths of these mysteries.

---

1   Józef Hurwic, "The Polish Contribution to Mathematical and Physical Sciences in The Years 1918–1970," *Organon*, 1976/1977, Vol. 12/13, p. 265
2   Douglas Clement, "Intelligent Designer," *Minnesota Economics*, Fall 2006, Department of Economics, University of Minnesota College of Liberal Arts, p. 7.

Leo also seriously pursued mastery of the piano, reveling in the complex and subtle melodies and rhythms of the great classical and romantic composers, particularly Chopin, under the watchful eye and vigilant ear of Maria Klimont-Jacynowa at the Warsaw Conservatory.

His tastes, however, were not limited to high culture. The cafes of liberated Warsaw pulsed with tango, foxtrot, swing, waltz, Charleston and New Orleans jazz. As the reborn nation leapt into modernity with a joyful vengeance, Leo leapt with it—and danced with it. He particularly loved jazz/swing. This, of course, also gave him the opportunity to socialize with other young Polish hep-cats and cool chicks.

This was an extremely full life; it could be exhausting at times. It is said that Leo coped, in part, by learning to sleep standing up on streetcars without missing his stop. He couldn't have gotten much sleep on the trams, though: the University and the Conservatory were only about half a mile apart, and the apartment on Graniczna just a mile or so from both. He often just covered the short distances involved at a speed-walker's pace, literally racing to get an education.

Despite these varied pursuits, it was not until his second year of law school (1935/36) that he discovered the vocation that would allow him to respond constructively to the disruptive economic, social and political forces that had marked his formative years. He found his inspiration not in Chopin, nor in legal training, nor even in physics, but in a "political economy" course.

CHAPTER 10

Economics and Einstein

Over the course of academic year 1935/36, Leo attended Professor Antoni Kostanecki's economics and taxation seminar. Kostanecki—an economist widely respected, not only in Poland, but throughout Europe—was an adherent of the historical school of economics, which looked at economic systems in the context of history and culture, with a focus on the particulars of time and place. As such, he valued accurate and representative statistics; he had in fact been the president of the Polish Society of Economists and Statisticians (*Towarzystwa Ekonomistów i Statystyków*) from 1917 to 1928.

The historical school also believed in state-sponsored programs of social uplift for the working class, especially through education. In fact, because of this, and because many of them were academics, they were sometimes referred to as "armchair socialists" (German: *Kathedersozialisten*, literally "lectern socialists"). In addition, Kostanecki was specifically an adherent of the Younger German Historical School, which held that economists should be engaged in politics through designing tools for businesspeople and policymakers.

British economist John Maynard Keynes, and before him Polish economist Michał Kalecki, were suggesting that governments should stimulate employment through public works, even though in times of depression that would mean deficit spending. (Keynes garnered more attention largely because he took the precaution of publishing in English, whereas Kalecki preferred Polish and French.)

Meanwhile, in Poland and around the world—in England, Sweden, Norway and America—economists were increasingly applying the scientific method and high-powered mathematics to their problems. Leo was galvanized. There had been so much arguing and fighting, killing and dying, over economic issues—socialism, capitalism, free markets, central planning—based on ideals deeply felt but usually only vaguely defined. What if the socially and politically engaged mission that Kostanecki espoused were to be combined with an approach based on the hard science and mathematical tools that Leo was being trained in by Professor Pieńkowski and other world-class researchers at the Institute of Experimental Physics? Might some lucky economic scientist discover the X-Rays that would reveal the bones and muscles of market cycles? Or, to take a different analogy, all the economic records and statistics, past and present, might be treated as one vast series of astrophysical observations—and the time now come, finally, to determine what really circles around what in these galaxies. The difference being that, in the economic universe, humans could surely have some significant influence on the orbits, perhaps even keep planets from colliding. And what mysteries and controversies might be resolved when, one day, some genius sitting in a patent office—or a university office—pierced through to the $E = mc^2$ of the economic cosmos?

Perhaps the most heated and high-flown of these controversies was between two sets of dedicated idealists: socialists on the one hand and what were then called "classical liberals" (translation: "free-market fundamentalists") on the other. The argument had been going on for decades and had only gotten more heated and seemingly intractable.

CHAPTER 11

Socialist Calculation

When Leo was less than three years old, in January 1920, Austrian economist Ludwig von Mises published a famous article, "Economic Calculation in the Socialist Commonwealth,"[1] in which he reasoned that state ownership of all the means of production—the essential definition of socialism—eliminated rational decision-making about productive resources. With only one owner, Mises argued, there can be no meaningful exchange (buying and selling) of the means of production. Because economic exchange is the means by which value is calculated and resources allocated in complex economic systems, socialism eliminates the only practical means of making rational, economically based decisions about how to allocate, deploy, decommission, upgrade, or expand the various means of production in a large-scale modern economy.

Many, noting the conspicuous failures of the Bolshevik economic program, found Mises's argument quite convincing. In fact, Mises concluded that "[e]very step that takes us away from private ownership of the means of production and from the use of money also takes us away from rational economics." (The Bolsheviks had also envisaged a money-free economy.) Mises and other classical liberals insisted that a free market, unhindered by governmental meddling, was essential to economic efficiency.

Perhaps the most prominent counterargument was championed by Polish economist (and committed socialist) Oskar Lange. Lange's *On the Economic Theory of Socialism*, a two-part article published in late 1936 and early 1937 (and brought together in a book in 1938) suggested combining central planning with something at least imitating a free market. Lange believed this could match and perhaps improve upon the performance of the capitalist system. Thus was born "market socialism."

---

1   Ludwig Mises, "Die Wirtschaftsrechnung im sozialistischen Gemeinwesen," Archiv für Sozialwissenschaft und Sozialpolitik, Mohr, Vol. 47.1920/21, p. 86–121, https://mises.org/library/economic-calculation-socialist-commonwealth

In what became known as "Lange's model," a free market would be simulated via a dialog between a Central Planning Board (CPB) and producers, prior to any production taking place. The CPB would produce a schedule of hypothetical prices for produced goods; producers would indicate how much they would produce at that price. Thus, production would be managed via a market-like system, even though those managing the production facilities would not own the means of production.

Classical liberals such as Friedrich Hayek, a professor at the London School of Economics and one of the leading economic theorists in the world, objected that this required firms to know their production technologies and costs without necessarily ever having produced the items in question. Real-world competition was learn-as-you-go, he said, with firms learning about production technologies and costs by producing goods.

No one leapt to implement Lange's system. But then, had anyone implemented socialism as envisioned by Marx and Engels: a system free of coercive social relations and material scarcity, where people would work to fulfill their creative or humanitarian desires, rather than just to survive? Or, for that matter, the "perfect competition" model that underlay the liberal faith in free markets? That, too, represented a rather utopian ideal, a system in which people can switch jobs with no problem, firms can enter or exit the market without cost, all competing firms are selling the same product and cannot influence the market price of their product, where market share has no effect on costs or profits, where one can be assured that an optimal and stable equilibrium can be reached, where each economic agent is so tiny compared to the market as a whole that no single agent can have a meaningful effect on supply or demand, where economic agents cannot form coalitions and buyers have complete and perfect information about products and prices—past, present and future! For now, in the context of the socialist calculation debate, at least, both "socialism" and "free market" were abstractions, perhaps approachable but not attainable.

In November 1936, shortly after being elected president of the London Economic Club, which met at LSE, Hayek presented a lecture to the club titled "Economics and Knowledge," later published in the journal *Economica*.[2] The background for Hayek's analysis was General Equilibrium Theory (GET) as expounded by Léon Walras, who envisioned the market operating in the manner of an auctioneer announcing prices and available quantities. If there was more demand than available product at the announced price, the price would

---

2   F.A. Hayek, "Economics and Knowledge," *Economica*, February 1937, pp. 33–54.

go up until some of the buyers dropped out of the market. On the other hand, if there was excess supply, the price would go down, stimulating buying. An underlying assumption of GET was that participants had information such as prices, costs, and how to obtain and use various commodities. In reality, Hayek observed, such knowledge is dispersed among many people, with each person having only a portion of it, and some even having mistaken beliefs. This was Hayek's "knowledge problem."

In a sense, he didn't really think it was a problem: a free market, he believed, was uniquely fitted to efficiently and accurately share knowledge that was inherently private. Thus, where Mises focused on the market's role in establishing value, Hayek added to that a focus on its role as a communication system. Once people grasped this, he hoped, they would stop trying to fix something that wasn't broken. As he had written:

> It . . . is not necessary for the working of this system, that any-
> body should understand it. But people are not likely to let it work
> if they do not understand it.[3]

A critical glance at actual attempts to significantly curtail the free market—for instance, in the Soviet Union—did indeed seal the doom of socialism in the minds of many. On the other hand, the stubbornly lingering Great Depression was not a great advertisement for capitalism, either.

More importantly, perhaps, when it came to actually trying to solve problems using a scientific approach, how well did the assumed models of socialism or the free market approximate real governments or economies? How would one model Poland's complexities, for example?

Reflecting its history of partition, Russian Bolshevism vied with Austro-German social democracy. Right-wing Polish nationalists sought to reduce the influence of minorities. Left-wingers wanted to nationalize major industries. Peasants agitated for land reform. Workers demanded an eight-hour day and the right to strike, while industrialists looked for secure investments and often, finding none, left factories idle. Parliament considered nationalizing some businesses, but never did. By necessity, the government did immediately take over the railway system, which had previously been under the control of occupying forces; it was a system that had been designed for partition and largely lacked the connections needed for a unified Poland; in addition, it had been decimated by

---

3   Friedrich Hayek, *Collectivist Economic Planning*, Routledge & Kegan Paul LTD, 1963 reprint of the1935 original, pp. 7–8.

war, with many bridges blown up and tracks often in extremely poor condition, to the extent that it was not unusual for trains to have to proceed at 5km/hour.

The immediate result was political and economic chaos. This in turn led to the coup of 1926. Piłsudski, for the sake of stability and unity, tried to accommodate the various points of view. Though he had been a socialist, he did not attempt to force a socialist revolution. Private industry continued to function. At the same time, massive government projects assisted recovery from war and depression, and prepared the country for likely conflicts. There was some land reform, with large estates cut up into smaller parcels and distributed to landless peasants.

Amazingly, under Piłsudski's leadership, with no external loans or economic aid, Poland managed to recover from the massive destruction of the Great War and from the 1929 crash. Massive government four-year plans implemented projects such as the Gdynia seaport, which allowed Polish coal exports to bypass the port city of Gdańsk (which became increasingly subject to German aggression and boycott of Polish shipping from the early 30s); the 500-kilometer Polish Coal Trunk-Line carrying coal from Upper Silesia to Gdynia; and the central industrial district (*Centralny Okręg Przemysłowy*) encouraging industry in the heart of Poland, where it was least vulnerable to attack from hostile neighbors. Of course, one could argue that private firms would have done the job more efficiently. More likely, private enterprise would have been intimidated by both the sheer size of these projects, and the risks—such as the possibility of renewed hostilities inflicting recurring damage to ports, railways and industrial facilities.

In order to be truly useful, Leo reasoned, economic models had to take such complexities into account. He was determined to contribute to that enterprise. There were, however, two major factors militating against Leo achieving the influence he dreamed of: his caste (Jewish) and his politics (socialist). The most serious of these was caste.

CHAPTER 12

Brown Shirts and Ghetto Benches

In the middle and late 30s, when Leo was at college, antisemitism rose to new heights in Poland, and in the region as a whole. Hitler became Chancellor in Germany in 1933, and Nazification was proceeding apace, stripping Jews of their civil rights and legally barring them from holding positions in the civil service, and as doctors, lawyers and teachers. Boycotts of Jewish-owned businesses were encouraged, and books by Jewish authors were burned.

Especially after Piłsudski's death in May 1935, Poland tilted towards fascism. Anti-Jewish and National Socialist parties emerged in Poland advocating excluding Jews from political life, confining them to ghettos and eventually expelling them from the country. Violence against Jews became more common.

In the eyes of the nationalists and fascists, being Jewish had nothing to do with religious belief or practice: it was a race, a nationality, and a caste one was born into and remained in for life.[1] The Hurwicz family would have been glad to be accepted as loyal Poles of Jewish descent. They were ready to fight for their country against Germany and Russia. All this was irrelevant to the nationalists and fascists who were now coming to dominate Polish society.

The Hurwiczes did not particularly "look Jewish" (as it was perceived in Poland at that time) either in dress or in physical appearance: their features did not fit the Jewish stereotype. Adek was blond and blue-eyed; Henry was blond; Leo had dark blond hair. All this somewhat protected them from random street violence.

For instance, in 1937, when he was around 15, Henry came out of a Walt Disney movie on Marszałkowska Street to find "brown shirts" beating up Jews on the street. These were members of the violent, antisemitic Falanga National Radical

---

1   See Aleksander Hertz, *The Jews in Polish Culture*, translated by Richard Lourie, Northwestern University Press, 1988.

Camp political party (Polish: *Ruch Narodowo Radykalny-Falanga*. "Falanga" is Polish for "phalanx"). They did not recognize Henry as being Jewish, and he was not targeted.

Even before going to college, Leo could not escape similar experiences. Now, at university, he was much more engaged with the larger society—and much more exposed to its prejudices and dangers.

Professors at UW tended to be socially and politically conservative, as well as nationalistic. Jews were widely thought of as a national group (albeit without a state), and one likely to oppose Polish national interests. Even Professor Kostanecki—with whom Leo chose to work intensively over a period of three years (academic years '35-'36-'37), and who gave Leo a glowing recommendation—had signed on to a document in 1919, "The Polish Nation's Open Letter to the Allied Nations," which painted Jews as inevitably antagonistic to Polish interests. The "Open Letter" asked, for example:

> Do Allied governments place less trust in their own delegates, the English, American, French and Italian, than in the unavoidably biased and partisan Jews, Germans, Ukrainians and our other antagonists?[2]

The University of Warsaw was not as bad for Jews as some other institutions. In the late '30s, nationalist-radical student groups at the Main School of Commerce in Warsaw perpetrated brutal attacks that school authorities did not effectively act to curb.[3] The University of Warsaw and especially the leftist Free University experienced less antisemitism. Leo was never physically attacked on campus. But even at UW there was antisemitic harassment, an atmosphere of threat, and occasional incidents of violence against Jews.

In addition, he was directly affected by an attempt to segregate Jews in class at the University. The reason, or at least the excuse, for this attempt was that many if not most Jews would not donate corpses to the medical school, believing this was not allowed under Jewish law. Somehow this led to an attempt to seat Jewish students in a separate part of the classroom. Leo's *indeks* (student identity document) was stamped *Miejsce w ławkach nieparzystych* ("position in odd benches,"

---

2 *Free Poland: Devoted to the Presentation of the Cause of a United and Independent Poland to the American People*, Volume 6, October 16, 1919, Chicago, IL, published semi-monthly by the Polish National Council of America.

3 *A Discipline Divided: Polish Economists and the Communist Regime, 1945–1960* Aleksandra Witczak Haugstad (Doctoral thesis, 2008), p. 27.

i.e., seating in benches with an odd number) showing that he had permission to sit in lectures and classes, but only on odd number benches, which would be all on the left side of the room as seen from the lectern. In other places, this type of segregation (termed "ghetto benches") had turned out to be a prelude to violence against Jewish students. In response, Leo and other Jewish students did not sit down in class for a whole academic year: they stood in the back of the room, leaving the designated Jewish section empty. Some non-Jewish Poles, including some professors, stood in solidarity with Jews in cases like these. In March 1936, fifty Jewish students at the University of Warsaw were injured, two seriously, because they refused to sit in ghetto benches; the whole university was temporarily closed because of the incident.[4] In other towns, Jews were stabbed and died during this time of increasing terror. Eventually, the segregation attempt at UW was abandoned.

The ghetto bench policy was heroically opposed by some professors, tolerated by many, and actively supported by a few. One of the latter was Roman Rybarski, a Polish patriot who would later fight in the Polish underground under Nazi occupation and be executed in Auschwitz for organizing resistance among the prisoners. When Leo knew him, however, Rybarski was dean (*dziekan*) of the law school and professor of economics at the University of Warsaw. As such, Rybarski promoted "all-Polish education"—meaning, primarily, no Jews. He believed Jews could never be loyal to Poland. He also refused to sign the register (document verifying attendance) of any student who stood. This was serious: typically a student was only allowed to miss a certain number of lectures, after which, at the discretion of the professor, the student might not be allowed to finish the course, take the final exam, or get a grade.

Law student and chairman of the anti-ghetto committee, Gustaw-Szmuel Auscaler, who enrolled at UW in 1936, reported that "Professor Rybarski refused to give us the necessary signatures because we did not take seats in the benches assigned to us. For this reason we were unable to take exams. Professor Rybarski was a well-known Endek and therefore his position did not surprise us."[5]

---

4   Mary V. Seeman, "Cadavers for dissection," *Hektoen International Journal*, Winter 2016, https://hekint.org/2017/01/22/cadavers-for-dissection/. Accessed October 13, 2022.
5   Natalia Aleksiun, "Together but Apart: University Experience of Jewish Students in the Second Polish Republic," *Acta Poloniae Historica*, 109, 2014, p. 135, citing "Yad Vashem Archives (YVA), Testimonies O3, 1644, Dr. Gustaw-Szmuel Auscaler, 8. He was born in Warsaw, May 31, 1917. He graduated from Mikołaj Rej Gymnasium and enrolled at the Warsaw University to study law, ibid., 5." http://rcin.org.pl/Content/55755/WA303_75899_A295-APH-R-109_Aleksiun.pdf

Students had a great deal of freedom in choosing classes and therefore professors. Leo felt no discrimination from his professors.[6] Apparently, he took no classes with Professor Rybarski. Nevertheless, as dean, it was Rybarski who signed Leo's graduation certificate in 1938.

While antisemitism was certainly the main threat at the University of Warsaw, there was another reason why Polish academia may have looked inhospitable as a long-term home for Leo: his leftist leanings. Leo's socialist background would pose a problem if he sought employment in Polish academia, because any adherence to socialism—no matter how peaceful, democratic, gradual or loyal to Poland—constituted a serious impediment to academic career advancement in interwar Poland. As a result, in most institutions of higher learning, socialist faculty were few and far between.

As an example, in the early 1930s, Oskar Lange had his "habilitation" thesis, ("Statistical analysis of economic cycles," *Statystyczne badanie koniunktury gospodarczej*) which qualified him to hold a professorship in Poland, recognized by the Józef Mianowski Fund as the best academic work on economics in Poland. Later, he obtained a Rockefeller Foundation scholarship to study at Harvard and the University of California at Berkeley. He lectured at the University of Michigan; became a vice-director of the highly influential Cowles Commission for Research in Economics and editor-in-chief of *Econometrica*, the house organ of the Econometric Society and a leading journal for economic theory and theoretical econometrics; and finally became a professor at the University of Chicago, while turning down a professorship at UC Berkeley—both among the top economics departments in the United States.

At the same time, with the assistance of the Polish Ministry of Religious Denominations and Public Enlightenment, his career in Poland was stymied due to his leftist political views.

If Leo was unable to secure an academic post in Poland, could he fall back on lawyering? This, too, was looking less and less hopeful: in February 1937, the Polish legislature proposed a law for the "regulation of the structure of the legal profession," the main purpose of which was to make it much more difficult for Jews to be admitted to the bar, or even to become law clerks. This law went into effect in May 1938; Leo graduated on June 13.

---

6   "Leonid Hurwicz's Game," by Ann Bauer, *Twin Cities Business* magazine, March 1, 2008, quoted with permission from the author and *Twin Cities Business* magazine, and reproduced at https://www.leonidhurwicz.org/tcb/ with similar permission.

Meanwhile, Germany had begun expanding eastward, annexing Austria in March 1938, with Austrians outdoing even the Germans in their brutality towards Jews. (The more organized aspects of this brutality were orchestrated by soon-to-be-infamous Austrian, Adolf Eichmann.) At the same time, Germany demanded possession of German-speaking areas of Czechoslovakia.

Adek decided that Leo should get out of Poland.

Antisemitism made this not only prudent but also *possible*. Though a young man of his age normally could be drafted into the Polish infantry, high school graduates had to go to officers' school. Not wanting Jewish officers, the military authorities instead always counted Jewish high school graduates as "supernumeraries" or some other classification that ensured that they would not be drafted. As a result, after graduating, Leo was excused from serving in the Polish Army.

Accordingly, in early July, Leo began looking into the possibility of studying at the London School of Economics. The LSE was popular among Poles: Oskar Lange, who had studied there in 1929,[7] was just the most prominent among a number of economic theorists emerging in Poland during the 1930s, mathematically trained and conversant with Anglo-American economics. Most of them were connected with the London School of Economics.[8]

Leo wrote to the University Bureau of the British Empire:

> Having passed the final exams of the Law Faculty of the Joseph Pilsudski University in Warsaw (which gave me the right to the MAGISTER JURIS title), I should like to deepen my knowledge of ECONOMIC matters.
>
> I suppose the best school for that aim would be the London School of Economics.
>
> Therefore, I should be glad to get, if possible, following informations [sic]:

7   https://www.encyclopedia.com/social-sciences/applied-and-social-sciences-magazines/lange-oskar. Accessed October 15, 2022.

8   Tadeusz Kowalik, "Economics – Poland," in Max Kaase, Vera Sparschuh, Agnieszka Wenninger, Informationszentrum Sozialwissenschaften (eds.): *Three social science disciplines in Central and Eastern Europe: handbook on economics, political science and sociology (1989–2001)*. Berlin, 2002, 135–151. https://nbn-resolving.org/urn:nbn:de:0168-ssoar-278806. Accessed May 27, 2021.

(1) under which conditions may I obtain the Doctorate or the Diploma of London School or other school of the same kind?

(2) have I to passe [sic] any entrance exams?

(3) are there specially easier conditions for bearers of foreign (Polish) university degrees?

I thank in advance for all informations [sic].

Yours truly
(signed)[9]

Also in early July, Leo wrote to the Graduate Institute of International Studies in Geneva, asking about courses, costs, and whether his law degree from the University of Warsaw would qualify him to become a regular student. He quickly received a favorable reply.[10] Tuition: 100 Swiss francs per semester. The GIIS was closely associated with the League of Nations and, like the League itself, dedicated to international institution-building to resolve and avoid conflicts: an appealing mission for someone whose family and country had been repeatedly battered by war.

Nevertheless, the LSE was more prestigious and would give Leo stronger credentials for an academic career. The Graduate Institute was probably a "back up" in case the LSE didn't work out or the situation in London began looking too risky. For, just as Leo was making his plans, London was planning for war: the civilian population was being issued gas masks, primitive trenches were being dug in parks for "air raid precautions" and arrangements were being made for evacuating children from the city.

---

9   "The Postgraduate File of Leonid Hurwicz at the London School of Economics 1938–1939: A Summary," p. 2, by Jim Thomas, Research Associate, STICERD, London School of Economics, dated May 26, 2009, emailed to the author on Jan. 4, 2019.

10   July 5, 1938. https://www.leonidhurwicz.org/geneva-response-1938/

CHAPTER 13

Graduation Getaway

———

After Leo's inquiry to the LSE in early July 1938, there were a number of administrative delays, some resulting from LSE sending the wrong forms, and even more from Polish passport authorities in Warsaw requiring that Leo be accepted at LSE, as opposed to just having applied for admission. On September 26, after some discussion with a Mr. Dobryszycki in London, the LSE registrar, Miss E. V. Evans, sent Leo the documents required by the Polish authorities.[1] Finally, with Kostanecki's enthusiastic recommendation, Leo was admitted to LSE for the Michaelmas term starting in early October. However, LSE could not accept him as a PhD candidate without a personal interview. He was registered initially as an "Occasional Student" pending an interview after his arrival in London.

In the last two days of September, Hitler and Mussolini signed the Munich Agreement with France and England, giving Germany what it demanded in Czechoslovakia, and supposedly securing "peace for our time." The Munich Agreement cleared the way for Germany to march into Czechoslovakia's Sudetenland, the border areas that contained most of the Czech defensive infrastructure. The Czechs would now be helpless to resist if the Germans decided to overrun the rest of the country, which would in turn put Germany at Poland's door. In late September, the news was of Polish Army units moving to secure the Polish border with Czechoslovakia.

Under normal circumstances, Leo would have had an overnight trip from Warsaw to England: westward by train across Germany, through the Netherlands and Belgium to the northern tip of France, and finally by ferry across the English Channel. Since German policy at that point was still merely to (savagely) "encourage" Jewish emigration from Germany, the Hurwiczes could hope that, as long as Leo's passport and transit visa were in order, he wouldn't be affected by official German efforts to expel Jews. In fact, perhaps by going to England, Leo would only be doing what the Nazis wanted.

———

1   "Letter from LSE Registrar to Leo in Warsaw," https://www.leonidhurwicz.org/dobryszycki/

On the other hand, there were plenty of reasons not to be overly optimistic. Since 1933, when Hitler had taken power, the Hurwicz family had followed the news as the German government issued hundreds of decrees and regulations restricting the rights and activities of German Jews, and as businesses and properties owned by Jews were confiscated or sold at bargain prices under duress. They had watched as the campaign to force Jews to the fringes of society, both economically and socially, ramped up viciously during 1937 and 1938, with attacks intensifying throughout Eastern Europe on Jews, their property and businesses, cemeteries and synagogues.

Leo was supposed to be in London for the start of the Michaelmas term in October 1938. Adek and Zina watched and waited, imagining sending their 21-year-old son out alone through unfriendly and unstable territory—with a likely change of trains in Berlin.

As it happened, there was a less nerve-wracking alternative: from the Polish port of Gdynia on the Baltic Sea, less than 200 miles north of Warsaw by rail, the Polish steam merchant *S.S. Warszawa* sailed every week, leaving Poland on Friday and arriving in England the next Tuesday. There was a huge advantage to this slower, more circuitous means of travel: the ship plied a northerly arc, several hundred miles from the troubles to the south. Unless full scale war broke out, there was little chance of interference en route. Though the steamer would actually spend about eight hours in German waters as it passed from the Baltic to the North Sea through the Kiel Canal in far northern Germany, passengers would stay aboard the whole time, insulated from local populations and authorities. If war did break out and the canal became unavailable to Polish ships, there was a longer, still more northerly route that avoided Germany completely: up around the tip of Denmark, through the Kattegat Sea and Skagerrak Strait to the North Sea. (In 1939, as part of the famous *Kindertransport* operation, the *Warszawa* would carry Jewish children to safety in England, using these same routes.) The Hurwiczes booked Leo's passage on the *Warszawa* for an October 28 departure.

On October 27, the Nazis began rounding up thousands of Polish Jews living in Germany and forcibly transporting them across the border into Poland. Just one tiny Polish village, Zbąszyń, within a few miles of the track Leo would have traveled on had he gone west by train, saw an influx of around 8,000 Jews. These were part of a torrent of some 17,000 Polish Jews expelled from Germany over the course of the next few days. This "Polenaktion," as it was called, had been triggered by a new Polish law that threatened to invalidate the passports of these Polish Jews, which would frustrate Nazi plans to expel all Jews from

German-controlled territories. The Nazis were taking preemptive action while the passports were still valid.

Perhaps—even probably—all this would not affect a passenger on a train with a proper passport and transit visa. But there was no way for the Hurwicz family to know for sure. They were thankful that Leo would go far to the north before heading westward.

On the quay at Gdynia, along with hundreds of other passengers (many of them emigrating Jews), Leo boarded the *Warszawa* on October 28. He spent the next five days in relative comfort and safety aboard the little black packet ship, steaming first across the Baltic Sea; then through Kiel Canal, where giant swastika flags waved atop massive German warships; and finally across the North Sea and up the River Thames, arriving at the Port of London on November 1.[2]

---

2   The dates of his travel are established by his responses on Form J-7-17-39-1000, April 15, 1940, submitted to the American Consulate in Zurich, Switzerland. Leonid Hurwicz Papers, David M. Rubenstein Rare Book & Manuscript Library, Duke University, Box 23, File: Correspondence 11-21-1938 to 9-10-1940. It is also from these dates that the author has deduced that Leo took the *Warszawa*.

CHAPTER 14

Math, Models and Mechanisms

Leo was admitted to the UK "for the purpose of study only" under the conditions that he not accept any employment, paid or unpaid, and that he not remain beyond August 1, 1939.[1] As he could not finish the PhD is less than two years, he was counting on getting his visa extended when that time came.

Without much delay, Leo's initial "supervisor" (equivalent to "advisor" in an American university), Mr. P. Barrett Whale, interviewed him for admission into the economics PhD program. Despite what Leo himself described as rudimentary English skills, he handled himself well: Mr. Whale noted that young Leo impressed him "extremely favourably."[2]

Leo enrolled for five lecture courses and a seminar, taking classes at night as well as during the day.[3] Then he began, as he described it, "inhaling knowledge."[4]

There was no time to waste: with all the delays in the application process, he had missed the first four weeks of the nine-week Michaelmas term. He wanted to proceed as quickly as possible, since the world situation was precarious and capable of interrupting—violently interrupting—his studies.

On November 11, 1938, less than two weeks after Leo's arrival in London, the papers reported *Kristallnacht*, a two-day eruption of state-sponsored terror, looting, arson, and mass murder targeting Jews throughout Germany and Austria. The clouds of war grew darker as the U.S. recalled its ambassador. Other countries severed diplomatic relations with Germany. Hundreds of thousands of Jews fled Germany and Austria. The British Cabinet authorized the *Kindertransport*,

---

1   Leonid Hurwicz Papers, David M. Rubenstein Rare Book & Manuscript Library, Duke University, Box 23, Folder: lh academic docs 1930s-1940s 2.

2   Nov. 3, 1938, in "The Postgraduate File of Leonid Hurwicz at the London School of Economics 1938–1939: A Summary," p. 3, by Jim Thomas, Research Associate, STICERD, London School of Economics, dated May 26, 2009, emailed to the author on Jan. 6, 2019.

3   "Leo's LSE Classes," https://www.leonidhurwicz.org/lse-classes, based on Leo's LSE Postgraduate File and the LSE Calendar, 1938/39, at https://lse-atom.arkivum.net

4   Douglas Clement, "Intelligent Designer," *Minnesota Economics*, Fall 2006, Department of Economics, University of Minnesota College of Liberal Arts, p. 8.

allowing thousands of unaccompanied Jewish children into Britain. Still, the British public debated the merits of appeasing Hitler. Leo was unreservedly opposed: his family in Warsaw would likely be among Hitler's next victims if German expansionism was not stopped, and quickly.

When he focused on his studies—the world-class concentration of economics knowledge and passion that was LSE—Leo felt at home. Professors were, of course, of the highest caliber. Students, too, were world-class. The atmosphere was friendly, collegial, challenging and inspiring, both in and outside the lecture hall, with long discussions at all hours of the day and night, during meals, walks and weekends,[5] about socialism, liberalism, planning, business cycles, war, equilibrium, econometrics, oligopoly, monopoly, mathematics, modeling, mechanisms . . .

In January, around the beginning of Lent term, with Mr. Whale's recommendation, Leo was admitted to the PhD program with registration retroactive from October. Four out of five of his Michaelmas term courses carried through to Lent term, and he added six more. Ten simultaneous courses and a seminar!

It was February before he caught his breath enough to continue indulging his passion for the piano. Leo applied for use of the piano in the Founders' Room, noting that he had been a student at the State Academy of Music in Warsaw from 1935–38. As required by the university, he promised to play "serious music only, e.g., Beethoven, Mozart, Haydn, Schumann, Chopin."[6]

Leo also briefly encountered Oskar Lange at LSE. Lange, an associate professor at the University of Chicago at the time, had been in Poland from mid-March to early May, settling the affairs of his mother, who had died.[7] One imagines the two left-leaning Polish exiles conversing in their native tongue, no doubt delving into economic issues, and the problems and perils of their homeland, with the famous and significantly older Lange (35 at the time) proposing market socialism as at least one pattern for a prosperous society without big winners or losers. Lange concluded that Leo was "one of the ablest of the graduate students" he met at LSE.

Leo also attended the lectures of Friedrich Hayek, though he did not officially enroll in any of the illustrious professor's classes. If he had not already done so,

---

5   Nicholas Kaldor, "General introduction to Collected Economic Papers," in Kaldor, *Essays on Value and Distribution*, 2nd edn, Duckworth, 1980, p.xi.

6   Feb. 7, 1939, From Leonid Hurwicz [from 26 Lambolle Road, London NW3] to the Secretary, in "The Postgraduate File of Leonid Hurwicz at the London School of Economics 1938–1939: A Summary," p. 3, by Jim Thomas, Research Associate, STICERD, London School of Economics, dated May 26, 2009, emailed to the author on Jan. 6, 2019.

7   Lange biographer Jan Toporowski in an email to the author, January 7, 2019.

Leo now embraced Hayek's "knowledge problem," rejecting the assumption of market-omniscient economic agents (a key element of the "perfect competition" model) and substituting the more realistic assumption that people knew only what they directly experienced, such as market "signals" (local pricing and availability), or what they were told by other agents.

However, if Hayek succeeded in advocating for the knowledge problem, he failed spectacularly, in Leo's case, in his broader goal of inspiring a "hands-off" attitude towards markets. One reason may have been Hayek's own willingness to entertain some "hands-on" ideas such as state intervention to deal with public health threats, chronic unemployment and extreme poverty due to disability.[8] Hayek also favored a supranational authority, a world government which he hoped could create the conditions under which *laissez faire* could work at the national level—as well as possibly creating a framework within which the gold standard could be revived. At the same time, the supranational authority would offer a peaceful forum for addressing international economic problems that otherwise lead to war.

In this, Hayek followed Mises, who had written in 1927:

> The liberal . . . demands that the political organization of society be extended until it reaches its culmination in a world state that unites all nations on an equal basis. For this reason he sees the law of each nation as subordinate to international law, and that is why he demands supranational tribunals and administrative authorities to assure peace among nations in the same way that the judicial and executive organs within each country are charged with the maintenance of peace within its own territory.

Mises expressed the hope that from the "extremely inadequate beginnings" of the League of Nations, "a world superstate really deserving of the name may some day be able to develop that would be capable of assuring the nations the peace that they require."[9]

If even Mises and Hayek were not one hundred percent committed to a "tough it out" stance toward economic downturns, others had moved much farther

---

8   Friedrich Hayek, *The Road to Serfdom*, The University of Chicago Press, 1944.
9   Ludwig von Mises, *Liberalism: The Classical Tradition*, Foundation for Economic Education, 1996 (reprint of 1927 original), pp. 148, 150. https://mises.org/library/liberalism-classical-tradition/html/p/47. Accessed June 6, 2021.

toward an interventionist philosophy. Nicholas Kaldor, a lecturer and reader in economics at the LSE, and at one time a disciple of Hayek's, was a moderate socialist by the time Leo encountered him. The most prominent British economist at LSE, Lionel Robbins, though as recently as 1934 advocating solutions for depression such as rapid liquidation of unsound businesses and "reshuffling" the labor force (for example, from agriculture to other occupations)[10] had, by the time Leo arrived in London, realized that mass bankruptcy and unemployment (even when called "reshuffling") would be, as he later put it, "highly unpalatable as regards practical action."[11]

Leo and his classmates were in general moving even more quickly to the front lines of economic activism. Raised on grinding depression in the aftermath of horrific, pointless warfare, these young economists desperately aspired to become the architects of peace and prosperity. As a result, in thinking about intervening in the economy, they had to go well beyond just pointing out difficulties and pitfalls, and look for practical ways to address them. There were so many moving—or stalled, or broken—parts: the economic system itself, institutions and organizations, people, their expectations and communications, the things they could change, the things they couldn't, the policymakers' goals—all to be modeled objectively, scientifically, mathematically, and in ways that suggested realistic solutions!

Leo took a particular interest in the socialist calculation debate. How might it be approached in a more objective manner? There was something particularly unsatisfying about ideologues who already knew the "right" answer (whether it be socialism or free markets) advancing arguments proving that they had been right all along.

Much of the education Leo received at LSE had to do with "market failures," situations in which the simplifying assumptions of "perfect competition" do not hold up, and therefore the "invisible hand" of the market may need a helping hand. Kaldor's "Theory of Production" course explored industries that tend towards monopoly, potentially giving one company, or a small coalition, massive influence over prices. Roy Allen's course took a deeper mathematical plunge into the same waters that Kaldor was navigating. Joan Robinson's *The Economics of Imperfect Competition* was on the reading list for both courses, as was Edward Chamberlin's *The Theory of Monopolistic Competition*. (Aside: Władysław Marian Zawadzki's book on mathematics for political economy was also on Allen's

10   Lionel Robbins, *The Great Depression*, Macmillan, 1934.
11   Lionel Robbins, *Autobiography of an Economist*, Macmillan, 1971.

recommended list, confirming Poland's contribution to these intellectual currents.) Kaldor's course on "Public Finance and the Trade Cycle" covered "the question of state stimulation of employment by budgetary deficit, the creation of public works and subsidies"[12]—the core of the Keynesian prescription for recovery from the depression.

In "Economic Theory (Statics and Dynamics)" Kaldor looked beyond processes that reach a stable (static) equilibrium to consider those that might seesaw up and down periodically in a way that is nevertheless understandable and predictable. The reading included Kaldor's "A Classificatory Note on the Determinateness of Equilibrium" (1934), in which he gave the example of a "cobweb" process triggered by a bad harvest, leading to high prices for a particular crop, which in turn caused farmers to plant more of that crop the next season, leading to a surplus at the next harvest, depressing prices and causing farmers to plant less of the crop, and so on. If demand was more elastic (volatile/reactive) than supply, then demand would flexibly adjust to supply, and prices would not change much when supply changed; producers, reacting to smaller price changes, would adjust quantities less and less in each growing season, and both prices and quantities would converge over time, as in Figure 1 below. If supply and demand were equally elastic (i.e., if farmers increased and decreased production exactly in proportion to prices, and prices adjusted exactly in proportion to production), then the process would go around and around endlessly. On the other hand, if demand was inelastic, people would be willing to pay higher prices when supply was low, but would not increase consumption in proportion to falling prices. In that case, farmers would change prices out of proportion to changes in crop yield (to profit in times of low supply and dump their surplus in times of oversupply), and the cobweb would theoretically spiral ever outward.

Here was yet another universe of possibilities for Leo to consider—and perhaps a pattern suggesting counter-cyclical intervention by the government, moderating price swings by buying when there was excess supply and selling when there was excess demand.

---

12   LSE Calendar 1938/39, p. 120, https://lse-atom.arkivum.net

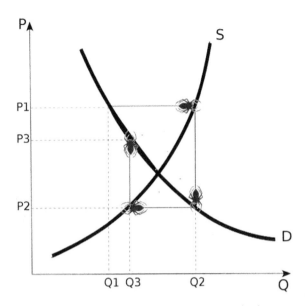

Figure 1. In the upper left, price is high (P1), because supply is low (Q1). In the upper right, quantity has gone up (Q2) to take advantage of the high price (P1). In the lower right, the increased supply (Q2) drives down the price (P2). In the lower left, the lower price (P2) depresses supply (Q3). In the upper left, reduced supply (Q3) raises prices (P3). Because in this example demand is more elastic than supply at the equilibrium point (where the two lines cross), the "cobweb" converges.[13]

One did wonder whether in reality the insanity would stop when the farmers realized what was happening. Observing the pattern of alternating oversupply/undersupply, might not one clever farmer start planting more in years of over-supply to take advantage of the next year's excess demand, and less in years of undersupply in order to avoid having to sell during the next year's glut? As long as it was pursued by a limited number of suppliers, such countercyclical activity would tend to moderate swings. If pursued too widely and enthusiastically, it could actually intensify and prolong the oscillations. Such expectations and conjectures about competitors' strategies, however, didn't hold much hope for building more reliable models. They seemed like a wild card, and Kaldor and others could not find a comfortable place for them in their theories. Still, given the fundamental importance of competitive strategy in a market economy, it was troubling to feel limited to a framework that treated it as an afterthought.

---

13   Figure adapted from https://en.wikipedia.org/wiki/Cobweb_model. Creative Commons license.

CHAPTER 15

Government Intervention

The 1939 academic year was drawing to a close, and Leo's degree looked within reach. He had more or less completed two years of classes in one year. Continuing on the current track, he would be able to present his thesis in June 1940. There would then be an oral exam on the thesis and, if successful, he would have a PhD in economics from the London School of Economics. Just one more year.

However, while Leo was engrossed in his studies, moving as fast as he was able toward a PhD, and pondering the advantages and difficulties of government intervention . . .

Governments were about to intervene.

In the late spring of 1939, as the academic year was ending, Leo asked the British to extend his visa beyond August 1. They said he had to have his passport renewed; then they could extend his visa.

The Polish authorities would not extend his passport.[1] Perhaps Leo was supposed to come back to serve in the Polish army: with war looming, the policy of discriminating against educated Jews in the military had been relaxed.

He tried to get the British to permit him to stay a little longer. They said that was "not their custom." He had encountered the phrase before and knew that "not our custom" meant "if you stand on your head, they won't do it."[2]

No official document in Leo's LSE file mentions any visa or passport problems. Instead there are a number of "This Is To Certify" documents (TITCs) relating to a summer trip to France and Switzerland to collect information for his thesis on currency devaluation. This was perhaps the truth—but certainly not the whole truth.

Meanwhile, as Leo prepared to depart, England prepared for war: by July 25, LSE Director Sir Alexander Carr-Saunders had arranged with the Ministry of

---

1   Videotaped interview with author, 2007. Appendix E. Also https://www.leonidhurwicz.
    org/interview/
2   Ibid.

Works to take over the LSE buildings on Houghton Street in the event of war, while most LSE classes would move to Cambridge.

A handwritten note on the last TITC from LSE indicates that it was handed to Leo on July 31, 1939. He also had with him a letter of introduction, dated the same day, from the French embassy in London, asking librarians and archivists to help him with his research. Obtaining transit visas through France and Switzerland, Leo left London on August 2 and arrived in Paris the same day. His passport was close to expiring, and he was pretending to be returning to Poland, though he actually had no intention of doing so.

On August 23, Russia and Germany signed the Ribbentrop-Molotov non-aggression pact. Leo immediately recognized that war might break out at any moment, because the Germans, no longer having to worry about the Eastern Front with Russia, were now free to move their forces to the Western Front: the Netherlands, Belgium, Luxembourg, and ultimately France.

France was allied with Poland and England, and therefore against Germany. Switzerland, on the other hand, had maintained official neutrality and should be safe. The evening of Friday, August 25, he left Paris. He stepped off the train in Bern on Saturday.

On the overnight trip, to reduce visibility to possible enemies, there were only dim blue lights in the train. With no bright lights that he could read by, Leo had plenty of time to worry: about economics, about the world, about himself, about his family.

CHAPTER 16

A Lifeline

Bern, September 1. Having just ordered breakfast, Leo stepped over to a nearby newsstand to get a newspaper. They were sold out.[1] Rushing back to the restaurant, he borrowed a paper from a man sitting across the table from him. The headline screamed: WARSCHAU BOMBARDIERT.

The Germans were bombing Warsaw (as well as a number of other Polish cities and Vilnius). Ulica Graniczna had been almost entirely destroyed by bombs.[2] The German high command claimed that German troops had crossed the frontier, and that the German Navy had taken over the Baltic and "liberated" Danzig (Gdańsk) and Gdynia, Poland's only seaports. The French and British parliaments would meet later in the day: general mobilization was expected. The Poles claimed that Polish anti-aircraft artillery and the Polish *Brygada Pościgowa* (Pursuit Brigade) were shooting Luftwaffe bombers out of the sky.

Leo quickly sent his family a telegram (probably through the Polish embassy in Bern) saying he was coming home. Since this is what he was officially supposed to be doing, this message would be acceptable to various authorities, such as the Polish consul. It would pass any censorship that was in place and would let his family know where he was and that he was okay. Hopefully they would understand that he would do everything in his power not to actually come home.

That night, lying awake in the *Jugendherberge* (Youth Hostel) dormitory, amid the tosses, turns and snores of twenty or so other budget-conscious guests, Leo considered his immediate future. His family, if they were able to respond, would presumably send their message to Bern, so that was reason to stay there for the time being. He looked forward to moving on to Geneva, where hopefully the positive reply he had received from the Graduate Institute of International

---

1   "Hurwicz Family Stories: My Grandpa Leo's Story," by Leo's granddaughter, Lara Markovitz, based on her interview with Leo.

2   March 3, 1940, in "The Postgraduate File of Leonid Hurwicz at the London School of Economics 1938–1939: A Summary," p. 7, by Jim Thomas, Research Associate, STICERD, London School of Economics, dated May 26, 2009, emailed to the author on Jan. 6, 2019.

Studies back in July of '38 would still be valid—and where the population spoke standard French. He didn't feel motivated to master the Swiss-German dialect spoken in Bern, which would not be of use anywhere else in the world. In fact, even people in neighboring valleys in the Bern region had different dialects and may well not have been able to understand each other. On a positive note, he was told they clung to these dialects in part because avoiding the literary "High German" separated them from the German Nazis.

In Geneva, he would encounter Professor Ludwig von Mises, champion of free markets and *laissez faire* capitalism, and still an influential economic thinker, even if that influence was waning. To be able to have exchanges with him would no doubt be interesting.

Ultimately, Leo really needed to get out of Europe. Even Switzerland wasn't safe, with Germany to the north and Italy to the south. The United States would be ideal. However, the U.S. had quotas in place that made immigration problematic. It helped a lot to have a sponsor, preferably a relative, who had the means to support you, ensuring you would not become a burden on the public.

Morris' widow, Helen Kotzin (Aunt Helen) and her four sons—Sol, Ted, Adek and Bernard—were now in Chicago, having moved there from Canada in 1923.[3] But Leo didn't know if he should try to contact them. There was that old feud between the brothers, Max and Morris. Morris had extended the ban to Max's wife, Sara Lea. Perhaps it would extend to the whole Hurwicz family, including Leo? As far as Leo knew, the families had been out of touch for twenty years.

On the other hand, both brothers had passed away in 1927, and Sara Lea in Moscow in 1935. So, in 1939, could there be reason to hope that old grudges, too, might have passed away?

The next day, September 2, Leo got a telegram from his father, telling him the family was okay (though Leo suspected this was a bit of a simplification, with the Germans bombing Warsaw) and giving the address of the Kotzins in Chicago: 3605 Dickens Avenue.[4] From this, he knew it was okay to contact them.

He had a lifeline.

For the more immediate future, he had the address of the Beaulieu *Auberge de la Jeunesse* (Youth Hostel) in Geneva.

---

3   Katarzyna Kasia Kacprzak, "Kotzin Genealogy," https://www.leonidhurwicz.org/wp-content/uploads/2020/08/Kocyn_research_report_2018_07_10.pdf
4   Videotaped interview with author, 2007. Appendix E. Also https://www.leonidhurwicz.org/interview/

CHAPTER 17

Hurwiczes on the Run

On September 26, Adolph "Adek" Kotzin (Aunt Helen's son) wrote from Chicago saying that he was enclosing an affidavit and papers "which should enable you to obtain a satisfactory hearing from Our Consul in Switzerland." He added, "Everybody is looking forward with great pleasure to your speedy arrival and asked me to send you their love."

Adolph said it had taken him a little more time to get the papers ready than expected, but that he had been careful to get all the details correct. He concluded with, "If you should need anything at all, do not hesitate to let us know. Your loving cousin, Adolph."[1]

It turned out that the sisters, Helen and Sara Lea, had continued secretly corresponding with each other all along. The Chicago Kotzins held no grudge. Far from it. He was family. They would do everything they could to help him.

A subsequent letter dated October 24 illustrates the hoops the Kotzins jumped through:

> Dear Loluś:
>
> Your letter of October 10th was received yesterday, and we are accordingly mailing to you affidavit for the Swiss authorities; also certified copy of income tax return and photostatic copies of checks showing payment to the Internal Revenue Department of the United States.
>
> Undoubtedly, you received affidavit with other letters showing the amount of money deposited to my credit in the National Security Bank of Chicago, which was mailed to you on the

---

1   Letter from Adolph Kotzin to Hurwicz, 09/26/1939; Leonid Hurwicz Papers, David M. Rubenstein Rare Book & Manuscript Library, Duke University. https://www.leonidhurwicz.org/letter-from-adek-kotzin-sept-1939/

26th of September by registered mail, and you have one or two copies left which you could also present to the Swiss authorities.

Needless to say, we are all very much interested in you and most anxious to hear whether you received my papers, and what success you had with them at the American Consulate.

We made inquiries at the "Hias"[2] and they said that the papers we sent you should be entirely satisfactory and sufficient. However, if the American Consulate should demand anything more, cable us and we will send it to you without any further delay.

I am in a hurry to send the papers to you today, in view of the fact that the mail for the Clipper closes this afternoon.

Therefore will close this letter with regards and love from everybody.

Yours,
Adek

The "Clipper" refers to Pan American Airways' Yankee Clipper, a Boeing 314 Clipper flying boat, which carried airmail from Port Washington, New York, across the Atlantic. While Leo's letter had taken almost two weeks to reach the Kotzins, the Clipper would get the reply to Leo in a matter of a few days. This service had only begun on May 20, 1939.

On October 27, Adek Kotzin wrote again, enclosing an affidavit to the Swiss authorities guaranteeing a remittance of $75 monthly for Leo's maintenance, and reiterating that they all hoped that Leo would be successful in obtaining the visa, were "anxiously awaiting to hear" that he was on his way to the United States, and once again sending "love and best regards from everybody." The fact that this affidavit was for the Swiss authorities suggests that the Kotzins paid Leo's tuition at the Graduate Institute of International Studies, where Leo spent the academic year of September '39 to June '40 as a doctoral student in political science, specializing in international studies.

Leo also wrote to Oskar Lange at the University of Chicago. Lange responded on November 1, promising to help, asking for news about members of the PPS and the Bund, and requesting copies of socialist publications expressing

---

2   The "Hias" was originally founded as the Hebrew Immigrant Aid Society in 1881, but eventually became known simply as HIAS.

attitudes towards the war.[3] He also included this statement, on University of Chicago Department of Economics letterhead:[4]

> November 1, 1939
>
> To Whom it may Concern:
>
> I understand that Mr. Leonid Hurwicz is applying for a visa of entry into the United States. I know Mr. Hurwicz personally, and appreciate his intellectual and scholarly qualities. I am sure that he would qualify as a first rate graduate student at the University of Chicago, as well as any other American university.
>
> (Signed)
> Oskar Lange
> Associate Professor of Economics

The reference to knowing Leo personally no doubt reflects their meeting at LSE.

On November 25, 1939, Adek Kotzin once again wrote from Chicago, updating Leo on events relating to Leo's quest for a visa: the State Department had contacted Adek for some more information, and he had managed to get the governor of Illinois to write asking the American Consul in Geneva to expedite the visa.

In addition, Adek Kotzin had a favor to ask. His wife Leah's father, Nachum Lewartowicz, was living in Ostrów-Mazowiecka, then under German occupation. The Kotzins in America had not heard from Nachum since the war began. Adek asked Leo to try to contact Nachum and find out how he was doing.

Adek was hopeful that Leo could correspond with Nachum, because Leo had recently had news of his family in Poland. In fact, perhaps initially through messages carried by the Red Cross,[5] Leo had received some wonderful news about his family: they had somehow managed to get to the Russian-occupied zone of Poland. They were in Białystok—or "Belastok" according to the occupying Russians—a city with a large Jewish population.

It seemed like a dream. For one thing, the Poles had mobilized every male between 16 and 60; why were Adek and Henry not in uniform? Or perhaps lying

---

3   Lange biographer Jan Toporowski in an email to the author, January 7, 2019
4   "Oskar Lange," https://www.leonidhurwicz.org/oskar-lange/
5   Leonid Hurwicz Papers, David M. Rubenstein Rare Book & Manuscript Library, Duke University, Folder: correspondence_1938_Nov 21-10_Sept_1940_1; "Red Cross Letters," https://www.leonidhurwicz.org/red-cross-letters/

by the side of the road somewhere on the outskirts of Warsaw, blown to shreds by a German bomb? Even given that they had somehow survived, how had they managed to cross the Bug River, thus escaping from the Nazi-controlled part of Poland? Crossing would be forbidden. One would expect armed troops patrolling both banks, Wehrmacht on the west and Soviet Red Army on the east. And yet, somehow . . .

In Białystok, his family was presumably safe from the current German onslaught. Still, Leo worried about them, especially as winter closed in. In late December, a vicious cold wave hit everywhere from England to northern Germany and Poland, even up into Russia and Lithuania. Białystok, north of Warsaw, was bitterly cold. Did the family have funds for fuel and food? What was available? With the war, there would be shortages of everything, including basics like bread, flour, milk and sugar.

But then, did his family really intend to stay in Białystok? They couldn't mention it in writing, of course—the border crossing would be illegal—but perhaps they planned to continue north to Vilnius, Lithuania. Lithuania had been under Polish control since the end of World War I, but the Soviets had now granted control over Vilnius and the surrounding region to Lithuania. Although still very much under Soviet influence, Lithuania was now officially a neutral, non-Soviet country from which it might be possible to emigrate.

In Białystok, the family had already covered two-thirds of the distance from Warsaw to Lithuania. They were perhaps only 50 or 60 miles from the Lithuanian border. If caught trying to cross over, they could end up in prison—or worse. If successful, they could end up in Israel or the United States.

CHAPTER 18

An Intellectual Warrior
at the School for Peace

By late September, Leo had enrolled at the Graduate Institute of International Studies and moved into a room at 85 Rue de Montbrillant, chez Mme. Roch. The Institute was a fifteen-minute walk away, near the shore of Lake Geneva.

Although overall Leo found LSE a richer and more stimulating intellectual environment, there was one major advantage to being in Geneva: access to the "raw materials" of economic research, such as statistics relating to various countries, was unparalleled, due the presence of libraries maintained by the League of Nations, the International Labor Organization (ILO) and the GIIS.[1]

On the other hand, the GIIS was more career-oriented than LSE. In large part because of its location, but also because of its close association with the League of Nations, the GIIS attracted students planning careers in International Relations—certainly in its economic aspects, but equally in the social and political spheres. The Institute was especially attractive for students who needed both a degree and work experience: they could take classes from some of the most respected names in IR and economics, while at the same time interning with the League or one of the many international and non-governmental organizations in Geneva, such as the ILO, the International Bureau of Education, or the Women's International League for Peace and Freedom.

The hands-on tendency of the GIIS did not suit Leo as well as the more purely academic orientation at LSE. He confided in a letter to an LSE official that the conditions for "scientific work" in Geneva were "hardly comparable" to those at LSE, noting in particular that students did not tend to keep up with the latest

---

1   Letter from Leonid Hurwicz, Geneva, 85 rue de Montbrillant, to "Miss Ryder," i.e. Miss E. M. Ryder, Assistant Registrar at LSE, Mar. 3, 1940, in Leo's Postgraduate File at the London School of Economics

developments in economics in any systematic fashion, and contributed less in class.[2]

"The professors," he wrote, "are, of course, very good specialists (we have Prof. von Mises, Prof. Rappard and Mr. W. Roepke), but there are few students who make any serious contribution to the Seminar discussion. Moreover, the habit of reading new (or even old) publications is not very widespread. Therefore, the contact with the main currents of economic thought is rather superficial and not systematic."

At the same time, he understood that the LSE he had known was now an early victim of the war: students and faculty in large numbers had interrupted their academic pursuits to support the war effort. For the remainder, only greatly reduced night classes continued in London; daytime operations had moved to Cambridge in order to escape expected bombings.

On the positive side, Leo could still obtain a PhD at GIIS by the end of the year, if he could complete his thesis. Ludwig von Mises was Leo's advisor. Leo also attended Mises' seminars. He took advantage of this opportunity to argue against Mises' doctrinaire liberal assertions.

Another professor at the Institute, Wilhelm Roepke, offered similar opportunities to do battle concerning planning, mathematics and statistics. Leo participated in Roepke's seminar on "Economic Stabilization and Other Problems of Economic Policy" during the summer session. Though Roepke knowledgeably and insightfully discussed economic cycles and trends, shocks, crises, equilibrium, over-production, under-consumption, inflation, deflation, investment, savings, etc., he was absolutely opposed to using well-established mathematical and statistical techniques from the natural sciences to express, investigate and reveal the relationships among the many variables involved. He would say this was clear and that was obvious, and there were certainly numbers involved, but somehow it never got the point of a model which could be validated (or invalidated) by testing its predictions against real-world data. What were the essential variables in the equation? What were economic planners actually trying to stabilize? Employment/unemployment? Gross national product? And how to state the goal in measurable terms?

The Graduate Institute was far from being an indoctrination center for the Austrian school, or any other ideology. Better understood as the academic extension of the League of Nations, the Institute was founded as a school for international cooperation and peace. The founders, Paul Mantoux and William

2   Ibid.

E. Rappard, were both senior officials in the League. The core mission of Institute was to work out a scientific basis for the study of peace and the avoidance of war, especially through the design and implementation of better mechanisms for international relations.[3]

Liberals hoped that one aspect of ensuring peace would be ensuring a free market on the international level. Around the time Leo arrived in Switzerland, Hayek published an essay promoting an international federation that would encompass the political, legal and economic spheres:

> It is rightly regarded as one of the great advantages of interstate federation that it would do away with the impediments as to the movement of men, goods, and capital between the states and that it would render possible the creation of common rules of law, a uniform monetary system, and common control of communications. The material benefits that would spring from the creation of so large an economic area can hardly be overestimated, and it appears to be taken for granted that economic union and political union would be combined as a matter of course.[4]

Such ideas would also have come up in the seminars Leo took with Mises: "International Monetary Relations" and "Problems of International Finances" (in the winter semester 1939/40), and "International Monetary Problems" and "Contemporary Political Thought and International Economic Cooperation" (in the summer semester, probably starting in February 1940).[5]

Leo spent only about three hours a week in class with the icon of Austrian economics, out of a total of 13 class hours per week in the winter semester and 11 hours per week in the summer. In both semesters, Leo spent two hours a week with William Rappard considering *questions économiques internationales contemporaines*. Rappard was both a friend and an admirer of Mises. However, he challenged Mises' absolute opposition to state intervention in the economy.

---

3   "Rappard was also convinced of the need for studying peace—like war with its own strategy—in order to safeguard it . . . The Institute, directed by Rappard from 1928 to 1955, was to work out a scientific basis for the avoidance of war, and to encourage the study of international relations and institutions."

   Ania Peter, *The League of Nations in retrospect, a colloquium held November 6–9, 1980*, United Nations Library, Geneva: Series E, Guides and Studies, pp. 221–222.

4   "The Economic Conditions of Interstate Federalism," *New Commonwealth Quarterly*, V, No. 2 (September 1939), 131–49.

5   Based on class schedules from the archives of the Graduate Institute, https://www.leonid-hurwicz.org/giis/

Mises' argument assumed that most people will always want to improve their material well-being, and that overall improvement is equal to the sum of individual improvements. The logical conclusion was that maximal overall social welfare would result if people were simply left free to seek their own individual welfare—especially given that each individual is more familiar with his or her own situation and preferences than anyone else can be, and therefore more able to make sound, fact-based decisions.

Rappard questioned Mises' assumption that individuals primarily maximize material gain: "Does the British voter, for instance, favor confiscatory taxation of large incomes primarily in the hope that it will redound to his material advantage, or in the certainty that it tends to reduce unwelcome and irritating social inequalities? In general, is the urge towards equality in our modern democracies not often stronger than the desire to improve one's material lot?"[6]

Leo, of course, knew from his time at LSE that there were a number of assumptions underlying the idea that individuals or firms seeking to maximize their own profit would necessarily lead to maximized overall profit. And he knew that these assumptions by no means held universally. Again, this provided ample opportunity to engage in spirited discussions with Mises and other liberal-minded professors such as Roepke.

Mises was also theoretically opposed to tariffs of any kind, because they prevented individuals from making exchanges that they desired to make based on their perception of their own welfare. He reasoned, therefore, that such tariffs would, by limiting individuals' ability to pursue their own welfare, reduce overall welfare.

Rappard brought up the counterexample of Switzerland's tariffs on agricultural products:

> My country, in which farmers represent less than 20 per cent of the population, has in the course of the last generations repeatedly favored this small and dwindling minority by protectionist measures on corn, dairy products, and wine. The urban industrial and commercial majority have done so, neither in what would obviously be an absurd belief that they were thereby increasing their real income, nor out of what would be a no less absurd desire to hurt foreign producers. Quite deliberately and

---

6   "On Reading von Mises," in Mary Sennholz, *On Freedom and Free Enterprise: Essays in Honor of Ludwig von Mises*, Princeton, N.J., D. van Nostrand, 1956, p. 17. Reprinted by the Foundation for Economic Education, 1994. pp. 32–33.

expressly, political parties have sacrificed the immediate material welfare of their members in order to prevent, or at least
somewhat to retard, the complete industrialization of the country. A more agricultural Switzerland, though poorer, such is the
dominant wish of the Swiss people today. It may be dismissed as
a myth or a dream. In fact it is a somewhat costly, but a sincerely
professed national ideal of a real democracy.[7]

Mises likewise opposed union activity or labor legislation for purposes such
as guaranteeing the right to collective bargaining, or a minimum wage, limited
working hours, legally imposed safe working conditions, or the elimination of
child labor. He argued that such measures would result in unintended negative
side-effects such as unemployment and that an unhampered market economy
would result in better overall conditions, and thus better conditions for both
workers and employers.

Rappard, on the other hand, would go on to represent Switzerland at the
ILO, which promoted collective bargaining, standards for minimum wages
and worker safety, limitations on hours of work, and elimination of child labor.
(In 1977, the ILO building in Geneva would be rechristened *Centre William
Rappard*.) Fundamental values of international cooperation, peace, democracy
and individual freedom united Mises and Rappard, despite sharp divergences in
economic theory and strategy.

In the summer semester, Leo took a course on the League of Nations, taught
by an American, Pitman B. Potter, formerly a professor at the University of
Wisconsin. The League, though it would continue to exist on paper until 1946,
had been functionally suspended a few months earlier, in December of 1939.
Even before that, in July 1938, Professor Potter was publishing articles like,
"League Publicity: Cause or Effect of League Failure?"[8] Perhaps, in addition to
the content of the class, which must have been a bit depressing, Leo wanted to
tune his ear to an American accent?

Economists associated with the League, but not the Institute, also gave seminars which Leo was able to attend. Here, he would have been exposed to a wide
variety of economic thinking, much of it left-leaning. One such seminar, for
instance, was given by James Meade, Ragnar Nurkse and Tjalling Koopmans,

---

7   Ibid., p. 33.
8   Pitman B. Potter, "League Publicity: Cause or Effect of League Failure?," *Public Opinion
     Quarterly*, Volume 2, Issue 3, July 1, 1938, pp. 399–412

all of whom were employed by the League at the time.[9] Meade was a British economist with a strong egalitarian ethic, a Fabian Socialist in his youth, later belonging to the Social Democratic Party, but still a believer in free markets. In 1948, he wrote a book, *Planning and the Price Mechanism*, with the subtitle, "The Liberal—Socialist Solution."[10] This was "liberal" in the European sense of the word. So for American readers, Meade's subtitle might have the flavor of "The Libertarian—Communist Solution." Nurkse went on to distinguish himself in development economics, the study of how poor nations can be helped to escape a vicious cycle of poverty. Koopmans, born in the Netherlands, had followed an intellectual path somewhat parallel with Leo's: he had studied mathematics, switched to theoretical physics in 1930, and finally in 1934 decided to pursue mathematical economics, under the influence of Dutch economist Jan Tinbergen, a leader in this emerging field.[11] Thus, Koopmans was on the scene in the infancy of econometrics, the branch of economics concerned with the use of mathematical methods, especially statistics, in describing economic systems.

Meanwhile, as Leo was studying, working on his thesis and engaging in these intellectual conflicts, a far less rational and more deadly conflict threatened to intrude.

---

9   "At the same time he participated in an economic seminar given by Meade, Nurkse, Koopmans and others who were connected with the League of Nations." Memo on University of Chicago letterhead, from "Prof. Lange" to "Prof. Leland," dated January 8, 1941, recommending Leo for a scholarship. Memo sent to the author by Roger Myerson, attached to an email, on May 24, 2018.

10 A.B. Atkinson and Martin Weale, "James Edward Meade, 1907–1995," The British Academy, 2000, https://www.thebritishacademy.ac.uk/documents/1436/105p473.pdf Accessed October 13, 2022.

11 Herbert E. Scarf, "Tjalling Charles Koopmans, August 28, 1910–February 26, 1985," https://www.nap.edu/read/4894/chapter/14 Accessed October 13, 2022.

CHAPTER 19

Leo Hurwicz:
"Excess Foreign Population"

In late 1939 and into 1940, it was widely expected that Germany would eventually invade Switzerland. The Swiss, famous as a country of marksmen where every male was trained as a soldier, mobilized furiously, to the point where they could have quickly fielded an army of 600,000, out of a total population of only about four million.

A joke that Leo heard at the time—but which dated to at least to World War I—had someone pointing out that, the prowess of the Swiss soldier notwithstanding, the enemy could field a force twice the size of Switzerland's. The calm reply: "Then each of us will have to shoot twice."

Realistically, the Germans could have conquered Switzerland, but it would have cost them dearly and hampered other war efforts that were more important to them at the time.

In addition, it was by no means assured that Leo would be allowed to stay in Switzerland: in December 1939, citing *surpopulation étrangère* (excess foreign population), the Swiss authorities refused to extend his *permis de séjour* (residence permit) and ordered him to leave the country. As a result, Leo wrote this letter to Professor Rappard, who at the time was President of the Graduate Institute of International Studies:

> 85, rue de Montbrillant, Genève
> December 18, 1939
>
> Dear Professor Rappard,
>
> I have hesitated a good deal before I made up my mind to write this letter which you may find very improper.
>
> But I have found myself in a difficult, not to say tragical, situation and you seem to be the only person who perhaps might help me.

What has happened is simply that the Swiss Authorities have refused me a prolongation of the "permis de séjour" and ask me to leave this country by March 1, 1940. The motive given by the Authorities is "surpopulation étrangère."

Now, on the one hand, there is at present no country where I could go. On the other, however, even if I did succeed in finding such a country, it would mean for me, needless to stress, the end of my studies.

I am, of course, quite aware of the fact that—for various reasons—you may not be in a position to help me in my difficulties. I even expect that this will be the case.

But, should it not be so, i.e. should you be willing and in a position to help me somehow, I would be grateful to you really more than I can say. I am hardly exaggerating in saying that my whole future depends on whether I shall or shall not be allowed to continue my studies in the Institute.

I hope you will excuse my worrying you with such a trifle and remain, Professor,

Yours very faithfully
(signed)
Leonid Hurwicz

"My whole future" may have been his understated way of saying "my life." If deported into the genocidal insanity that was exploding in his home country, not to mention just across the Swiss border in Germany, he might not live long enough to make his contribution to the socialist calculation debate or help unravel the technicalities of imperfect competition. Nor was it by any means certain that the Swiss would take that into account: in fact, Switzerland had exhibited many of the same antisemitic and xenophobic tendencies seen elsewhere in Europe. In 1938, even before the war, the Swiss government had asked the Nazi authorities to stamp the passports of German Jews with a "J" so that the Swiss could reject their requests for asylum. Thousands were sent back to Germany, even though the Swiss knew they were consigning them to almost certain death.[1]

---

1   "Switzerland, National Socialism and the Second World War," *Final Report of the Independent Commission of Experts Switzerland—Second World War*, Pendo Verlag GmbH, 2002,

While trying to get his *permis de séjour* extended, Leo was working feverishly to get out of Europe. The desire of the Swiss to get rid of him ended up working in his favor.

The U.S. Consulate in Zurich required "certificates of good conduct" from each of the countries Leo had lived in during the previous five years, namely, England and France. (It technically included Poland, but the Americans were willing to make an exception there due to the Nazi occupation.) When Leo wrote the French, they quickly issued a certificate—a routine procedure for them.

The British, on the other hand, responded that they were "not in the custom" of issuing certificates of good conduct—a polite refusal. Leo thought about his dilemma and came up with a plan of action: he went to the office of the chief of police in Geneva and pointed out that if he was unable to get some kind of statement from the British indicating that he had conducted himself well during his stay there, he would not be able to emigrate to the U.S., and would be a burden on the Swiss taxpayer.

The chief of police was sympathetic but said, "How do you expect me to do anything about it?"

Leo suggested he write to the police in London, as if investigating a suspect, asking if they had anything against him. Such requests were not uncommon, and the police in Western European countries generally maintained collegial relationships and supported one another in this manner.

The chief said he would try it.

A few weeks later, the chief received a letter from the Assistant Commissioner of Police of the Metropolis, New Scotland Yard:[2]

> With reference to your letter of the 28th February, 1940, respecting Mr. Leonid Hurwicz, I am directed by the Commissioner of Police of the Metropolis to say that this man was properly registered with the Police when resident in this country and that nothing is known by the Police to his detriment.
>
>   I am, Sir,
>
> Your obedient Servant,
> (Signature)

---

https://www.uek.ch/en/schlussbericht/synthesis/ueke.pdf. See also "Bergier commission," https://en.wikipedia.org/wiki/Bergier_commission#Refugee_policy

2   "Letter from Scotland Yard," https://www.leonidhurwicz.org/scotland-yard/, from "The Collected Papers of Leonid Hurwicz," Volume 1, Chapter 1, p. 7, edited by Samiran "Shomu" Banerjee, Emory University

This satisfied the U.S. Consulate, and Leo was now able to start the process of applying to enter the U.S. under the Russian quota. This was easier to get on than some other quotas, since it was extremely difficult to leave Russia. Nevertheless, he was warned that it would be some time before the quota number would be available.

When filling out forms for the American Consulate in Zurich in April, Leo indicated that he planned to embark for the U.S. from Genoa, the largest Italian port, and the closest seaport to Geneva. However, the general expectation was that Italy would enter the war before long, on the side of the Axis, making that a risky choice. An alternative was to get to Portugal, where he could book a berth on an ocean liner from Lisbon to the U.S. If he could fly directly to Spain and then take a train to Portugal, his travel would be restricted to neutral countries (Spain and Portugal) that—unlike France—were not in immediate danger.

Civilian air traffic in and out of Switzerland had been suspended in August 1939, in response to the same events that hastened Leo's move into Switzerland, namely, the Molotov–Ribbentrop Pact which foretold Germany's invasion of France. In January 1940, the Swiss Army Command authorized the resumption of scheduled Swissair civilian service to Barcelona and Rome from the Locarno-Magadino airfield on the southern side of the Alps—and about as far from both Germany and France as one can get and still be in Switzerland. Locarno is less than ten miles from the Italian border, but Italy—though known to favor the Axis—was still officially neutral.

Negotiations between Swissair and the Italian and Spanish authorities were protracted: flights to Rome began on March 18, to Barcelona on April 1. Leo made plans to fly from Locarno to Barcelona.

He had to go through some machinations to get Spanish and Portuguese transit visas, as he explained: "But all these consulates were corrupt. But I think it was the Spanish or Portuguese consulate, they said he needed to consult with his head office and I had to pay him supposedly for a telegram. When I came back a week later, they said they hadn't heard anything and needed money for another telegram. So I said, 'Well, are you sure you'll get an answer?' He said, 'Yes I'll have an answer this afternoon.' So it was made obvious that all these telegrams were a fiction."

On April 19, Leo requested permission from the Consulate General of Poland in Geneva to travel to the United States. He was hoping to leave for America as quickly as possible after the end of the academic year, as indicated by a request to the Institute to present his thesis at the end of the 1939/1940 academic year.[3]

---

3   "I think it is superfluous to add that, under the present circumstances, I would be very happy if I were permitted to present my thesis after the two semesters of the 1939/40 academic

On May 10, 1940, the Germans invaded Holland and Belgium, driving toward France. If France fell, Switzerland, along with Liechtenstein, would be a tiny dot of neutrality, hemmed in by Germany, its allies and its puppets. Ludwig von Mises' wife, Margit, describes how she "really became frightened" at this time and implored Mises to make plans to emigrate to the United States. Mises, however, "did not want to leave. He never had been so happy as he was in Geneva, and he did not feel any fear."[4]

Leo was more realistic: he did feel fear. He only failed to panic because he couldn't afford it.

Meanwhile, he had no news from his family. He did know that, in general, Jews in Poland were not doing well: a postcard that Leo wrote to Leah Kotzin's father, Nachum, in Ostrów-Mazowiecka, dated May 8, 1940, was returned with the ominous inscription "he departed in an unknown direction" (*wyjechał w niewiadomym kierunku*).[5]

In late May, while Leo was still preparing to leave Switzerland, Hitler invaded France, driving almost 340,000 British and French soldiers up against the English Channel, where they gazed longingly from Dunkirk in northern France to Dover in England. Even in England, safety might be temporary: it was clear that Britain would be next on the menu for Hitler.

Leo left Geneva on May 31,[6] traveling by rail from Geneva to Locarno to catch his flight. He had left a little before the end of the summer term. Most of his class certificates were not ready, and he didn't stay to pick them up.

In addition, it would appear that he left without presenting his thesis on devaluation in the gold bloc countries. This despite the fact that, in his application letter to the Institute at the beginning of the academic year, he had mentioned his desire to complete his thesis, on which he had made "significant progress." This may be the earliest recorded example of Leo's recurring tendency to complete

---

year." Author's translation from the French: "Je crois superflu d'ajouter que—mi les circonstances présentes—je serais extrêmement heureux s'il m'était permis de présenter ma thèse déjà après les deux semestres de l'année académique 1939/40." Genève, le 31 Octobre 1939, Leonid Hurwicz "A la Commission Mixte de l'Institut de Hautes Etudes Internationales et de l'Université de Genève."

4   Margit von Mises, *Our Escape From Europe*, https://mises.org/library/our-escape-europe. Accessed June 4, 2021.

5   On September 10, 1939, the Germans had beaten Nachum till he was "covered with blood and could not see where he was going." JewishGen, testimony from Abraham Jakubowski, translated by Judie Ostroff Goldstein, https://www.jewishgen.org/yizkor/ostrow/ost429.html. Both Nachum and his wife Chaya died in the Holocaust in 1942.

6   Based on the date stamped on a Wagons-Lits | Cook receipt among Leo's papers at the David M. Rubenstein Rare Book & Manuscript Library at Duke University.

written projects in something between a long time and forever. In this particular case, he did have a solid excuse: "World War II ate my homework."

Leo didn't know exactly what he was going to do when he got to the United States. On forms for the American Consulate, he indicated that his destination might be Chicago or Berkeley. (Berkeley may have been suggested by Oskar Lange, who had studied there in 1934 and 1935.) This uncertainty may explain why, on June 20, his class certificates were mailed to a Miss Eleanor K. Taft in Cincinnati, Ohio. Miss Taft, a granddaughter of President William Howard Taft, had spent '39–'40 in Geneva working at the ILO. She was about a year younger than Leo, so perhaps she took a class or two at the Institute? In any case, the fact that he had the certificates mailed to her instead of to his relatives in Chicago reflects his uncertainty about his destination.

Another indication of this uncertainty is a letter written on May 28 by Professor Rappard to a friend, Professor James T. Shotwell of Columbia University (emphasis added):

> Dear Shotwell:
>
> I am enclosing copy of a general introduction I am giving to one of our students who is suddenly leaving for America. Knowing your kind heart, I am sure you would be good enough to give him your advice in case he should need it on his trip through New York. **He intends to go to California, but may be detained on the way.**
>
> It was a great delight to see you in New York and Philadelphia. In the terrible days we are living through, memories of the past are a particularly precious comfort.
>
> With warm regards,
> Ever yours,
> William E. Rappard

New York, Chicago, Berkeley: he really had very little idea how he would manage in any of these places. As he prepared to leave Geneva, one imagines him with both feet planted firmly in mid-air, his parents and brother lost in the fog of war, his old life blasted out from under him, and a new one only dimly perceived or hoped for.

Soon, he was literally in mid-air—also, as it turned out, a frightening experience.

CHAPTER 20

Geneva to Chicago
by Way of Locarno, Barcelona
and Lisbon

———————

Leo described his departure from the Locarno airport: "We got into the air-plane. It got dark. They circled somehow or other, trying to take off from that airport. I wasn't really worried. But that was the first time in my life I had been in an airplane. Then they gave up. They said it was too dark and so on."

The airline put the delayed passengers up in a nearby Ritz Hotel—an unfamiliar luxury for Leo, who was more accustomed to Youth Hostels.

The next morning, after boarding the plane, Leo looked out the window. It appeared, once again, that a great deal of hard-won economic knowledge might be about to go down in flames.

"I really got frightened. Because this was just a small flat area with huge mountains all around. How an airplane would expect to gather enough speed to take off!"

But take off they did, and soon the prospects for unravelling the mysteries of imperfect competition were looking much brighter.

Spain being officially neutral in the war, it was possible to fly there from Switzerland. They landed safely in Barcelona. Later in the war, Spanish dictator Francisco Franco was pressured into acting somewhat neutral; for example, some German planes that for one reason or another violated Spanish airspace were "interned"—seized at least for the duration of the war. However, Franco's personal leanings were pro-Axis, and in June of 1940 he was still allowing refueling and/or repairing of German planes that crashed or were forced to land on Spanish soil.

That probably explains why, riding in a little shuttle bus after landing in Barcelona, and chatting with a Portuguese businessman who was sitting next to him, Leo looked out the window and saw planes with swastikas on their tails. He commented that he didn't know that there were Nazi planes in Barcelona. The businessman replied emphatically, "Here, we don't notice these things."

Surprisingly, however, Franco was also favorably disposed towards Jews. Why? Back in 1924, when Franco was evacuating Spanish garrisons from Morocco, the Sephardim (Spanish-speaking Jews) were the only locals who supported him. Jewish men had been enlisting in the Spanish army since the late nineteenth century. In 1924, they supported Franco with both money and manpower. Jewish soldiers helped him fight his way to the coast of Morocco. Many gave their lives for Spain and for Franco, and he never forgot it.[1] From June 22, 1940 to December 31, 1941, Franco was instrumental in saving the lives of at least 15,000 Jews. That count is based largely on the records of ships that came to New York from Spanish and Portuguese ports.[2]

From Barcelona, Leo went by train, first to Madrid, then to Lisbon. In Lisbon, he received an answer from the Polish Consulate in Geneva. It had been mailed to Leo's address on Rue de Montbrillant in Geneva on May 31, the day Leo left the city, and forwarded to Lisbon general delivery on June 1. The Polish government had refused his request to travel to the U.S. Based on his age, he was told he should report to the Polish Army in France.[3] He decided not to do that.

However, there were other impediments in store. Continuing Leo's narrative: "At some point the Kotzins sent me some money, after I lost my wallet in the post office." (This misadventure in the post office in Geneva is something Leo mentioned several times but never went into detail about. Losing one's wallet is bad enough under any circumstances. It must have been devastating in this situation.)

Leo booked passage on an Italian boat, the *Augustus*, scheduled to sail from Lisbon to New York on June 4. "This was early June. And just at that time Italy joined Germany as partner in the war. So, of course, they couldn't operate ships between Europe and the United States. So I was stuck again without money. I couldn't ask Kotzins for money a second time."

Italy didn't declare war on Britain and France until June 10, 1940. However, on May 25, the Italian navy sent a warning through Italian diplomatic missions

---

1   Lawrence H. Feldman, *Escape: The Evacuation of Jews from German Territory. 1940–1941*, Preface. http://www.academia.edu/34698509/Escape_The_Evacuation_of_Jews_from_German_Territory._1940_-_1941. Accessed June 4, 2021.

2   Ibid.

3   Leonid Hurwicz Papers, David M. Rubenstein Rare Book & Manuscript Library, Duke University, Box 23, File: Correspondence 1938 Nov 21-10 Sept 1940 1 https://www.leonidhurwicz.org/polish-consulate-refusal/

overseas to merchant ships outside the Mediterranean, ordering captains, in the event of war, to make stealthily for Italy or neutral ports, and to scuttle their ships if capture seemed imminent. In late May it would already have been obvious to the captain of the *Augustus* that war was imminent and that, if he tried to make the trip from Lisbon to New York, the Royal Navy would most likely intercept and take possession of the *Augustus* for the transport of British troops.[4]

> First I went to the Italian shipping lines and I asked for my money back. They just laughed at me. They said, "Yes, you are an enemy, and come back after the war." That was not a good solution. Then I went to the harbor police, and essentially I used a variant of my trick in Geneva. I explained to them that if I cannot go to America, I cannot work in Lisbon, I'll be a public burden.
>
> So he said, "What do you expect me to do?"
>
> I knew that Portugal was a dictatorship. (The dictator was an economist.) And the police could do anything they wanted. So I told them, "Just tell them you'll take away their license."
>
> And within two days I got my money back.
>
> But how I got these inspirations, I mean, I really acted as if I was an experienced person. I never had . . . It was really desperation. But finally then I bought a ticket on a Greek boat. I was 23. The world was totally changed. The rules of the game were changed. But I somehow found if you sort of think through logically from the point of view of the other person . . . And everybody wanted to get rid of the refugees.

Desperation, and perhaps a facility inherited from centuries of refugee ancestors: some long-ago doctor from Padua whispering in his ear?

The Greek ship on which he booked passage was the *Nea Hellas*, scheduled to leave Lisbon on August 2, 1940. (Greece had not yet entered the war.)

For the intervening months, he found a way to use his math skills to make a little money:

---

4   "But the Augustus survived (presumably held back in port in Italy) to begin conversion in 1941–2 into Italy's second aircraft carrier, which (like the first) was unfinished when Fascism collapsed and the country was occupied and fought over by Germans and Western Allies from Julyct–September '43." Based on an email dated March 19, 2019 to the author from MacGregor Knox, Stevenson Professor of International History emeritus, The London School of Economics and Political Science.

When I got to Lisbon, you know, I had some money, but not really very much. And I found that there was a place in a suburb called Estoril, that was sort of like a Monte Carlo, you know, a gambling place. And I found that there were many French families there in this casino who had escaped the Nazi invasion. They were very worried because it was just when their kids were supposed to take these final examinations to graduate from high school. So I got to talking to these people, I told them I could keep them in good shape in things like mathematics and so on. So that's how I earned small change.

On June 10, Italy declared war on France and Britain and began bombing raids over France. The next day Swissair stopped flying to Barcelona from Locarno.

Leo had left Switzerland just in time: later travelers bound for Lisbon—like the Miseses—would have a much more difficult and dangerous journey, over-land across France. Margit von Mises describes how immediately "every line of communication between Switzerland and that country [France] was closed. Starting June 11, no cars were allowed, no trains were running, no planes were flying, no buses were moving, no letters or telegrams came through."[5]

On June 12, Winston Churchill told his chief military assistant, General Hastings Lionel Ismay, "You and I will be dead in three months' time."[6]

On June 14, the Germans broke through the Maginot line and marched into Paris unopposed.

On June 18, in a speech to the House of Commons, Churchill captured the desperate mood of the hour and tried to inspire the heroism it demanded:

> The whole fury and might of the enemy must very soon be turned on us. Hitler knows that he will have to break us in this island or lose the war. If we can stand up to him, all Europe may be free and the life of the world may move forward into broad, sunlit uplands. But if we fail, then the whole world, including the United States, including all that we have known and cared for, will sink into the abyss of a new Dark Age made more sinister, and perhaps more protracted, by the lights of a perverted science. Let us therefore brace ourselves to our duties, and so

---

5   Margit von Mises, *Our Escape From Europe*, https://mises.org/library/our-escape-europe
6   David Reynolds, "Churchill in 1940: The Worst and Finest Hour," in Robert B. Blake and William Roger Louis, *Churchill*, Clarendon Press, 1993, pp. 249, 252, 254–255.

bear ourselves that, if the British Empire and its Commonwealth last for a thousand years, men will still say, "This was their finest hour."[7]

Had Leo been able to join the 55,000 Polish soldiers fighting in France, within a few days he could have been one of the 16,000 taken prisoner by the Germans or the 13,000 interned after fleeing into Switzerland. Otherwise, ironically, he would most likely have been evacuated to England.

The Miseses finally began arranging visas and transportation to emigrate to the U.S. France formally surrendered to Germany on June 22. The Miseses didn't manage to leave Switzerland until July 4; then, instead of flying over France like Leo, they had to cross it by bus, dodging German military control posts as they went. The bus got them as far as Cerbère, France, near the Spanish border. Even then, their troubles weren't over: attempting to enter Spain, they were turned back twice and had to get new visas in Toulouse before finally, on the third try, they were allowed to enter Spain.

Leo was still in Lisbon on July 4, when Germany started bombing ships in the English Channel. In the following weeks, the Battle of Britain intensified, as the Germans bombed RAF airfields and radar stations in England, attempting to eliminate British defenses against the planned German sea-based invasion, "Operation Sea Lion." In response, the RAF began bombing German invasion barges, in what became known as "The Battle of the Barges." By the beginning of August, it was clear that everything hinged on whether the Luftwaffe or the RAF would dominate in the air.

Leo boarded the *Nea Hellas* on August 2, arriving nervous but excited in Hoboken, N.J., on August 11. The Kotzins had sent a New York relative, Madzia Solowiejczyk, to meet him and arrange his train trip to Chicago.

(Margit and Ludwig von Mises had passed through Hoboken on the day Leo departed from Lisbon: after their nail-biting trip across France and difficult entry into Spain, they made it to Lisbon, boarded a boat on July 24 and arrived in New Jersey on August 2.)

Leo apparently remained in New York for a week or a bit more. A letter was addressed to him on August 15th in New York at an address just a block or so east of the Columbia University campus. It seems probable that Leo

---

7   In 1953, Churchill would be awarded the Nobel Prize for Literature "for his mastery of historical and biographical description as well as for brilliant oratory in defending exalted human values." "The Nobel Prize in Literature 1953," https://www.nobelprize.org/prizes/literature/1953/summary/. Accessed October 13, 2022.

went to James Shotwell with Rappard's letter of introduction. Apparently, nothing came of it: later, Leo would say that he had ". . . no contacts worth speaking of in N.Y."[8]

In a letter to "Mrs. Morgan," Leo mentions seeing three of their "Genevese acquaintances": Jane Braucher, Helen Fisher, and Mrs. Jacqueline.[9] Also in Manhattan, he visited the parents of a young American woman, Ruth Schechter, whom he had met in Europe.

He then proceeded from New York to Chicago and took up residence on the couch at Aunt Helen's apartment—the fabled 3605 Dickens Avenue, an address that would remain firmly lodged in his memory until his final days. The Kotzins continued their extraordinary kindness and generosity. As he wrote to a friend he had met in Estoril ("Miss Janka"), "I can not complain, the more that I live with my family, who treat me like a newborn baby. And for a long time I was (from necessity) adult, so I rest a little."[10]

To a large extent, this "rest" may have consisted in letting go of the uncertainties of his recent past and focusing on the much less threatening present. Writing to Mrs. Morgan, he said:

> The description of your trip in June is very thrilling, too. But all that seems now such a long time ago, does it not?
> I myself feel as if I had never been in any country but the U.S.

As always, he channeled most of his energies into academics, still pursuing the elusive PhD. He enrolled for the Fall quarter at the University of Chicago, taking "Economics 371—International Economic Policies" from Jacob Viner.

In addition, though he did find relief and comfort with the Kotzins, one must not imagine him lounging about on the couch all day: he wrote to Madzia

---

8   "I am afraid I shall have to stay here—for various reasons. The chief one is that I have no contacts worth speaking of in N.Y." Hurwicz, writing from Chicago to Ruth Schechter, 9/18/1940, Leonid Hurwicz Papers, David M. Rubenstein Rare Book & Manuscript Library, Duke University, Box 23, File: Correspondence 1940.

9   Hurwicz to "Mrs. Morgan," 9/12/1940; Leonid Hurwicz Papers, David M. Rubenstein Rare Book & Manuscript Library, Duke University, Box 23, File: Correspondence 1940. https://leonidhurwicz.org/letter-to-mrs-morgan/

10 Hurwicz to Ms. Janka ("Panno Janko"), 9/12/1940; Leonid Hurwicz Papers, David M. Rubenstein Rare Book & Manuscript Library, Duke University, Box 23, File: Correspondence 1940. In Polish, typed on an American typewriter, so without diacritical marks: *"Tak wiec nie moge sie uskarzac, tym bardziej, ze mieszkam u rodziny, ktora mnie traktuje jak nowonarodzcne bobo. A ja juz przez dlugi czas bylem (z musu) doroslym, wiec troche odpoczywam."* Scan of original letter: https://leonidhurwicz.org/panno-janko/

(in Polish) on September 12 that he was "literally never at home," that he was running around to the university and "various statistical institutions" and going out every evening as well, having made some friends at the university. He mentions giving a speech at "the Zionist organization" with Sol. All this in addition to playing the piano and spending two or three hours a day in transit. "If I had a little more free time, I would be happy," he concludes.[11]

The "statistical institutions" likely included the Cowles Commission, a small, prestigious economic research institute associated with the University of Chicago, created in 1932 for the "sole purpose of applying the science of econometrics to current economic problems[12] . . ."—like the stock market crash of 1929 and the Great Depression that followed. The Cowles Commission was dedicated to fostering rigorous logical, mathematical, and statistical methods of analysis in economic research. The fact that Alfred Cowles III, founder of the Commission, used the term "econometrics" in 1932 showed how forward-looking he was, since this was an approach whose beginnings many would date only to the early 30's, when the Econometric Society was founded and the term "econometrics" was first used in its modern sense—apparently by Ragnar Frisch.

Leo's introduction to the Cowles Commission came through Oskar Lange, who was then a researcher at Cowles as well as a professor at the University of Chicago. Lange saw Cowles as a good fit for Leo. True, 23-year-old Leo had no employment history and no academic credential except a law degree from the University of Warsaw. But perhaps if they got to know him . . .

Overall, Leo was quite happy: "The University is very pleasant," he wrote to Jane Braucher (now in Red Hook, Brooklyn), "and, as far as economics is concerned—probably <u>the</u> one in the U.S."[13]

Only finances prevented him from taking more classes: Oskar Lange, in recommending him for a scholarship in January 1941, said, "He is very anxious to do graduate work at the University of Chicago, but during the last quarter had to limit his work to taking only one course because of the lack of resources to pay tuition for additional courses."

---

11 See https://www.leonidhurwicz.org/leo-letter-to-madzia-sept-1940/

12 From the announcement of the creation of the Cowles Commission for Research in Economics, 1932, 7. Quoted in *A Colorado College Reader*, Chapter 12, "The Cowles Commission: the Early Years," by Vibha Kapuria-Foreman, p. 145. https://faculty1.colora-docollege.edu/~bloevy/ccreader/CC-Reader-012-Kapuria-Foreman-Cowles.pdf, retrieved January 26, 2019.

13 Hurwicz to "Janie" [Jane Braucher], 10/27/1940; Leonid Hurwicz Papers, David M. Rubenstein Rare Book & Manuscript Library, Duke University, Box 23, File: Correspondence 1940. He had met Janie (sometimes spelled "Janey") in Geneva. At the time he wrote to her, she was in Red Hook, Brooklyn, https://www.leonidhurwicz.org/braucher/

Although Leo told Mrs. Morgan that his plans were "not quite clear yet," he added, "It is very likely that I shall settle down here. The University here is very good and I have made very good contacts, so that I can have either a scholarship or some sort of research assistanceship [sic] in statistics."

Despite his praise for the University, he did have a few criticisms: in September 1940, writing to Ruth Schechter, he noted that he found the U of Chicago "rather nice tho' very reactionary and orthodox. I met [Jacob] Viner, [Frank] Knight and other local celebrities and . . . didn't think very much of them."

About a month later, he wrote to Jane Braucher: "I am now a student of the Un. of Chicago, and quarrel with Prof. Viner and Knight just as if it was another Mises or Roepke." On the same day, he wrote to Ruth Schechter, "I am working with Viner which requires a good deal of patience on my part. Maybe on his too . . ."

Viner and Knight were associated with the emerging Chicago school of economics, which opposed the Cowles Commission project of creating tools for centralized economic management, as well as the Commission's Keynesian goal of demand management; along the same lines, the Chicago school was suspicious of the Commission's mathematical and econometric methodologies that supported this mission. Theoretical conflicts aside, Leo was not alone in having problems with Viner. Others have noted that he was thought to be "vicious";[14] students held that his teaching methods derived from the Spanish Inquisition.[15] That Leo merely mentioned needing patience is perhaps a testament to his own good nature, or his talent for understatement.

Leo's "very good contacts" started with Oskar Lange. In another letter to Ruth Schechter, he noted that though he didn't have a job yet, Lange thought his prospects were good.

A major reason that his plans were "not quite clear" in September was that, as he wrote to Schechter, he had a choice to make about the draft:

> You ask me whether I am "draft'able." I really don't know. I think
> that I have, as it were, my fate in my hands. Namely, if I apply for
> the naturalization papers I shall be, but not otherwise. In other
> words—I don't have to marry (I wouldn't even if I were liable,
> but that is, as they say, another story). Most of my friends and

---

14 Roger Backhouse, *Founder of Modern Economics: Becoming Samuelson, 1915–1948*, Oxford Studies in History of Economics, Oxford University Press, 2017, p. 581.
15 Hyman P. Minsky, "Beginnings," *PSL Quarterly Review*, Vol. 62 Nn. 248–251 (2009), 191–203, p. 199.

acquaintances advise me not to apply, but maybe . . . I will in
spite of all. What do you think of it? You see, it seems that in a
country at war being soldier [*sic*] is safer than being a civilian . . .

He ultimately decided that the United States had taken him in when no one else
would, and it was only right that he be willing to serve as every American was
expected to. He did apply for naturalization, but his number didn't come up in
the next draft lottery on October 29, 1940.

He continued to suffer one agonizing anxiety during this period, which even
the study of economics could not relieve: lack of any communication from or
about his parents and Henry. Eventually, however, he did get news, probably
from Roza. He wrote to Ruth Schechter on October 27, 1940:

I also had news about tho' not from my parents. They are now
together with my brother near Archangelsk, i.e. much nearer the
North Pole than any other habitable region. How and why they
got there, I don't know. One possibility is that they were forced
to go there on account of being refugees (i.e. from the German
occupied areas). My father's political affiliations may have played
a role, too. One of my uncles has been arrested for almost half
a year (presumably for trying to cross the Lithuanian frontier).

Blood-curdling accounts had reached the West of these deportations from
Russian-occupied Poland: masses of people, hundreds of thousands, herded
into cattle cars, overcrowding, stench, darkness, hunger, cold, sickness, even
death.

But they had not died: his family was alive.

CHAPTER 21

Chicago and MIT

———

When Leo came to Chicago, he had no employment and few prospects. Calling on his Conservatory training, he was able to contribute something to the Kotzin household by giving piano lessons to Aunt Helen's granddaughter, Rhoda, who was about seven at the time. Once again, learning turned out to be the safest investment. Even though forced to flee to a distant land with only what he could carry, he still had treasure in his head (and fingers).

Around the same time, Leo was trying to convince Americans that a Nazi victory would be bad for the United States economically. He wrote to "Nonie" (Eleanor Taft) on September 12, 1940:

> Yesterday I gave a talk to a group consisting mainly of very serious business people. The topic was: the implications for the U.S. economy of a Nazi victory. I was as gloomy and pessimistic in my forcasts [sic] as I only could be and most people were duly impressed. But there were some voices in the discussion which terrified me. I tried to convince them, for example, that the British Dominions and the South American countries would naturally tend towards Europe (whether Nazi-dominated or not) because the U.S. is competing with them, whereas Europe is a "complementary" organism. But they told me not to worry because "after all the U.S. is not asleep." Like it, don't you?

The Blitz of London began on the afternoon of September 7, 1940, with 348 German bombers, escorted by 617 fighters, blasting London and leaving many parts of the city in flames. The first assault continued from 4:00 PM to 6:00 PM, the second from around 8:00 PM until 4:30 in the morning.

London was bombed for the next 57 days, either during the day or the night. Fire destroyed many parts of the city. As many as 177,000 would seek shelter in the Underground stations during the night. In one incident, a bomb hit a school being used as an air raid shelter, killing 450 people.[1]

The U.S.—while still not a combatant in the war—was determined to be, as FDR announced in December 1940, "the arsenal of democracy." Congress prepared to quadruple the annual military budget. The question now presented itself: how could the U.S., quickly and efficiently, switch huge segments of manufacturing over to military production, while preserving a decentralized, free-market economy, without massive inflation and/or shortages in the civilian sector? It was not enough to simply wave the money and hope that manufacturers would come around. Business leaders, including William Knudsen, President of General Motors, consulted with FDR and lobbied for tax incentives and advance payments to encourage businesses to retool factories and retrain workers. Socialist calculation debates notwithstanding, when it was urgent to redirect the economy with accuracy and efficiency, it turned out that even Big Business agreed that this required . . . central planning!

Leo Hurwicz and the Cowles Commission were waiting in the wings.

Meanwhile, Lange helped Leo get his first job in economics, working with Paul Samuelson at the Massachusetts Institute of Technology. "The job was as a teaching and research assistant for only one semester [from January to June 1941] – a term no self-respecting graduate student would accept. But I had no other offers. In fact, it was a miracle I had this one," Leo said.[2]

Lange, recommending Leo to Samuelson in December 1940, wrote:

> He has an excellent mind, and is in my opinion, the best of the candidates on this list. He has quite a background in mathematical statistics, and has quite extensive knowledge of analysis. Before becoming an economist he was a theoretical physicist. He also did numerical work in experimental physics. He is really one of the very best I have had among students. In addition, he needs a job very badly, because he has no income at all.

---

1   "The London Blitz, 1940," http://www.eyewitnesstohistory.com/blitz.htm. Accessed October 11, 2022.
2   Ann Bauer, "Leonid Hurwicz's Game," *Twin Cities Business* magazine, March 1, 2008. This article was also the basis for Leo's bio at nobelprize.org. https://www.leonidhurwicz.org/tcb/

Samuelson was known for his "conviction that . . . economics had much to learn from physics and the laws of thermodynamics."[3] So touting Leo as a "theoretical physicist" was a good move from a marketing perspective. In fact, as far as formal training went, Leo had only minored in physics while studying law. Still, he no doubt had the mathematical skills implied by Lange's recommendation. Leo could never have known, back at the University of Warsaw, as he was plunging into experimental physics and differential calculus that, a few years on and some four thousand miles away, he would get his first paying job in economics—working with famed economist Paul Samuelson at MIT—based at least in part on a recommendation emphasizing his experience in mathematical statistics and theoretical physics.

In any case, 1941 found "twenty-three-year-old Leo as research assistant to twenty-five-year-old Paul Samuelson, at the very beginning of MIT's economic renaissance."[4]

Samuelson would later recall the process by which Leo was selected, beginning with a conversation between Samuelson and MIT Economics Department chair Rupert Maclaurin, which took place sometime in the period from late September to December of 1940, and then proceeding to describe how Samuelson himself was lured to MIT.

> MIT's Rupert Maclaurin asked new arrival Paul Samuelson, "Who's the world's greatest economist?"
>
> "Ragnar Frisch," I suggested.
>
> "Okay, let's get him here at MIT."
>
> "No, we can't do that. He's a Norwegian patriot, sequestered right now in a Nazi concentration camp, where he's reduced to studying Darwinian bee genetics."[5]

---

3 "Paul Samuelson," *The Economist*, December 17, 2009
4 Used by permission of the Paul Samuelson estate. Appendix B contains a transcription of Ket Richter's reading on the occasion of a celebration of Leo's 90th birthday. The version in this chapter reflects a document in the Samuelson papers at Duke University: "P.A. Samuelson, Undated, The Hurwicz 1940–41 year when MIT launched its graduate degree rocket," Paul A. Samuelson papers, David M. Rubenstein Rare Book and Manuscript Library, Duke University, box 39. Differences between the version in the appendix and the one in this chapter are slight. Although the document is undated, the celebration took place on April 17, 2007 (a little more than four months before the actual birthday), and one can surmise that it was written not too long before that.
5 "Frisch's most important hobby was bee-keeping, for which Frisch performed genetic studies." Wikipedia, https://en.wikipedia.org/wiki/Ragnar_Frisch

So to speak, therefore, I had to palm off on go-getter Maclaurin twenty-three-year-old Leo Hurwicz, instead of Frisch or Tinbergen, or for that matter Keynes.

There's a story behind this story. Whilst Harvard was keeping in its court the ball that was put there by an October 1940 MIT invite to 25-year-old Paul to levitate three miles down the Charles River, frenetic Maclaurin phoned me nightly. One warm evening, he dangled before me what follows: "If you come to MIT, for your research you will have at your disposal the Roger Babson Grant to study how Newton's Second [*sic, but should be third—M. H.*] Law of Action and Reaction applies to macroeconomics."

Babson, who personally owned only two New England colleges, won Andy Warhol celebrity fame for—now listen to my words—correctly predicting in advance the Great Wall Street Crash of October, 1929. Never mind that Babson made that prediction in 1925, when the Dow Jones Index was about one-tenth of its 1929 peak. (Maybe Newton had told him, "What goes up must fall down.")

The rest is history: I quit my late September Harvard lecturing on Econ I abruptly at the mid-hour. Arriving by Massachusetts Avenue streetcar, what I found awaiting me at MIT were both half a secretary and my own telephone. (Ten years later, Schumpeter at Harvard still hadn't attained that affluence.)

While I couldn't fetch Frisch for Maclaurin, I still could deliver to him some new star. But who? Oskar Lange, then at Chicago or Berkeley [*It was Chicago. Berkeley came—M. H.*], narrowed down the field for me. He suggested two names: Hungarian Tibor de Scitovsky or a young Pole, Leonid Hurwicz, late of Warsaw, Geneva, Barcelona and Lisbon—always one step ahead of Hitler's mobile tanks.

Tibor's work at LSE I knew and admired. But applying Lange's needs test, Hurwicz was the one in more desperate financial need.

Think of it this way: suppose Niels Bohr could choose between say, Heisenberg or Pauli. My die was cast and MIT was the beneficiary.

Historians of stochastic intertemporal U.S. time series, and Isaac Newton in his dissenting Anglican Valhalla, must know how we did early spectral analysis of Frickey's aggregate U.S. output for the timeslot 1865–1935. [*Edwin Frickey was a former professor of Samuelson's at Harvard, who had compiled data on which one could perform mathematical searches for regularly recurring patterns—M. H.*]

When I say "we" I do not refer to Leo and Paul only. Instead, I can still see in my mind's eye Leo, whip in one hand, slide rule in the other, marshaling his crew of mostly young female National Youth Administration galley-slave computers. *Parallel* computer computation thus merits a marble marker at the northwest corner of Massachusetts Avenue and Memorial Drive. Leo began that there.

Even more melodramatic was the new Hurwicz-Samuelson grading system for my first regular statistics course. MIT engineers have always been notorious whiners. They are grade chasers beyond Philadelphia barracks lawyers anywhere.

One of us—I will point no finger—said: let's add a hard extra-credit exam question, with the proviso that it can only *raise, but not lower* your grade.

All hell broke loose when undergraduate commerce course nerds learned that their exam mark of 115 put them below the median of the class grades. It did not help when Leo explained that this was the famous Chicago grading system. Leo had little to lose: the Babson pittance was already spent; it was my tenure and future life-time career that dangled on the razor's edge.

Fortunately, Japan at Pearl Harbor saved my bacon as well as that of Hitler-hating Franklin Roosevelt.

Can anyone doubt creative design's superiority over atheist Darwin?

Best of all, the Leo MIT year was a fun year. You know you're a has-been when you hear yourself saying, "I gave Goethe his first job." Well, damn it, I did give Leo his.

The Roger Babson grant was a "pittance" of $500 (around $9,295 in 2020 dollars). Roger Babson (1875–1967), an MIT graduate and wildly successful entrepreneur, had developed a pseudoscientific theory based on the idea that Newton's third law of motion (for every action, there is an equal and opposite reaction) could be applied to the analysis of economic cycles. In order to justify using the Babson grant, Samuelson had to hint that his research had some relation to Babson's idea. (It didn't.)

It's also somewhat curious that Samuelson mentions only two names suggested by Lange. In reality, there were four, the other two being Grace Gunn and Rutledge Vining. Apparently, Scitovsky and Hurwicz were the ones he seriously considered, and therefore the ones that lodged in his memory.

Another open question is what Leo actually did during his short tenure at MIT. His Nobel biography says that he "tested a hypothesis about how businesses arrive at prices for their goods and services." Presumably, that was Leo's memory. However, "spectral analysis" involves mathematical examination of regular fluctuations—for instance, analysis of the spectrum of colors (i.e., frequencies or rates of variation of the electromagnetic waves) comprising a beam of light. The idea was that regular, periodic variations in economic activity (business cycles) might be analyzed using some of the same mathematical tools (e.g., Fourier analysis) that physicists use for analyzing light. (Samuelson mentions Isaac Newton because Newton is generally considered to be the founder of spectroscopy.) It was such patterns that the "galley-slaves" were searching for. Again, the crossover of analytical tools from physics to economics explains why Leo's physics background was significant.

These two descriptions could actually be referring to the same project, with Leo describing the ultimate goal and Samuelson the methodology: for instance, they may have been looking for patterns where a cyclical variation in the cost or availability of some raw materials (e.g., iron, aluminum) would be followed by a similar variation in the cost of producing goods, and therefore the prices of those goods. Or perhaps cyclical variations in demand would trigger price changes.

In any case, whatever research they labored at so diligently for six months, there is no indication that it had any lasting significance. There is evidence that such spectral analysis was in general not successful. For example, the paragraph below seems to describe an attempt (after Leo returned to Chicago from MIT) to use the same mathematical approach:

> One year Lange had a research project in which Leonid Hurwicz, Bernard Zagorin and I were the assistants. The aim was to decompose the observed time series of economic data into its simple cyclical components. The project was not a success.[6]

---

6   Hyman P. Minsky, "Beginnings," *PSL Quarterly Review* Vol. 62 Nn. 248–251 (2009), p. 202, https://rosa.uniroma1.it/rosa04/psl_quarterly_review/article/view/9448. Accessed October 13, 2022.

If their project turned out to be of little importance, the same cannot be said of a manuscript shared with Samuelson and Leo around this time by a young Norwegian economist, Trygve Haavelmo, who was at Harvard on a Fulbright scholarship. Haavelmo's "On the Statistical Implications of a System of Simultaneous Equations" had to do with constructing predictive models of interrelated economic activities, such as total consumer expenditures and investment. He demonstrated how economists' models often made logically inconsistent assumptions about "error terms" (random variations) and how they would manifest in real-world statistics. He also showed with a simple example how errors should be modeled in such cases. Enthusiastic about Haavelmo's observations, Leo made "valuable comments" (Haavelmo's words) on the manuscript.

When Leo returned to Chicago in mid-June 1941, it was with increased sophistication, knowledge and experience in a statistical and mathematical approach to economics, and with insights from Haavelmo's paper to which few other economists had been exposed. His employment prospects were greatly improved now that he had worked for the highly respected Samuelson and absorbed the groundbreaking lessons of Haavelmo. (He had also taken courses at Harvard in mathematical economics, advanced economic theory and economic cycles, receiving two As and an A+ respectively.) He was hired as a research assistant to Lange and Theodore Yntema. The latter was a professor of statistics in the School of Business at the University of Chicago and director of research at the Cowles Commission.

His statistical skills also helped him land a teaching assistantship. "Strangely enough," he wrote his friend Jane Braucher, "the field will be statistics, a thing I would never have forseen [sic]." No doubt he would have preferred economics: after all, the socialist calculation controversy was not going to solve itself; thinking about imperfect competition, while often ingenious, remained piecemeal; and models of business cycles still seemed at best incomplete, if not downright contradictory.

Still, he thought about these things in his spare time, when he wasn't busy worrying about his family. At some point before leaving MIT, he did receive "one short postcard" from Zina "alluding to their tragic conditions",[7] namely,

7   Hurwicz to "Dear Mr. Lash" [Joseph P. Lash], Leonid Hurwicz Papers, David M. Rubenstein Rare Book & Manuscript Library, Duke University, Box 23, File: Academic records, 1930s-1940s.

that they had been exiled to the north of Russia—or as Leo would put it, "not Siberia, but just as good."[8]

Leo also made an effort to get Eleanor Roosevelt to intervene to rescue his family. Apparently, his friend Ruth Schechter knew Joseph P. Lash, a journalist and political activist who was in turn friends with Eleanor Roosevelt. On June 7, 1941, Leo wrote to Lash, asking him to ask Eleanor Roosevelt to ask the U.S. Ambassador in Moscow to help the Hurwicz family in the "Northern Russian swamps" get visas to the U.S., or anywhere in the western hemisphere. Or, for that matter, even to Japan—basically, anything to escape the life-threatening situation they were in: "[h]ardest conceivable labor, lack of most basic foods, clothing and hygienic facilities" amid the marshy forests and damp, cold tundra climate of the Archangelsk district.[9]

There is no record of any reply from Mr. Lash or action on the part of Mrs. Roosevelt.

However, on June 22, 1941, in violation of the Ribbentrop-Molotov nonaggression pact, Germany invaded Russia. Their aims: repopulate western Russia with Germans; put Slavs to work as slave labor for the Axis war effort; seize oil reserves in the Caucasus; and take possession of crops and farmland, particularly in Ukraine.

Białystok was one of the first cities that Nazi armies captured. During the battle, both invading Nazis and retreating Russian troops committed atrocities against local civilians.

Jews were particular targets. On June 27, 1941, Nazi troops surrounded the square by the Great Synagogue of Białystok, forced people from their homes and shot many on the spot. Around 800 men, women and children were locked in the synagogue, which was then set on fire; all perished. Perhaps 5,000 Jews were killed on that one day. Between July and August 1941, about 50,000 Jews from Białystok and the surrounding area were enclosed in a ghetto. Most became forced labor for the German war effort in large textile, shoe and chemical plants, either inside or close to the ghetto. This likely would have been the Hurwicz family's fate, had they remained in Białystok.

To repel the Nazi invasion, Russia wanted the help of the Polish Army, much of which had fled into Russia and ended up in some form of detention. Accordingly, on July 30, Russia and Poland signed the Sikorski-Mayski Agreement, which declared the Ribbentrop-Molotov Pact null and void and normalized relations

---

8   Nina Shepherd, "The Wisdom of an Economist's Economist," *University of Minnesota Update*, October 1987, Volume 14, Number 9.

9   Ibid.

between the Soviet Union and the Polish government-in-exile. Part of the agreement was freeing Poles in the gulags and other forms of exile.

A few months later—probably in August or September 1941—Leo got a telegram from Adek asking "Where is mother?" The telegram came from Fergana, Uzbekistan, in the easternmost reaches of the USSR—about 2800 miles from Archangel. How had Adek ended up there, almost in China?

When the Germans attacked Russia, many Russian industries, along with their workers, had been relocated to Uzbekistan for safety. Perhaps Adek had also headed for this area because it was one of the last locations in the USSR that the Germans would be likely to reach? Or he may have had no choice about his destination. Leo had many questions and few answers, including the answer to Adek's question about Zina.

But about ten days later, Leo did get a postcard from Zina. She and Henry were in Kutaisi, Georgia, in the Caucasus region, near the Black Sea.

Leo sent telegrams back to both Adek and Zina. Now at least they knew they were both alive—though 2300 miles apart. What would they do now? What *should* they do?

What even the immediate future held was anybody's guess. Over the past several months, the Germans had continued their drive into Russia, overrunning Ukraine and now turning toward Moscow and perhaps Leningrad—but also surely not forgetting about the oil fields of the Caucasus.

If Hitler succeeded in conquering Russia . . .

CHAPTER 22

Surprise Attack

———

Leo now had his first permanent, full-time job, at the Cowles Commission. After a brief stint as a research *assistant* to Lange and Yntema, he had moved up (in July 1941) to a research associate position at Cowles. While not an exalted position in the Cowles hierarchy, it did give Leo a seat at the table with a group of adventurous economists, many of them European refugees like himself, ambitious to play a part in fomenting a more mathematical and statistical science of economics.

This emphasis was met with skepticism and even hostility in many quarters of mainstream economics. One such skeptic in the University of Chicago economics department was Frank Knight, particularly known for his hostility toward quantitative techniques. His famous comment on the Kelvin Dictum ("When you cannot measure, your knowledge is meager and unsatisfactory") was that it very largely meant in practice, "If you cannot measure, measure anyhow!"

Along with his anti-quantitative philosophy, Knight was opposed to the whole idea of economics as science, at least in the sense that it was being pursued at the Cowles Commission. He wrote that it was a fallacy "to believe that social science should or can be a science in the same sense as in natural science."[1] Thus he opposed the fundamental mission of the Cowles Commission.

Though it is usually less emphasized, people at the Cowles Commission tended likewise to be more or less unappreciative of at least some of the denizens of the University of Chicago economics department. (As noted in an earlier chapter, Leo was "not impressed" by the "local celebrities.")

The Cowles Commission was created from a desire to better understand and address "current problems" (i.e., The Great Depression)—the same desire that drew Leo into economics. By the time Leo came to Chicago, however, World War II had largely sidelined that project, while creating new priorities. For one

———

1   Frank Knight, *Freedom and Reform*, 1947, p. 226

thing, the war ended the Depression. At the same time, it created significant economic issues of its own.

On the positive side, the war nearly eliminated unemployment. Many people who had previously not been working now entered the workforce. In addition, people were often working better-paying jobs: farm workers came to the cities to work in shipyards and factories, while domestic workers transitioned to factory jobs.

In normal times, new suppliers or products might have come into the market, or existing suppliers might have expanded, to give those people something to spend their money on. But in 1941, any potential excess production capacity was going either to the U.S. military or across the ocean to support the British in their fight for survival.

Without some kind of intervention from the government, more money chasing fewer products would have caused prices to skyrocket. Price controls and rationing prevented a situation where only the richest would have been able to afford meat, fresh fruit, a new pair of shoes, and many other basics. But the price control system was clearly imperfect: there were shortages, empty shelves, long lines, black markets.

A Committee on Price Control and Rationing was organized, with Leo as its Associate Director, to determine what was working and what wasn't, with a view to improving the system. Operating under the joint auspices of the Cowles Commission and the Conference on Price Research of the National Bureau of Economic Research, a private nonprofit research organization, the committee was headed by a psychologist, George Katona.[2]

Leo's involvement with this study was probably a result of his lowly position on the Cowles totem pole: both in subject matter and in investigative/analytical approach, this was not what anyone at the Commission really wanted to be doing. As far as subject matter goes, they would have preferred to be studying business cycles, figuring out how to mitigate against the next Great Depression. More importantly, their organizational mission was to apply advanced mathematical and statistical analysis tools to economic problems, while the study—reflecting Katona's psychological orientation—was based on extended

---

2   Findings were published near the end of the war in a book-length report, with Katona as the author: *Price Control and Business: Field Studies among Producers and Distributors of Consumer Goods in the Chicago Area, 1942–44.* Published as Cowles Commission for Research in Economics, Monograph No. 9, by The Principia Press, Inc., Bloomington Indiana, 1945.

interviews with a small sampling of businessmen, better suited to discovering motives than to compiling quantitative data.[3]

In addition, it seems that what Leo was actually doing may have been as much leg work as brain work: "Mr. Leonid Hurwicz, the first Associate Director of the Committee, conducted its first surveys,[4] ..."

Leo's direct, hands-on role in the price controls study was short-lived: he moved into a "consulting" role after only about half a year because ...

On December 7, 1941, at 7:48 AM local time, Japan launched a surprise attack on the U.S. naval base at Pearl Harbor, near Honolulu. Coming in two waves over a span of just 90 minutes, three hundred fifty-three Japanese fighter planes, bombers and torpedo bombers hit all eight U.S. Navy battleships in the harbor. Four of the ships went to the bottom. Also sunk or damaged were three destroyers, three cruisers, a minelayer and an anti-aircraft training ship. One hundred eighty-eight U.S. aircraft were lost, 2,403 Americans killed, and 1,178 wounded.

The next day, Roosevelt gave a now-famous speech to Congress. ("Yesterday, December 7, 1941—a date which will live in infamy . . .") Eighty-one percent of American homes tuned in to the live broadcast—the largest radio audience in U.S. history. An hour later, Congress declared war on Japan. On December 6, the nation had been deeply divided on the question of entering the war. On December 8, it was united in shock and outrage. On December 11, Germany and Italy declared war on the U.S., and the U.S. returned the favor.

Leo had long been disgusted and depressed by attempts to appease the Fascists in order to avoid war, a policy that had encouraged Hitler to invade Poland, and that had offered no resistance when he did. Now the whole might of America—and its massive ability to manufacture tanks, planes, ships, shells, bombs—would be unleashed against the Axis. It was a turning point that could well save his family.

At the same time, the German assault on Russia seemed to have stalled on the outskirts of Moscow, partly because of the onset of winter, but perhaps just as much due to the absolute refusal of the Russians to stop fighting, even at the cost of incredible destruction and loss of lives.

While thousands of Americans rushed to enlist, Leo went to his statistics professor (perhaps Theodore Yntema?) and asked what he could do to help the war

---

3   Katona, *op. cit.*, p. 4
4   Katona, *op. cit.*, vii

effort.[5] This got him involved, before long, in something almost as crazy and unpredictable as the economy: the weather.

Perhaps one of the lesser-known aspects of the war effort was the need to quickly train thousands of military personnel as weather forecasters. More than 6,000 weathermen and women were trained over the course of the war—though Army Air Forces (AAF) Brigadier General Harold McClelland, director of AAF Technical Services, estimated the need at 10,000. The magnitude of this effort becomes apparent when one considers that there were only 377 weather forecasters in the entire nation as of July 1940. Five prestigious civilian universities were involved: UCLA, MIT, NYU, the California Institute of Technology, and the University of Chicago.[6]

However, for the first half of 1942, Leo continued working at the Cowles Commission, still focusing on price controls and rationing. Cowles Commission researchers went out and interviewed Chicago businessmen to find out how price controls and rationing were affecting them. Leo "was the associate director of the project; during the first half of the year he was actively in charge of its administration, and during the latter part of the year he continued to act as consultant and advisor."[7]

This research turned out to be a real-world course on the vicissitudes of central planning. The report's chapter titles suggest that the attempt to prevent price increases was less than entirely successful:

- Legal Direct Price Increases
- Illegal Direct Price Increases
- Indirect Price Increases: Quality Deterioration
- Reduction in Number and Size of Markdowns
- Uptrading: Shift to Better-Grade Merchandise

To add a bit more detail:

Some people found ways to raise prices within the law, either because some commodities were not controlled, or because current prices were below those allowed. If the control price of a particular line was too low, a merchant might discontinue that line and start selling, at higher prices, another line not sold previously. Some processors and wholesalers also discontinued unprofitable lines.

---

5   Ann Bauer, "Leonid Hurwicz's Game," *Twin Cities Business*, March 1, 2008, p. 5, https://www.leonidhurwicz.org/tcb/

6   J.M. Lewis, "WAVES Forecasters in World War II," p. 2187, *Bulletin of the American Meteorological Society*, November, 1995.

7   Cowles Commission for Research in Economics, *Report for 1942*, p. 2.

In some cases, a "similar product" was sold (as allowed under the price control legislation), but of inferior quality, thereby effectively raising the price. In the shoe industry, the report said that "the government had reserved the best sole leather for military use and that tanners were selling low-grade leather at high-grade prices." In other cases, previously common sales and markdowns were eliminated, again effectively raising prices. In general, all this was within the letter of the law.

Then again, some people, either knowingly or unknowingly, sold goods above the legal "ceiling price." For instance, an interviewee at a large shoe chain that also sold handbags said, "There is no ceiling on handbags, and they've gone up terrifically in price." This individual was "greatly surprised" to find out that handbags were indeed price-controlled.

In some cases, mainly involving meat and produce, the law was just flagrantly violated:

> Some merchants also maintained their customary pricing procedures in deliberate violation of the law, but only with great scruples and only when they considered the resultant price increases "justified."

One might be tempted to conclude that price controls just didn't work. In fact, however, the report concludes they actually worked fairly well for some things and not so well for others, and better at some times than others. (See the graph below, based on the Bureau of Labor Statistics cost-of-living index.) Katona said in his 1942 book, *War Without Inflation*, that "in general the OPA was successful in stabilizing those few prices which it singled out for action . . ." Note that the graph shows prices leveling off overall, and in the case of food falling significantly, after the summer of 1943, when controls became more pervasive, more enforceable (largely because they were simpler), better enforced, and more widely understood and accepted. For meat and butter, the government enforced a ten percent price "roll-back" with subsidies to middlemen and processors to make up for their losses. Favorable weather also played a role in increasing supplies of hogs, cattle and milk.[8] Nevertheless, "new price regulations and better compliance also played a substantial role in stabilizing food prices."[9]

---

8   Maury Klein, *A Call to Arms: Mobilizing America for World War II*, p. 592. Bloomsbury Press, 2013.
9   George Katona, *Price Control and Business: Field Studies among Producers and Distributors of Consumer Goods in the Chicago Area, 1942–44*, p. 87.

(The graph below is from George Katona, *Price Control and Business: Field Studies among Producers and Distributors of Consumer Goods in the Chicago Area, 1942–44*, p. 26.)

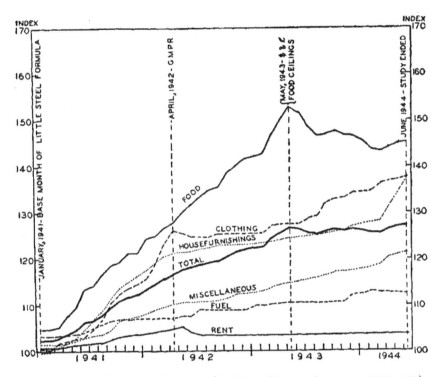

Figure 2. Prices paid by Ultimate Consumers (BLS Cost-of-Living Index; August, 1939 = 100).

One of Katona's most salient points was that attitudes played an important role in the success of price controls and rationing. For example, patriotism made many willing to "play by the rules" even if it meant personal sacrifice. On the other hand, a perception that the regulations were unfair, poorly managed, or impractical made others unwilling to cooperate. Katona proposed education that would go beyond mere propaganda to give people an understanding of how and why the system worked. (Katona was a psychologist by training. His book was subtitled "The Psychological Approach to Problems of War Economy.")

Although the price controls study was not Leo's ideal job, this street-level contact with the business world gave him a gut-level feel for the motivations behind cheating and idealism in economic systems. Later, he would speak of "intervenors" as a potential key to ensuring the proper functioning of economic mechanisms; intervenors were individuals or groups that would act to make sure rules were followed, irrespective of personal benefit, just because they believed in the rules.[10]

After being actively involved in the price controls study for about half of the year 1942, Leo taught for a time at the Illinois Institute of Technology, in the electronics program of the U.S. Army Signal Corps. There, he taught prospective Army and Navy inductees the statistics, mathematics and physics needed to analyze weather data generated by radar. He then joined the faculty of the Institute of Meteorology, teaching statistics and engaging in "statistical and other research activities."[11]

Wanting to do as much as he could to help the war effort, he asked a colonel if he should volunteer for the army. The colonel told him it would be the worst thing he could do: the army bureaucracy would make it impossible for him to do anything.[12]

Leo also stayed involved with the Cowles Commission: he "moved back and forth between the Institute of Meteorology and the Commission and worked on similar ideas in both places."[13]

Meanwhile, the situation in Europe was looking very dark. On November 25, 1942, multiple American newspapers reported that two million Jews, many of them German and Polish, had already been murdered. Though the Nazi plan to exterminate the Jews of Europe had been reported months earlier, many had dismissed it as "war rumors." Now the U.S. State Department, after months of investigation, confirmed the truth of these rumors.

The Jews of Białystok were liquidated from February to November 1943. When the Nazis entered the ghetto on August 16, 1943, resistance fighters met them, and the ensuing battle continued for about a month. After the Białystok Ghetto uprising was crushed, all the remaining inhabitants (around 40,000 people) were either killed locally or transported by train to the Majdanek and Treblinka death camps. How many of the estimated 50,000 Jews who had been in Białystok in June 1941, eventually survived? A minuscule percentage.

---

10   Leonid Hurwicz, "But Who Will Guard the Guardians?" Nobel Prize Lecture, December 8, 2007, https://www.nobelprize.org/prizes/economic-sciences/2007/hurwicz/lecture/. Accessed May 7, 2021.

11   Cowles Commission, *Report for 1942*, p. 5, https://cowles.yale.edu/sites/default/files/files/pub/rep/r1942.pdf. Accessed October 15, 2022.

12   *Longfellow/Nokomis Messenger*, "Nokomis Resident Wins Nobel Prize," December 2007, p. 14. Leonid Hurwicz Papers, David M. Rubenstein Rare Book & Manuscript Library, Duke University, incorrectly filed under National Medal of Science 1990.

13   Olav Bjerkholt, Memorandum 26, "Trygve Haavelmo at the Cowles Commission," 2013, p. 45, https://www.sv.uio.no/econ/english/research/Memoranda/working-papers/pdf-files/2013/memo-26-2013.pdf. Accessed October 13, 2022.

Adek, Zina and Henry had escaped the fate of the Białystok ghetto. They had survived persecution by a Russian autocrat. Had they gone through all that only to now face death at the hands of the German dictator?

Now together in Georgia where Adek had joined Zina and Henry, they could gaze across the Black Sea, knowing that on the opposite shore, though hundreds of miles away and out of sight, was Nazi ally Romania, a country that had exterminated tens of thousands of its own Jews and helped Hitler invade Russia in 1941. Georgia itself, though under Russian control, had its fascist sympathizers. In fact, a Georgian Legion, currently supporting Nazi efforts elsewhere, had as its expressed purpose returning to "liberate" their home country and implement Nazi policies, including ridding the country of Jews.

Now that everyone knew what was going on, would the Allies finally launch rescue operations? There was much talk about "bloody cruelties" and "cold-blooded extermination," many promises that perpetrators would be punished after the war. Very rarely did anyone in an official capacity mention actually doing something right now to save intended victims. Even when Polish underground hero Jan Karski met personally with FDR on July 28, 1943 and described the horrors he had seen with his own eyes, he was assured only that the Allies would win the war. How many millions of innocent people might die before the day of victory? He was given no reassurance on that score.

In the winter of 1943, Leo went to Washington, D.C., to consult with the government on long-range weather prediction. While in D.C., he got an emergency call from the executive secretary at the Institute of Meteorology: the teaching assistant for his meteorology class had quit. He needed to return immediately to begin the process of hiring a new one. Or . . . there was an economics undergrad named Evelyn Jensen, who seemed very bright, and had just finished working on a project having to do with electrical storms in the Midwest.[14] Leo talked with her on the phone and asked her if she could type. She said no. He asked her if she could learn. She said yes. He hired her.[15] Then he came back to Chicago, they fell in love and . . .

. . . that starts a new chapter.

---

14 *Longfellow/Nokomis Messenger*, "Nokomis Resident Wins Nobel Prize," December 2007, p. 14. Leonid Hurwicz Papers, David M. Rubenstein Rare Book & Manuscript Library, Duke University, incorrectly filed under National Medal of Science 1990.

15 As told by Carla Rosenlicht to her daughter Giovanna. Carla was at the University of Chicago from 1940 to 1943 and became a friend of Evelyn's and then a lifelong friend of the family.

CHAPTER 23

Honey

———

I attribute it all to Evelyn. Without her, you could not have survived so long. I heard that the book finally got finished because she would not go traveling with you until it was finished.
— Harvard statistician, colleague and friend Herman Chernoff, in an email congratulating Leo on winning the Nobel Prize

Evelyn Jensen, later to become known as "honey" (by Leo) and "mom" (by the rest of the family), was born into a Lutheran Wisconsin farm family on October 31, 1923. Her stories of her early life, though probably typical of rural America at the time, have something of the flavor of *Little House on the Prairie.* To take a bath, they had to carry water into the house by the bucketful, heat it on the stove and pour it into the tub. (Whether the source was a well or a pump, getting the water was probably hand labor, since few farms had electricity until the '30s.) One of Evelyn's teachers told the class that they should bathe every day, but with no indoor plumbing and a family of six (Evelyn, three brothers, two parents), one bath a week each was a practical limit.

There was no heat in the house except the wood cookstove in the kitchen, so on winter nights that's where they would all gather until bedtime. The stove was also used to heat bed warmers, which took the chill off their beds so that they didn't have to climb into freezing sheets. Horse-drawn wagon was a common conveyance. Evelyn told of a neighbor, a bachelor farmer, who would go into town on weekends to drink with his friends. Coming back, he'd often fall asleep at the reins. The horse would take him home, and he'd wake up when the horse stopped at his front door.

Both her parents were born in Wisconsin. Her grandparents on her father's side were born in Denmark, on her mother's side in Sweden.

Her mother's maiden name was Smith, not a typically Swedish name. Evelyn said that originally her maternal grandparents' surname was Peterson. But there were so many Petersons in Wisconsin at that time, that mail kept getting misdelivered. So they changed their name to Smith, giving her grandfather the unusual and distinctive name "John Smith."

Her family, as she described it, were "farmers and factory workers ... [T]he generation before me—in fact I think even my generation—didn't have college degrees. I'm the only one of four children in my family who got a college degree. ... My mother worked for years in a Chinese laundry. ..."[1]

So, coming from this background, she naturally ended up marrying a lefty Polish-Jewish refugee economist!

Actually, they did have at least two things in common in their backgrounds: the Great Depression (which in both cases led to an interest in economics) and a society permeated by socialism—and a similar brand of socialism, at that.

The 1920s were tough times for rural Americans, with the prices farmers could get for crops falling steadily, and the prices they paid for most non-farm products staying the same. By the early '30s, the price of corn fell so low that in some places farmers were burning their corn crops to heat their homes, because it was cheaper than buying coal.[2] In the '50s, the Hurwicz family record collection would include Pete Seeger's *American Industrial Ballads* album, with songs like "The Farmer is the Man" ("His pants are wearing thin, his condition it's a sin"). But in the '20s and '30s, Evelyn's family lived those songs.

Evelyn's father, John Arthur ("Art") always seemed to be having a tough time on the work front. He never owned his own farm. When Evelyn was just a few months old, Art was working the Smith family farm (belonging to John and Elizabeth Smith, the parents of Evelyn's mother, Hazel). He wrote to his brother George, "We need a new plow and mower and if I'm to have them why I expect I'll have to buy them myself and I won't invest in machinery until I own some land myself." In early February 1924, he was in the hospital having his appendix out. The doctor said his gall bladder was in bad shape, too, but he didn't dare to remove it, because he thought it would be too much for Art's heart.[3] (Art, though he did not know it, had leaky heart valves, a condition that results in fatigue and lightheadedness, among other symptoms.) In early March, Art took off for Duluth, Minnesota, looking for work, and by late March, he was

---

1   Appendix A.

2   "The Great Depression Hits Farms and Cities in the 1930s," Iowa Public Television, https://www.iowapbs.org/iowapathways/mypath/2591/great-depression-hits-farms-and-cities-1930s Accessed October 13, 2022.

3   Florence (Jensen) Smith, sister of Arthur John Jensen, writing to her brother George R. Jensen, from Almena, Wisconsin, on February 4, 1924.

working on a farm 80 miles north of Duluth.[4] In April he got work in a steel plant in Duluth.[5] By May, he was working for a contractor, operating a large cement mixer, 10- and 11-hour days, making 45 cents an hour (less than $7 an hour in 2020 dollars).

In any case, the difficulty of making a living by farming was probably the reason that, before Evelyn was seven, her family moved from their farm near Almena, Wisconsin, to West Allis, an industrial suburb of Milwaukee, where Art could put his experience with farm machinery to good use working for the Allis-Chalmers Manufacturing Company, famous for its poppy-colored ("Persian orange") tractors. The town was growing by leaps and bounds: from a population of 6,645 in 1910 to 34,671 in 1930.[6] The company was doing well, too, even after the depression hit.

In the 1930 census, Arthur gave his occupation as "inspector" in the "tractor parts" industry. In these years, "Wisconsin workers joined unions in droves, making Wisconsin one of the most unionized of states on a percentage basis . . . Wisconsin employers, however, fought back and resisted unionization."[7] Arthur was a victim of that resistance: by 1940 he was an elevator operator in a hospital, making $1,200 a year (according to the 1940 census) at a time when an average wage in manufacturing was around $1,350 a year.[8] According to Evelyn, he had lost his previous job due to union activity.

The union that was eventually recognized at Allis-Chalmers in 1937 was Local 248 of the UAW-CIO. The largest, most influential labor union in Wisconsin, it has been described by researcher Yu Takeda as "communist-oriented."[9] Later, in the McCarthy era, the company used this communist orientation against the union, while suggesting that the communist leadership had led the innocent

---

4   "Hazel had a letter and card from Art. He is working on a farm at Buhl, Minn, That is 77 miles north of Duluth. But I guess he plans on coming to Duluth when the steel plant opens." Florence (Jensen) Smith, sister of John Arthur Jensen, writing to her brother George R. Jensen, from Almena, Wisconsin, on March 28, 1924.

5   "We haven't heard anything from Art lately. But Hazel says he is back in Duluth working in some Carbon plant." Alfred Sandberg and Nellie (Jensen) Sandberg ("Al and Nell") writing to her brother George R. Jensen, from Almena, Wisconsin, on April 16, 1924.

6   "West Allis, Wisconsin," https://en.wikipedia.org/wiki/West_Allis,_Wisconsin

7   Ken Germanson, "Milestones In Wisconsin Labor History," Wisconsin Labor History Society, August 20, 2012.

8   *Handbook of labor statistics / U.S. Department of Labor, Bureau of Labor Statistics, 1941 edition.* https://babel.hathitrust.org/cgi/pt?id=uiug.30112018120003;view=1up;seq=15

9   Yu Takeda, *The Allis-Chalmers Strike in 1941 and the Issue of Communism,* June 25, 1982 (on file with Osaka Kyoiku University).

members astray.[10] Takeda, however, concluded that "[t]he sympathy for communists and communist ideas reflected a general left-wing orientation of the membership and not just the machinations of a few leaders."

Arthur Vidich, a friend of Evelyn's—they skipped school together to go see *Gone with the Wind* in Milwaukee in 1939—said in his memoir, "Others—including Finns, Scandinavians, and Eastern Europeans—who were or had been socialists became communists or Soviet sympathizers; underpaid and underemployed Allis Chalmers workers were radicalized."[11]

In fact, all during the '30s and for decades before, Wisconsin, and particularly Milwaukee, was a hotbed of socialism/communism. In 1910, Wisconsin's 5th congressional district elected a Socialist, Victor Berger, to the U.S. House of Representatives—the first time in history any state had sent a Socialist to Congress. (The 5th district was a Milwaukee district at the time. It was gerrymandered beyond recognition in 2000.) Thanks largely to the leadership of labor and the Socialist Party in Milwaukee (and progressives elsewhere in the state), Wisconsin in 1911 hatched a communist plot called "workers' compensation"—the first state in the nation to do so.[12] In 1932—again, first in the nation—the state instituted unemployment insurance. From 1910–1912, from 1916–1940, and from 1948–1960 the Mayor of Milwaukee was a member of the Socialist Party of Wisconsin. Milwaukee had the first Socialist mayor in the U.S. (Emil Seidel) and the last (Frank P. Zeidler).

The mayor while Evelyn was growing up was Daniel Webster Hoan, who could boast the longest continuous Socialist administration in U.S. history. His radical left-wing programs included public housing, a city-owned bus system, and municipal ownership of the sewage system, street lighting and water purification. The "Sewer Socialists," as they were sometimes called because of their focus on public works, had little concern for Marxism, social theory or revolutionary rhetoric. Instead, they focused on honest government, grassroots democracy and public health.

10   "The Next Five Years: A Story of the Contract Between Allis-Chalmers Manufacturing Company and Local 248 United Auto Workers-CIO," 1950, https://leonidhurwicz.org/allis-chalmers-red-baiting/, https://fau.digital.flvc.org/islandora/object/fau%3A4547. Accessed October 11, 2022.

11   Arthur J. Vidich, *With a Critical Eye*, p. 112, https://trace.tennessee.edu/utk_newfound-ebooks/11/. Accessed October 11, 2022.

12   "WLHS Primer on Wisconsin Labor History," revised November 2018, WLHS = Wisconsin Labor History Society.

Arthur Vidich describes the politics of West Allis:

> In West Allis, as in Milwaukee, under a socialist ideology that
> presupposed governmental responsibility for social welfare,
> civic benevolence fell under the purview of public adminis-
> tration. The well-being of the mass of workers and small mer-
> chants was to be aided and abetted by enlightened social policy.
> Milwaukee's socialism was a moral and civic socialism created by
> Lutheran capitalists. When I was growing up, a socialistic infra-
> structure—including schools, playgrounds, parks, and a refor-
> matory—was already in place.[13]

So the Milwaukee socialists Evelyn grew up with believed in democracy, cooperation among all elements of society, and working through peaceful means such
as unions as opposed to violent revolution—much the same views that forced
the Menshevik Hurwicz family to run back to Warsaw after Lenin took power in
Russia. Thus, it was natural that Leo and Evelyn shared a worldview founded on
peaceful, inclusive, democratic, lefty social and political values. In fact, this was
the worldview that provided the basis for Leo's professional mission, because if
governments were going to design and implement institutions with economic
functions, with the intention of benefitting both specific groups (such as children) and society overall, it was important that the designers have not just good
intentions, but good understanding and tools.

Evelyn was an excellent student. In her senior year of high school at West Allis
Central High School, she was a valedictorian, was on student council and also
won a forensic (competitive speech) award and a Latin award.[14] She wanted
to be a teacher and, after high school, attended the Milwaukee State Teachers
College and the University of Wisconsin at Madison. The family story is that
one of her teachers, impressed with her intelligence, submitted her as a scholarship candidate to the University of Chicago. Records there show that she started
classes on January 4, 1943.

Her major was economics—another interest in common with Leo. In fact, a
little-known family secret is that she was better at economics than he was: she

---

13 Arthur J. Vidich, *With a Critical Eye*, p. 82, https://trace.tennessee.edu/utk_newfound-
    ebooks/11/. Accessed October 11, 2022. Download this free book for more about West Allis
    in the 1924-1940 era.
14 "Wamago" yearbook, West Allis Central High School, 1941. https://www.leonidhurwicz.
    org/evelyn-hurwicz/; https://www.classmates.com/siteui/yearbooks/171856?page=64

handled all the family finances, and—by buying houses, fixing them up and reselling them in an era when that could be quite profitable—may have made more money than he did. Her money-management capabilities were also recognized by her high school classmates: in her junior year, she was class Treasurer.

The war was going better now. In January 1944, the Soviet army ended 872 days of German bombardment when it lifted the German siege of Leningrad, a siege that resulted in starvation and even cannibalism, with Russian casualties larger than combined American and British losses for the whole war. Following up on the surrender of Italy in September 1943, the Allies liberated Rome from the Germans in June 1944.

On June 6, the beginning of the end for the Axis: D-Day, the Allies' massive attack on German forces in Normandy in Western France. Planned for June 5, the attack was postponed to June 6th based on a somewhat more favorable weather prediction. Note the importance of accurate meteorology! Inaccurate meteorology also played a role: because the Allies controlled the Atlantic, German meteorologists had difficulty getting good information on incoming weather patterns, and had predicted two weeks of stormy weather. Many military personnel were given extended leave. Field Marshal Erwin Rommel returned to Germany.

Leo and Evelyn were married in Chicago on July 19, 1944. She converted to Judaism. They had a Jewish marriage ceremony: the *ketubah* (Jewish marriage contract) was prominently displayed on the wall in their home. Klara says Evelyn even did the ritual bath (*mikvah*) a traditional part of conversion to Judaism and also for brides before the wedding.[15]

Evelyn had tendencies toward religious search: she had been raised Lutheran and at some point converted to Catholicism. In addition, at a time when Hitler had done and was still doing his best to stamp out Jewish people, Jewish culture, Jewish traditions, the Hurwicz family made it clear from its inception that they were not going to allow that. Later, Leo was fond of quoting, as a summary of every Jewish holiday: "They tried to kill us; they failed; let's eat!" They would celebrate Passover and Chanukah, as well as Christmas—with a tree, presents and carols—and Easter—with an Easter egg hunt and bunny-shaped chocolates: Leo's principle was "all of the feasts, none of the fasts." Klara mentions that her family had a Christmas tree in Warsaw before World War II, so this was not an unknown or unique pattern.

---

15   Klara Samuels, *God Does Play Dice*, BainBridgeBooks, p. 31.

Below is a picture of Evelyn and Leo with some friends at the Hotel Bismarck in Chicago, just a few days later, on July 23. (They're the ones who are totally in love and can't stop looking at each other.)

CHAPTER 24

A Little Bit Unruly

In early 1945, while the Allies were making breakthroughs in Europe, Leo had another kind of breakthrough: the possibility of his first permanent academic position, as an associate professor at Iowa State College (now Iowa State University) in Ames, to begin in the fall semester. This would be a tenured position, just one step below a full professorship.

Normally, one would not expect to become an associate professor without first being an assistant professor. Iowa State's interest no doubt reflected the high opinion the department had of Leo and the strong recommendations he would have received from well-known economists like Lange and Samuelson.

In addition, however, the Economics and Sociology department at Iowa State had an unusual number of higher-level positions to fill, having recently been struck, blindsided and capsized by . . . butter and margarine. Actually, it was a 35-page pamphlet *about* butter and margarine.

Since the early '30s, Iowa State had been building a highly regarded economics department under the leadership of Theodore W. Schultz, who joined the department in 1930, became acting head of agricultural economics in 1932, and permanent head of the Economics and Sociology department in 1935. An "Ames School" of economics had arisen, known for rigorous science and fearless, impartial policy recommendations.[1]

The fateful pamphlet, "Putting Dairying on a War Footing," authored by graduate student Oz Brownlee, was initially released in April 1943, under the imprint of the Iowa State College Press. It was fifth in the college's Wartime Farm and Food Policy series. The pamphlet suggested various ways of addressing the shortage of dairy products for soldiers—among others, consuming more

---

[1] This and subsequent descriptions of "The Butter-Margarine Controversy" are primarily based on the author's reading and interpretation of David L. Seim, "The Butter-Margarine Controversy and 'Two Cultures' at Iowa State College," p. 47 ff, https://pubs.lib.uiowa.edu/annals-of-iowa/article/id/14081/. Accessed October 11, 2022.

margarine and less butter at home. It also suggested that margarine was equal to butter in nutrition and palatability.

Unfortunately (for Oz and the department), Iowa was second in the country in dairy production at that time, and had a powerful dairy lobby—which exploded in indignation, demanding that the pamphlet be retracted and the faculty members involved dismissed. Among other things, the lobbyists suggested that a state-funded institution should not be making recommendations that would harm the state—or perhaps should not be making policy recommendations at all.

In other words, the question was essentially, "At an Iowa cow college, which should come first: winning the war, or selling butter?" (Or should winning the war even enter the picture?)

To be fair, Iowa Farmers Union president Donald Van Fleet did speak out against what he called a "witch hunt . . . to smother free thought at our state schools."[2] The American Association of University Professors (AAUP) and the ACLU threatened to investigate.

University President Charles E. Friley tried hard to stave off attacks from all sides (academics, free speech advocates and the dairy industry), while balancing principles of academic freedom with the need to stay on good terms with those who could (through the legislature) have a powerful influence on the school's budget. It proved an impossible task. The revised report that was ultimately released was substantially equivalent to the original, although a few points had been finessed. (It turned out, for example, that margarine was merely "nutritious" and "acceptable by many consumers as a spread." The comparison with butter—in that particular sentence at least—had disappeared.)

Schultz, the guiding light of the department, resigned unexpectedly on September 15, 1943, accepting an offer to go to the University of Chicago. The best of the younger economists in the department followed him. In the end (around May 1944), nobody was happy and "ISC's Department of Economics and Sociology was in shambles."[3] Ultimately, 16 out of 26 economics faculty members left the school between 1943 and 1945, and more in the next few years. Within three years or so, while the department remained, the school of thought that had grown up there had vanished.

Leo's position at Iowa State would pay $4,300 a year—well over $60,000 in 2020 dollars. This would perhaps be irresistible to the newlyweds looking to start a family and straining their budget to send food packages to Adek, Zina and

2   *Des Moines Register*, 5/25/1943, as quoted in Seim.
3   Seim, *op.cit.*, p. 47.

Henry. Even more important was the need to assure American authorities that Leo's family would not become a public burden if granted immigration visas: Leo's number one priority at that time was getting Adek, Zina and Henry out of their current situation, ideally by getting them into the U.S. Leo and Evelyn may also have wanted to get out of Chicago, where thefts and assaults were common in the University district.[4]

Even though Leo had not received a firm offer from Iowa State, Cowles Commission research director Jacob Marschak, who had known Leo since 1942, started plotting to keep him involved with the Commission. Marschak started by helping Leo get a Guggenheim Fellowship for 1945/1946. (The other three references listed on a draft of the application were Oskar Lange, Paul A. Samuelson and Theodore O. Yntema.) Marschak's opinion of Leo was reflected in this comment in support of the Guggenheim:

> He is without any doubt one of the most creative and brilliant men of his generation in his field. His particular gift is that of quickly discovering the essentials of a problem, piercing through the cloud of verbiage, side-issues, lazy-minded vagueness and well-meant or malicious superstition which still surrounds most of economic discussion. His favorite words, to start a sentence in discussion are, "Essentially, the problem boils down to this," and what follows is, in most cases, essential indeed.[5]

Leo was particularly valued at Cowles for his ability to critique other people's work. Cowles economist Tjalling Koopmans (1975 Nobel Prize recipient, jointly with Leonid Kantorovich) had this to say:

> Our work is based on a division of labor, where the different parts are highly complementary. Marschak is the general manager, and participates actively in all matters except pure mathematics. In particular, he works on the theoretical economics side. Lawrence Klein drafts the equations, tries different assumptions and because of the tempo by which he moves through the

4   Clifford Hildreth, "The Cowles Commission in Chicago, 1939–1955," Cowles Commission Discussion Paper No. 225, October 1985, p. 4.
5   Letter from Jacob Marschak to the Guggenheim Foundation, The Jacob Marschak Papers, UCLA Library Special Collections, Charles E. Young Research Library. The letter is undated but begins, "I have known Leonid Hurwicz for more than 3 years, especially closely during the last year (1944) . . ."

different subsets of the system of equations, he gives the others no opportunity to lose themselves in theoretical or methodological details. Leonid Hurwicz is our critic, a role which fits his sharp and nimble spirit.[6]

A competitive offer from the University of Chicago was not an option: the Cowles Commission was not able to offer faculty positions to research associates. Accordingly, in June, 1944, Marschak suggested that, with the consent of Iowa State, Leo could continue working for the Commission, remotely for the most part, reading and criticizing papers by Cowles staff, presenting his own work for discussion, and attending regular conferences at Cowles.[7] Marschak was only able to offer Leo a $50-a-month honorarium for this work (around $740 a month in 2020 dollars).

In November 1944, Leo was in Ames, testing the waters and waiting to see if they would make him an offer. Marschak wrote to Leo discussing possible financial terms if Leo remained at Cowles, assuming the Guggenheim came through. He concluded by saying, "Don't let Ames snatch you away. We are poorer and cannot make splendid offers—as you know, our wealth is a spiritual one!"[8]

On December 1, Marschak wrote again, "Thank you for your letter of November 25. I agree with your suggestion. As you say, it will carry us, in the worst case, for a full year minus ten days. But favorable contingencies may be expected (such as the granting of a Guggenheim fellowship) which would extend our cooperation further."[9] (Note that Leo had calculated the time period to the day. Of course, one would expect no less.)

The remote participation arrangement suggested by Marschak was not immediately necessary, however, because Leo did get the Guggenheim. The $2,000 award, along with an annual salary from Cowles of just under $1,700,[10] permitted him to continue working full-time with the Commission for another year starting

---

6   Tjalling Koopmans to Jan Tinbergen, July 18, 1945; Jan Tinbergen Papers, Erasmus University, Holland, Jolink translation from the Dutch. Quoted in Philip Mirowski (2012), "The Cowles Commission as an anti-Keynesian stronghold 1943–54," p. 155.

7   Jacob Marschak to Leonid Hurwicz, June 26, 1944, The Jacob Marschak Papers, UCLA Library Special Collections, Charles E. Young Research Library.

8   Jacob Marschak to Leonid Hurwicz, November 22, 1944, The Jacob Marschak Papers, UCLA Library Special Collections, Charles E. Young Research Library.

9   Jacob Marschak to Leonid Hurwicz, December 1, 1944, The Jacob Marschak Papers, UCLA Library Special Collections, Charles E. Young Research Library.

10   $1,678.08. Box 148, folder: Cowles Commission Treasurer Reports, The Jacob Marschak Papers, UCLA Library Special Collections, Charles E. Young Research Library, reproduced in Philip Mirowski, *Machine Dreams*, 2002, Table 4.1.

in June of 1945, taking a leave of absence from Ames—where he had never actually started working. The leave of absence officially ran from September 16, 1945, through April 30, 1946. Final exams generally occur in late April and the first few days of May, so this was really the whole 1945/46 academic year at Iowa State.

Accepting a position and then immediately taking a leave of absence is perhaps an early example of Leo's tendency to be, as economic historian Olav Bjerkholt observed,[11] "a little bit unruly." It also had to do with priorities: what he really cared about was the opportunity to develop, test and share ideas. In that regard, Iowa State College, especially still reeling as it was from the blows of the butter-margarine controversy, could not compete with the Cowles Commission and its "staff meetings"—wide-ranging seminars in which new ideas were presented, or more graphically, where "everybody got together in a room with blackboards, and they spent the whole day talking at each other—about interesting things."[12]

Economist Herbert Simon gives a delightful description of these meetings:

> A visitor's first impression at a Cowles seminar was that everyone was talking at once, each in a different language. The impression was not wholly incorrect. . . . But the accents may have been more a help than a hindrance to understanding. When several speakers tried to proceed simultaneously, by holding tight to the fact you were trying to listen to, say, the Austrian accent, you could sometimes single it out from the Polish, Italian, Norwegian, Ukrainian, Greek, Dutch, or middle American. As impressive as the cacophony was the intellectual level of the discussion, and most impressive of all was the fact that everyone, in the midst of the sharpest disagreements, remained warm friends.[13]

Nobel prize-winner Ken Arrow, who started working with the Commission in 1946, described the meetings as "models of constructive intellectual violence"[14]

---

11 Olav Bjerkholt, in an email to the author, May 7, 2018.
12 Stan Reiter, Appendix B. Reiter also mentions staff meetings in Appendix A.
13 Herbert A. Simon, *Models of My Life*, MIT Press, October 8, 1996, p. 102.
14 Clifford Hildreth, associate professor in the Cowles Commission and research associate, associate professor in the Department of Economics, "The Cowles Commission in Chicago, 1939–1955," Discussion Paper No. 225, October, 1985, Center for Economic Research, Department of Economics, University of Minnesota, p. 7, citing a letter from Kenneth J. Arrow, November 24, 1982.

and on another occasion remembered "bubbling over with new ideas and shouting at each other."[15]

While visitors were sometimes taken aback by the seeming lack of respect exhibited by even the lowliest of grad students for the most distinguished of professors, Cowles Commission Director Jacob Marschak encouraged this no-holds-barred style of communication. "Of course," Arrow added, "Hurwicz, [Herman] Rubin, and I needed little encouragement for our freewheeling ways."[16]

A rule was instituted that a speaker could be interrupted only for a "clarifying question." All interruptions were thereafter dutifully labeled "clarifying questions."

According to one observer, at least, Leo was the interrupter-in-chief:

> Leo Hurwicz was for some of the time on the staff, and was always a regular attendee at our meetings. It is hard to recreate the total ebullience of our staff meetings and seminars—Arrow talking at his usual 200 words per minute, never getting very far before being interrupted by Hurwicz's gravelly voice saying, "May I ask a clarifying question" and then taking over the floor. (At Cowles, only clarifying questions were permitted during the expository part of a presentation; so, quite predictably and I would say inevitably with this group, all questions automatically became "clarifying" ones.) Just as famous as Hurwicz's interruptions was [Franco] Modigliani's unstoppability—a trait that all his friends will testify he did not leave behind when he moved on from the Cowles Commission. Nowhere have I ever experienced such a glorious intellectual melee as Arrow trying to expound, with Hurwicz regularly interrupting, and Modigliani simply taking over the floor any time he ever got the first word in, and finally with Koopmans and Marschak vainly trying to keep—sorry, I mean restore—order. All of us will remember those days as long as we live.[17]

---

15 "Interview with Kenneth Arrow," *The Region*, a publication by the Federal Reserve Bank of Minneapolis, December 1, 1995. https://www.minneapolisfed.org/article/1995/interview-with-kenneth-arrow. Accessed October 11, 2022.

16 Clifford Hildreth, *op. cit.*

17 Arnold C. Harberger, "Carl Christ: Youthful times with Carl," *Carnegie-Rochester Conference Series on Public Policy*, Elsevier, vol. 45(1), December 1996, pages 3–7.

CHAPTER 25

The Great Book Review

During this period, Leo did something that was arguably more important for his future than the Guggenheim, more decisive for his career than the job offer at Iowa State, more significant for his intellectual evolution than his encounters with Hayek and Mises. And this life-changing, career-boosting, intellect-inspiring event was . . . writing a book review.

In September 1944, Princeton University Press published *Theory of Games and Economic Behavior* (TGEB), by mathematician John von Neumann and economist Oskar Morgenstern. The purpose of the book was to show that the theory of "games of strategy" (e.g. chess, "matching pennies," poker, bridge) was "the proper instrument with which to develop a theory of economic behavior."[1] The book shows—in detail and sometimes rigorously—how mathematical techniques associated with game theory ("the study of mathematical models of conflict and cooperation between intelligent rational decision-makers")[2] can be applied to economics.

The Cowles Commission found this interesting enough that they invited von Neumann to present a two-day seminar on the book in May 1945. Leo reviewed the book for *The American Economic Review* the following December.[3]

The book specifically addressed economics. However, as Leo pointed out: "The techniques applied by the authors in tackling economic problems are of sufficient generality to be valid in political science, sociology, or even military strategy."

---

1   John von Neumann and Oskar Morgenstern, *Theory of Games and Economic Behavior*, Princeton University Press, 1944, p. 2.
2   Roger Myerson, *Game Theory: Analysis of Conflict*, Harvard University Press, 1991.
3   Leonid Hurwicz, "The Theory of Economic Behavior," *The American Economic Review*, Vol. 35, No. 5, December 1945, p. 909, published by American Economic Association. Appendix C of this book reproduces the entire review.

This generality also made these tools applicable to a wide variety of economic mechanisms—including, for example, both "perfect competition" and various forms of imperfect competition right up to a centralized socialist command economy. A common set of analytical tools also held the promise of objective comparisons of economic mechanisms, perhaps even a rigorous approach to the socialist calculation debate.

For instance, where perfect competition assumed large numbers of buyers and sellers, no one of which could have any effect on price, game theory could be applied to two-person rivalry, in which each player had a significant (though of course not absolutely controlling—that would be no fun) effect on the outcome. Where perfect competition saw market participants making simple yes-no decisions about buying or selling at a particular price, game theory envisioned players considering a wide range of possible outcomes and making strategic moves to limit possible damage and/or secure at least a minimum of gain.

For example, imagine a grid in which one player chooses a row, another chooses a column, and the outcome of this simple "game" is the intersection of these choices. It could, for example, be a payment from one player to the other. Thus, this would be a "constant-sum" game, where one player's loss is the other's gain. Neither player can definitively control the outcome, because neither can control the other's choice. However, the first player can choose a row with a limited number of options for the second player to choose among.

It turns out that a game of this sort has a very interesting property called a "saddle-point."[4] The name derives from the fact that, if points on the grid are mapped to vertical elevations, the grid become a "saddle" with *rows* disposed in the direction of the rider's legs and *columns* disposed in the direction of the horse's head and tail.

---

4 This makes a standard assumption, namely, that "mixed strategies" are allowed. See Appendix C, pp. 185ff.

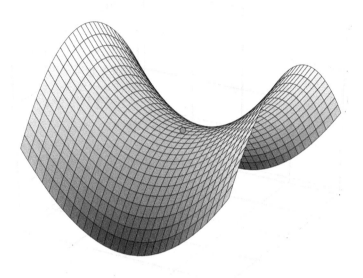

Figure 3. A saddle-point.[5]

If each point on this surface represents a possible payment from player A to player B, and player A first selects a row, after which player B selects a column, player A can minimize the potential payment by selecting the row in the middle of the saddle—the one with the dot on it. Player B, to maximize the payment, should then select the column that intersects that row at the dot, because that's the highest point on the row. Any other column will have a lower point on it, and thus a lower payment to player B.

The interesting thing about this solution is that they will end up with exactly the same point if player B makes the first choice. In that case, player B chooses the column with the dot, because that is the column with the "highest low" point. Any other column will be slightly down the side of the saddle and therefore have a lower elevation. Play A will then choose the row with the dot, because that is the row with the "lowest high" point—the lowest payment to B.

Saddle-point solutions are characterized by the fact that there is one point that is both the "lowest high" for one player and the "highest low" for the other. That point ends up being the only stable solution—the only one where neither party

5   Taken from https://commons.wikimedia.org/wiki/File:Saddle_point.svg. Public domain. Accessed June 11, 2021.

would change their choice once they found out the other party's choice. The saddle-point is a stable solution for both parties.

This kind of thinking offered hope for escape from scenarios like Kaldor's potentially unstable cobweb: under some conditions, at least, rational market participants, thinking ahead and acting strategically, would arrive at solutions which, while perhaps not ideal for either, would have to be accepted by both. Neither one, acting alone, could do better.

Game theory also modeled the knowledge problem well. The rules of the game, in a sense provided a "language." Players communicated, and the outcome was determined by that communication. Perfect competition fit within this model, but so did a wide variety of other economic mechanisms.

Leo's review, though it included strong praise ("a book of outstanding importance," "a highly novel analytical apparatus") and some criticism (primarily that the authors were prematurely dismissive of prior and current theoretical approaches in economics) was largely "of an expository nature." It attempted—in around 17 pages and using only simple arithmetic—to give a meaningful impression of what von Neumann and Morgenstern were proposing. Though not many economists made it through the book, quite a few did manage Leo's review, which became the gateway to game theory for those economists. Leo became recognized as an authoritative commentator and interpreter of game theory in its application to economics.

Initially, however, it seemed it was primarily mathematicians, not economists, who moved game theory forward. At the Cowles Commission specifically, game theory did not immediately lead to much in the way of published output. However, the absence of "output" may be more apparent than real, because much of the Cowles Commission's involvement with game theory was through the RAND (**R**esearch **AN**d **D**evelopment) corporation, a think tank serving the U.S. Air Force. John von Neumann's ideas, and von Neumann himself, were often center stage at RAND. Because of the military connection, not everything funded by RAND was published. Because RAND was largely devoted to winning the Cold War, they often found themselves having to make strategic moves with potentially dire consequences under incomplete or imperfect information.

Much like a Polish Jewish family who had fled into Soviet Georgia, in whose case, the maximum potential loss could include a slow and miserable death after getting sent back to the frozen northern swamps by the Bolsheviks for being the wrong kind of socialist.

CHAPTER 26

A Slow and Difficult Process

In the early '40s, when Russian-Polish relations were good (because the Russians wanted the Poles to help them against the Germans), Adek, ever the activist, had become a delegate in Georgia of the Polish government in exile. However, by 1944, with the Germans thoroughly crushed in Russia, it became clear that the Russians had no intention of supporting a strong or truly independent Poland: in fact, in the summer of 1944, the victorious Red Army deliberately and unnecessarily halted on the outskirts of Warsaw, giving the Germans time to regroup and stage a counterattack, killing thousands of Polish resistance fighters and murdering as many as 200,000 Polish civilians in mass executions.

At the same time, Germany was staring global defeat in the face. On August 24, French troops entered Paris, firing on German soldiers. Civilians broke out onto the streets singing *La Marseillaise*. ("Come children of the motherland, the hour of glory has arrived.") Within 24 hours, the German commander in Paris surrendered, and Charles de Gaulle became head of the Provisional Government of the French Republic.

In December 1944 and January 1945, the Allies beat back a German surprise attack in Belgium, northeast France and Luxembourg, in what became known as "The Battle of the Bulge"—the largest and bloodiest battle for Americans, and a decisive, crushing defeat for the Germans. Now the Russians no longer needed the Poles, and the Polish-Russian relationship soured.

The war officially ended in May 1945, with the Germans surrendering, first on the Eastern and then on the Western front. On May 1, 1945, Soviet General Zhukov accepted the German surrender of Berlin. On May 7, Germany signed an unconditional surrender at Allied headquarters in Reims, France; the surrender officially took effect the next day.

Shortly thereafter, Leo and Evelyn got a letter from Henry, who was now in the town of Łódź in Poland, around 80 miles from Warsaw, where he was staying with friends from Kutaisi and had enrolled at the Polytechnic Institute. He had been two months shy of 17 when the Germans and Soviets crushed Poland in September 1939. His education had been largely derailed for the past six years:

naturally, the family's first priority was to get Henry back in school. Perhaps they would have preferred Warsaw, but the city was 85% in ruins. On the other hand, the Germans had retreated so abruptly from Łódź that they hadn't had time to destroy it. For that reason, and because it was close to Warsaw, Łódź had now become the de facto temporary capital of Poland.

Given that it was a nearly 2,000-mile trip from Kutaisi to Łódź, Henry must have left Georgia even before the surrender. Why he would have been in such haste to leave, why he had made the trip alone, and indeed how he managed the journey at all, was not immediately clear to Leo. Perhaps the Hurwicz family, as Polish citizens, were now considered "unreliable" by the Russians—especially given Adek's official status. But then one might think that, if anything, Adek would be the first to leave, not Henry. It could also be that the Russians, having suffered so many millions of casualties during the war, were simply looking to latch onto as many able-bodied men as they could, and that 22-year-old Henry was a more attractive prospect in that regard than 54-year-old Adek.

Again, Henry could not explain everything in a letter that could be read by interested officials on both sides of the pond. In any case, Adek and Zina were not far behind: they joined Henry in Łódź in September.

The Hurwicz family correspondence from Łódź in those years is mostly in Polish, but it also includes a postcard, written in English by Zina on September 24, 1945. ("My" is Polish for "We"; Zina slipped up and used the Polish word instead of the English. "Varsava" is of course Warsaw.)

> My dear, Evelyn and Lolus!
>
> Yesterday we have received your telegramme [sic] and card from Niagara and were happy to see the first time your hand-writting [sic] after six long years. My [sic] are very eager to see you and dear Evelyn. I am sure you will do everything to fulfill our wish. To-morrow [sic] I am going to see professor Lange in Varsava. I think he will help us to fulfill our dream. We are well and waiting for good news from you.
>
> Please don't mock at my bad writting [sic].
>
> Kisses and love from me, father and Henry.
> Mother

"Professor Lange" was of course Oskar Lange, who had now returned to Poland. Lange, though naturalized as a U.S. citizen in 1943, had renounced his U.S.

citizenship. In September 1945, he either was, or was soon to be, the Polish Ambassador to the United States.

While visiting Lange, Zina saw that Warsaw was almost entirely in ruins, a sea of rubble. Their apartment on ulica Graniczna would have been just outside the Ghetto. Just across the street, where Stefan had lived at one time, would have been inside. Like most of the rest of the city, the entire area was a lunar landscape of ruined, empty shells of buildings. The destruction was so total that there was serious talk of permanently moving the capital to Łódź, leaving Warsaw as a war memorial.

Zina realized that they truly were displaced persons now: even if they had wanted to go back home, there was no home for them to go back to. Their home, their community, even the landscape had been destroyed. Warsaw seemed little more than a vast unmarked grave for their friends and relatives—and their own former lives.

On December 22, 1945, when Henry was about a month away from taking his first semester exams, President Truman issued the Truman Directive, instructing State Department consular officials to give preference to displaced persons, though only within the existing immigration quotas, which had been established in 1924. Truman believed Congress would be unwilling to increase the quotas, despite the urgent pleadings of the international and U.S. humanitarian community.

Zina visited Lange again in early January 1946. This second visit was to get an affidavit from Lange attesting that they were, in fact, the parents and brother of Leonid Hurwicz, a valued and distinguished U.S. citizen.

Lange's affidavit would support Leo's application, in January 1946, for "preference quota" visas for Adek, Zina and Henry. Leo's principled decision to apply for citizenship in 1940, which could have meant wartime military service, paid off now: he had become a citizen in 1944 and, as such, his immediate family should be given preference for immigration. Still, it was a slow and difficult process, with most of the impediments coming from the Americans.

CHAPTER 27

Just a Closer Walk with Stan

Leo's leave of absence from Ames officially ran until May 1, 1946, with teaching duties starting in the summer session. Thus, early May found him in Ames looking for housing. Initially, he stayed with Ken and Elise Boulding. Ken was an associate professor at Iowa State and a prominent economist and peace activist. Leo paid the Bouldings a handsome $1.50 a week for his "rather nice room." Breakfast and dinner ran "about fifty cents per day." Evelyn remained in Chicago doing "grading work" but joined him after he found an apartment.[1]

Their first child, Sarah, was born in December 1946.

In Ames, William Murray, the new department head, and John Nordin, assistant head, were working to rebuild their shattered department. Leo's energy and productivity became legendary.[2] Nordin called him "the best department I ever met."[3]

In addition to his position at Ames, Leo continued to work with the Cowles Commission. That meant taking a train 300 miles east to Chicago every two weeks to attend staff meetings.

On one of these visits in 1947, Leo took an historic walk in Hyde Park. Tjalling Koopmans, then a Research Associate with the Cowles Commission, and soon to become its Director, had introduced Leo to Stan Reiter, an economics graduate student and Koopmans' assistant. Koopmans had been trying, apparently with little success, to help Stan clarify and formulate some ideas.

---

1   Hurwicz to "Honey," undated, Leonid Hurwicz Papers, David M. Rubenstein Rare Book & Manuscript Library, Duke University, Box 23, File: Correspondence, 1945 Sept. 17, 1946 Feb. 13.

2   Peter Orazem, an Iowa State professor of economics, said that Leo was still being talked about when Orazem arrived in the 1980's. "Nobel Winner Taught in Ames in the Late '40s," *The Des Moines Register*, October 16, 2007, p. 5A.

3   Quoted in "Nobel Winner Taught in Ames in the Late '40s," *The Des Moines Register*, October 16, 2007, p. 5A, Prof. Peter Orazem, in an email to author on March 19, 2018, identified Nordin as the source of this quote.

He thought perhaps Leo could lend something to the conversation. Or, as Stan told the story:

> I started bothering him [Koopmans] with some ideas that I had . . .
>
> So he [Koopmans] said, "When he [Leo] comes, I'll introduce you, and you can talk with him." And this way he got rid of me.
>
> So Leo did show up. . . . Well, I was summoned to Koopmans' office. Leo was there. We were introduced, and Leo said, "Let's go for a walk."
>
> So we went out, and we spent the rest of the day walking around in Hyde Park and discovering that the ideas that I was groping toward, and trying to make straight, were similar to the ideas that Leo had about what we now call mechanism design. And that was the beginning of a long relationship[4] . . .

Usually, histories of mechanism design start with a 1960 article by Leo.[5] Even Leo and Stan in their career-crowning book, *Designing Economic Mechanisms*, note that the 1960 paper was the first "formal treatment"—the first rigorous mathematical presentation—of economic mechanisms and mechanism design. But, in fact, Leo and Stan had been noodling these ideas even before that auspicious stroll in 1947. This is further evidenced by the fact that, though unpublished, some version of the 1960 paper was actually completed in 1948. It was finally published as part of the proceedings of a June 1959, conference on mathematical methods in the social sciences, held at Stanford University.[6] The organizers invited Leo to present in part to force publication of the article he had been perfecting for the past decade or so.

The essence of the idea was simple: that the economic system, or mechanism, could be the "unknown" of a mathematical problem. Whereas in the past, the

---

4   Appendix B. There is a similar version in Appendix A.
5   Leonid Hurwicz, "Optimality and informational efficiency in resource allocation processes," in *Mathematical Methods in the Social Sciences,* Arrow, Karlin and Suppes (eds.), Stanford University Press, 1960.
6   Kenneth J. Arrow, "Leonid Hurwicz: an Appreciation," remarks delivered at a luncheon meeting of the American Economic Association, January 3, 2009, honoring American recipients of the Nobel Memorial Prize in Economic Science for 2007. Retrieved June 4, 2008, from Kenneth Arrow Papers, David M. Rubenstein Rare Book & Manuscript Library, Duke University.

procedure was typically to assume a particular economic system and use mathematics and statistics to determine an outcome, mechanism design proposed to turn that on its head: to assume an outcome and use mathematics and statistics to determine what system would produce that outcome. Indeed, there might be a whole set of systems, any one of which could produce the postulated outcome.

The approach had grown out of the socialist calculation debate, and more generally the debate about unregulated free markets versus regulation and planning.[7] Leo, unsatisfied with the lack of precision and rigor in this planning-versus-free-market discussion, realized that one prerequisite of a more precise discussion would be to define mathematically the desired outcomes, that is, the criteria by which the systems were to be judged. Desired outcomes would be expressed in a mathematical function, a *goal function*.

Of course, other things would probably have to be taken into consideration. For instance, Leo and Stan wanted to take Hayek's knowledge problem into account and require mechanisms to be privacy-preserving; each economic "player" (or economic agent) would have private information that others could not know unless the player revealed it. This also implied that players could strategically lie or conceal information. Ideally, the "rules of the game" would incentivize players to tell the truth, at least to the extent necessary to ensure the desired outcomes.

They also wanted to take into account the difficulty of operating the system; for example, if agents had to exchange or process huge amounts of information for every transaction, that "cost" of operating the system might make it unworkable.

Finally, there were "givens" that the designer could not change or influence, such as the preferences of the economic agents or the technologies available to accomplish various economic goals. Such givens formed an "environment," and there might be many different environments to deal with. For example, managers of a non-profit company, a for-profit company, a government agency and a military unit might each have different preferences and different technological capabilities.

Given a set of economic mechanisms, one could determine to what extent each satisfied the goal function, what its costs would be, and so on. However, if one's whole purpose was to find the best mechanism for a given purpose, it would be unnecessarily limiting to assume in advance the set of mechanisms to be considered. For example, one could compare free market "perfect competition" with an economy controlled by some type of Central Planning Board. But surely this would not represent all the possibilities. A means was necessary to

---

7   Stanley Reiter, "Two topics in Leo Hurwicz's research," *Review of Economic Design* Vol. 13 No. 1, April 2009, pp. 3–6.

generate the set of economic mechanisms that satisfied a given goal function for the desired environments, given the economic agents, their preferences and the technologies available to them.

The goal was not only to model known economic mechanisms, but to generate models of all conceivable mechanisms that fulfilled certain requirements, to identify their relevant characteristics, and to state precisely the standards by which one proposed to compare them, with the goal of choosing the preferred mechanism—possibly one which had never before been considered.

For this reason, mechanism design is often referred to as economic engineering: instead of *assuming* any mechanism or set of mechanisms, one seeks a means of *constructing* the set of mechanisms that meet the stated requirements. (For more on mechanism design, see Appendix G. Eric Maskin's and Roger Myerson's Nobel lectures are also great introductory material.)

Overall, 1947 was a good year for Leo. In addition to meeting Stan, a lifelong friend and collaborator, Leo got his family back: they managed to smuggle themselves out of Poland and into France[8]—among tens of thousands of Jews emigrating from Poland illegally or extralegally, with the tacit support of the Polish government. Henry would remain in France until September. Adek and Zina arrived in the United States on February 11, 1947.

Upon seeing Leo for the first time, fulfilling a vow he had made a world away, in the frozen north of Russia, Adek crumpled up the pack of cigarettes he was carrying and threw it away. He never smoked again.

Leo had received only a few letters outlining his family's harsh odyssey. Now, they were focused on their new lives, not on reliving the traumatic past. For example, Adek was so determined to become proficient in English that he generally refused to speak Polish and scolded others when they spoke to him in Polish; initially, however, his narrative abilities remained somewhat limited. (When he first arrived, his entire lexicon consisted of "Thank you very much, you are very kind.")

Still, slowly, in bits and pieces, the stories came out.

---

8   Letter from Leo to his granddaughter Lara Markovitz, November 1, 1993, p. 1.

CHAPTER 28

Blood, Fire, Smoke, Exile and Human Kindness

———

On September 1, Warsaw woke up to the sound of explosions. Or was it just a violent thunderstorm? And why these masses of birds flying away from the direction of the sounds? The Nazis were attacking Warsaw. The sounds were exploding bombs.

Early in the second week of September, Henry and Adek Hurwicz, along with Roza's brother, Abrasha Salman, went to the main railroad station in Warsaw and boarded a train for an Army enlistment site east of Warsaw.[1] Jews throughout Poland rose up *en masse* to defend the country, and Henry and Adek were no different. Of course, the Jews knew that they had more to lose than anyone if the Germans conquered Poland. Zina, rather than stay alone, moved in with her brother Moses Salamon, his wife Roza and their daughter Klara, who lived just a few blocks away.

In the next 24 hours, due to constant bombing, the train managed to go maybe 15 miles. They decided a) they would be better off walking and b) they were never going to make it to the enlistment site.

Abrasha actually jumped out of a train window, as if diving into a swimming pool. He eventually made it to Vilnius, Lithuania, and from there to Israel.

Adek and Henry slept in a bakery—with their shoes on, in case they needed to make a run for it in the middle of the night. They were indeed hit by a bomb in the morning; Henry remembered the baker, alive but covered in flour and blood. And bodies on the street.

Adek and Henry ended up hiding out at the villa of a lawyer friend of Adek's in a place called Śródborów, around 17 miles southeast of Warsaw, and a couple

---

1   Much of the information in this chapter is based on Henry's testimony for the USC Shoah Foundation Institute: https://collections.ushmm.org/search/catalog/vha47655 The author is grateful for the permission to quote from this testimony.

of miles east of the Vistula River. In the morning the sun came up dark red in the west, engulfed in fire and smoke. During the day, they sheltered in trenches which they dug themselves, avoiding artillery barrages from both sides, which came several times an hour.

Warsaw surrendered on September 28th, and Adek and Henry headed back home—by horse and buggy, still an everyday conveyance in Poland in 1939. In Warsaw, they found that Zina and the Salamons had all moved into the Hurwicz apartment, since the Salamons' place had been destroyed by bombing; luckily, no one was hurt.

Now that Adek and Henry were reunited with Zina in Warsaw, the Hurwicz and Salamon families began making plans to escape Poland, and ultimately to escape Europe. Their immediate destination was Białystok. From there, they hoped to continue on to Vilnius and eventually the United States.

Despite the risks, there was already an established network of vehicles, drivers, guides, rowboats and peasants on both sides of the river to help people escape— for a price. The first person the Hurwicz and Salamon families paid disappeared with their money, perhaps using it to buy his own way to safety—or perhaps destruction.

However, the second time they tried, they were indeed transported out of the city. Each had just a small suitcase. They still hoped, and perhaps expected, to return to Warsaw sooner or later. Zina's non-Jewish maid, Cesia, and her boy-friend took furniture, lab equipment and other possessions, promising to return them on demand, their only payment being permission to use the items in the meantime.

The journey to the village of Sarnaki near the Bug included a stretch during which their bags were hauled by horse-drawn wagon while they walked, as well as portions by military truck and 1938 Chevy taxi. In Sarnaki, they were hidden in a wealthy peasant's home to wait for nightfall.

Suddenly, there was a rap at the door and a harsh, "*Raus! Raus!*" (Out! Out!)

It was *Wehrmacht* border guards, who marched them to a school building now being used as a military headquarters. There, they waited in terror. After a while, the soldiers engaged Adek in conversation: he spoke fluent German. It turned out that the soldiers were afflicted with lice, and what they really wanted more than anything was soap! This the travelers were able to provide in some quantity.

Upon receiving this treasure, apparently in gratitude (though likely also being on the payroll of the smugglers), the *Wehrmacht* soldiers used their inti-mate knowledge of Russian patrols on the other bank to alert the Hurwicz/ Salamon group when the time was right to cross; in fact, a soldier even con-ducted them to the boat. In addition, the *Wehrmacht* told them how to fool the

Russian authorities on the other side into allowing them to stay: "Tell them you have been visiting relatives in Russia and want to get back to German-occupied Poland; their orders are to stop anyone from crossing the Bug, so they will send you back where you supposedly came from."

Anyone watching from a distance might have thought that the *Wehrmacht* were doing their job, when in fact they were getting paid off and perhaps picking up a little extra soap on the side.

The night was blessedly dark and cloudy, and, with the oars wrapped in rags to soften the splashing, they were ferried over quickly and safely to the Russian side. There they hurried to a nearby hut. A Russian patrol soon appeared. This was no surprise; in fact, it was just what the Germans had told them to expect.

Here again something seemingly incredible happened. While most of the Russian soldiers went off to search other parts of the house and farm, the refugees were left alone with one young soldier, who quickly and quietly presented them with a kind of password used by Polish, Lithuanian and Russian Jews: the Hebrew word *amhu*. Literally, it means "his people." But *amhu* was used among Jews as a way of determining whether someone was Jewish or could be trusted: if the other person also answered "*amhu*"—they were okay. The soldier then told them, in not very good Yiddish, that they should say they were trying to get to the German side. This advice, of course, confirmed the instructions they had already received from the *Wehrmacht*.

They did as instructed, and the Russian authorities put them on a train "back" to Białystok.

The money that paid for all this was provided by Klara's father, Moses. He had owned the building in Warsaw where, until the German onslaught, the Polish-Jewish daily newspaper *Nasz Przegląd* ("Our Review") had been published. Now, he had sold the building for the equivalent of $24,000 cash in gold coins. Some of that money went to pay the people who smuggled them out of Poland into Russia. As for the rest of it, they were afraid if they carried it with them, they might be attacked or even killed for it. So Moses had stayed behind in Warsaw for the express purpose of smuggling it to the family once they arrived in Białystok. They then forwarded it to the relatives in Vilnius. It was a slow process, done in amounts equivalent to about $1,000, again to minimize the chances of foul play, as well as to reduce the loss if any one transfer failed to arrive. Letters had to be sent stating the amount to expect and then confirming that the correct amount had arrived.

The winter of 1939 was bitterly cold in Białystok. There were shortages of everything, including fuel and food. The single room the Hurwicz and Salamon families lived in was always freezing cold. Klara and her mother slept in one bed, all three Hurwiczes in another. Henry and Klara stood in lines to buy basics such as bread, flour, milk and sugar. They were sometimes successful, sometimes not, since the article on sale would run out before they reached the front of the line. But they were always painfully, numbingly cold, and often frostbitten.

On the positive side, you could get ice cream in the winter! In Warsaw, shops stopped selling ice cream in the winter and substituted other sweets. Białystokers, like Americans, were happy to eat ice cream any time of year.

By the end of the winter, the money had been transferred to Vilnius and forwarded to Roza's brother, Solomon Salman, in New York. (Only about a third of the initial $24,000 arrived there, due to the money-smugglers' commissions.) Moses now rejoined the family in Białystok. Border security had tightened by this time, and it took him three tries to get across the Bug.

In the spring of 1940 (perhaps March or April), the Russian authorities made the Hurwicz and Salamon families fill out a questionnaire opting for one of three choices: 1) remain in Belarus, but with severe restrictions on where they could live (they would have to leave Białystok, for instance, since they would not be allowed to live in a city of over 100,000 inhabitants), 2) move eastward into the USSR proper and find work there, or 3) return to Warsaw.

The Hurwiczes didn't want to go deeper into Russia, even though they had relatives there, because they were afraid they would get separated from Leo permanently. They didn't know what or how well they would do in a small town; even Białystok felt too small for them.

So, ironically, after risking life and limb to get out of German-occupied Poland, both families now opted for returning to Warsaw. In reality, they hoped to get to Lithuania before the Russians got around to deporting them. With the border officially closed, they doubted that any mass cross-border deportation would happen quickly, in any case. They had very little idea what was really going on in Warsaw, but if they had to go back, they would survive somehow. Hopefully, they wouldn't have to go back.

In any case, after the questionnaire, nothing happened immediately: life continued in Białystok.

Even in this difficult situation, both Henry and Klara were urged to continue their schooling. Klara enrolled in a public school conducted in Russian. (Poland no longer officially existed as a country, and the Russian government was doing its best to extinguish Polish culture and language.) At Henry's urging, she also graduated from children's books to literary greats like Joseph Conrad and Tolstoy.

Then, in pursuit of their plan to get to Lithuania, in mid-April, the Hurwicz and Salamon families left Białystok for the little town of Lida, about 20 miles from the Lithuanian border. Their guide couldn't smuggle six people into Lithuania at once, so the Salamons made the attempt first, in a horse-drawn wagon, disguised as peasants. But it turned out to be a fiasco, ending with Moses in a Russian jail in the town of Baranowicze and everyone else back in Białystok.[2]

Early that summer, rumors started circulating that everyone who had opted to return to German-occupied Poland was instead going to be deported to Siberia. In general, round-ups like this were conducted at night, when people were likely to be home in bed. So Roza and Klara started spending nights with a local friend. The Hurwicz family remained in the room where they had been since arriving in Białystok.

Then one night in June, around midnight, soldiers arrived. They gave the family half an hour to pack their suitcases, then loaded them onto trucks and delivered them to the railroad station. The three Hurwiczes waited at the train station long enough for Roza to find them and bring them some supplies. In addition, Roza realized she did not want to be left with no close family in Białystok. She turned herself in to the authorities, trying to get deported, too. But to no avail.

The Hurwiczes were loaded into cattle cars, each car officially denominated to hold either six animals or 40 humans. They always had something to eat, and the train stopped occasionally to let the deportees get out and relieve themselves by the side of tracks. Still, said Henry, "that was not really a very good trip."

The cattle cars took the Hurwicz family around 1100 miles northeast to Nyandoma in the Archangel Oblast. They were then hauled in trucks about 50 miles to Kargopol. There, Henry remembered being offered "minnows—fish soup" that he couldn't eat, even though they had received barely adequate food during their ten-day trip.

From Kargopol, they were taken by boat around seven miles south down Lake Lacha, and finally by horse-drawn wagon to a barracks near Nokola, not far from the village of Morshchikhinskaya. Their status here was officially "free exile"; but there was nothing free about it. Such settlements were also, and more appropriately, called "areas of compulsory residence."

Though a difficult place to live, it was less harsh than a prison camp. People still lived with their families. There were very few guards, and those few only occasionally rode around the edge of the village. There were a lot of rules, such as forbidding the inmates to meet in groups, and particularly for anyone to address a group: the authorities didn't want any leadership to develop among the prisoners. Henry recalled the terrible bed bugs.

---

2   For more details of this sad but interesting episode, read Klara's book, *God Does Play Dice*.

In any case, they weren't in Nokola long, due to an incident in which Adek's take-charge tendencies landed him in serious trouble. Henry recalled: "The people started really rebelling. Now these were maybe about 90% Jews. 'They *can't* do that to us! We are Polish citizens. They cannot do it to us!' Well, my father said, since he was familiar with the Bolsheviks from the year 1917, he says, 'Yes, they can do to you whatever they want to do, and you're really better off if you just don't.'"

Some said they could all just walk away from the village. Adek said that was ridiculous. Their location was so remote and isolated, where could they walk to? Where would they find anyone to help them or give them shelter?

A guard must have observed Adek addressing the small group that had gathered—or perhaps there was a "snitch" in the crowd. That evening, guards came to the barracks and said that the commandant wanted to speak with Adek. As the guards started to take him away, Zina ran out and handed Adek his coat. A guard assured her that he would not need it, that he would be right back, but she insisted.

The guard's assurance turned out to be totally false. The family did not see Adek that day, or the next or the next. In fact, he never did return to that place. He ended up in one of the many prison camps (gulags) near Archangel, around 350 miles north, close to the Arctic Sea. It was all men. Whereas in free exile, the family had its own room in the barracks, here there were many men in a large dormitory. It was farther north, and temperatures were colder: Adek remembered holding a bowl of soup, and the palms of his hands were warm, but the backs were numb.

Adek worked outdoors, with only whatever clothing he brought with him when taken to the commandant's office. He often worked straightening nails, with no gloves.

The camp was very much dog-eat-dog. For example, no prisoner had anything he would willingly part with. So two men would gamble for another man's coat. Whichever one lost had to try to get the coat and give it to the winner.

Any sign of weakness was a death sentence, since others would immediately target you as a victim. This meant that Adek, who was five feet tall and an intellectual—not a muscle-builder—often had to fight, whether he wanted to or not.

The inmates slept on wide planks, with several men on a plank. The best position was on the outside edge of a plank, where you had some freedom of movement, at least on one side. On one occasion, such a position opened up, and Adek claimed it. Another prisoner, a huge, powerful man, demanded the spot. Adek wanted nothing more than to give it to him, but that would have been a sign of weakness. So he loudly refused. The big man basically picked Adek up and threw him across the room. But other inmates saw that Adek would put up a fight, no matter the adversary.

Years earlier, Adek had promised his father he would quit smoking. Now, he started smoking again. He was likely to die in the camp: smoking would make no difference. At the same time, he made a vow that if he ever saw his Zina, Henry and Leo alive again, he would quit for good.

When Adek was arrested, Henry and Zina were moved about 10 miles from their first location, but still in free exile. Zina worked as a telephone operator. Their living quarters were small and rustic. The available foods were bread, soup and goat meat. Henry said that except for the initial trip by train and truck, "... we really did not starve ... I couldn't eat the goat. So we did sort of starve in a certain way, but eventually we sold a few of our things and we survived. Also they gave us a plot that we could seed the potatoes."

Although Henry says they didn't starve, they did become quite thin: on one occasion Zina's skirt fell off even though she had it fastened with a string.

Henry described how, after he did the back-breaking work of clearing stumps from their potato patch, their neighbor somehow claimed half of it. Henry went for an axe.

> All I could see was a red spot and his head. Fortunately my mother was somehow waiting for me coming, and she grabbed me, and other people. But I can see that you can be insane and murder somebody. I never really believed that you could do this. But yes, you can do it. ... That poor guy died, in the camp, trying to pick either wild strawberries or blueberries or something. I don't know why he died, but he did. I really didn't feel that sorry for him.

When they were freed, Henry and Zina were able to head directly south, ending up in the wine country of Georgia.

When he was freed, Adek had been in the prison camp about a year. He weighed 89 pounds. As the ID that was issued to him showed, his face was sunken, skeletal, eyes lifeless, skin like parchment—a typical "Zek" (forced labor camp inmate). He was about 52 but looked 80.

Adek had wanted to go south, and the most direct route would probably have been through Moscow. But the Germans were storming eastward, with Moscow as their goal, so Adek, traveling by train, took a route that went east of Moscow. For sustenance, he had a bag of dried olives. He chose this because it was nutritious, but also not very appetizing. He thought it unlikely that anyone would kill him for it. They were so salty that it was impossible to eat very many at any one time.

In Fergana, he didn't have money for food or lodging. He was standing on a street corner and made a motion to a passerby, asking if he could spare a cigarette. The man approached him, stared, and in a questioning tone addressed him, in Polish, using a respectful term for an attorney. The passerby was one of Adek's law clerks from Warsaw.

The law clerk took him in, fed him, and nursed him back to health. (Would it be correct to say that smoking actually saved a life in this instance? Smoking and human kindness.)

Subsequently, if he encountered a panhandler, Adek would always give them whatever they asked for. He never forgot his time on the street in Fergana.

When he was able to rejoin his family in Georgia, Adek found work teaching French in a teachers' college. Henry began working 15–16-hour days as a lumberjack, in winter snow, summer heat, and rain in autumn and spring. While working in the woods, he sometimes went whole days without eating, and weeks eating only ounces of dark bread with water, then slept on the floor with no blanket, often wet through and through. He was a porter cabman (driver of a horse-drawn taxi) with the worst horses he had ever seen. At some point he became a "grease-monkey," working 12-hour days lubricating ten large trucks a day in a manufacturing plant, then standing in line for 2–3 hours for "dinner"—hot water and potatoes. After a year of this, he picked up enough knowledge to become a mechanic.

Toward the end of the war, as the Germans were being driven back on all fronts, all Russian males were being mobilized for military service, and Henry as a foreigner was one of the few mechanics left "in the rear." So he began driving a three-ton truck, officially as an assistant truck driver, often driving for two days continuously, stopping only to repair the truck. (Drivers also had to be mechanics, since there were no mechanics anywhere to do repairs.) He wouldn't see a bed for two days at a time and would sometimes fall asleep at the wheel. The winter was especially hard, often one step from catastrophe.

Although the pay for truck-driving was not great, he also served as an informal bus service. Fuel was scarce and expensive, so people were often hitchhiking instead of driving. Henry particularly remembered people transporting their wonderful Georgian wine to market. He would pick them up, and they would give him a little money, some of which he would pass on to the truck driver he was assisting. The chief of police also got his fair share of the proceeds.

One day, Henry was called in from work to a Russian military/police unit which he described as being just like the Gestapo. The Russian authorities wanted Henry to accept a Russian passport. He said he didn't want a Russian passport and refused to sign anything. He insisted he was a Polish citizen. They also wanted to indicate on the passport that he was a Polish Jew, but he refused to say he was Jewish. He said he had no religion. They asked his father's religion. He said his father had no religion. (Emphatically true: Adek had rejected religion as a young man.) What was his grandfather's religion, they asked. Also no religion.

The interrogators told Henry that Adek had accepted a Russian passport, but Henry did not believe that Adek would ever do that. He knew the family was determined not to stay in Russia, because they feared that, if they did, they would never see Leo again. Then the Russian "Gestapo" did allow Henry to return home, but the family feared that ultimately the Russians would find a way to force them into Russian citizenship and thus keep them in Russia. In fact, soon thereafter, the Russians did actually issue Henry a Russian passport.

The family decided that Henry should get back into Poland immediately, even though there had as yet been no official German surrender. Henry's education had been largely derailed for the past six years. (He was exactly two months shy of 17 when the Germans and Soviets crushed Poland in September 1939.) So the family's first priority was to get Henry back in school.

The husband of one of Adek's students was a military doctor and managed to get Henry a permit to ride on a military train carrying wounded soldiers. Henry was dressed more or less like a Russian soldier: long coat, military shoes, even a military-style hat (though lacking the hammer and sickle insignia). So he blended in with the troops. In early May, 1945, traveling with a friend, he went through Lwów (southern Poland, now Ukraine) and ended up in Równo (northern Poland), a journey of over 2500 miles from Kutaisi.

In the train station in Równo, it was announced that the Germans had surrendered on May 7, 1945. A Red Army officer fired celebratory shots into the air, accidentally severing some overhead telephone wires—something that would have taken incredible skill to do intentionally. Afraid he'd be punished, he ran away.

Henry decided to return to the town of Łódź.

On the train, a Polish partisan sitting next to Henry was unhappy. Perhaps he saw that, after all the sacrifices they had made, Poland was going to be a puppet of the Russian behemoth. No freedom, no sovereignty. No Poland for the Poles. He also had a more personal reason for mourning. During the war, he said, he could go anywhere and be welcomed and taken care of. Now what would become of him? He took out a grenade and indicated that if he just pulled the pin...

People started scattering. But Henry sat with him, talking, telling him why he really didn't want to do that. Eventually, the partisan put the grenade away again.

Henry was even able to smile, telling these stories. After all, he said, the important thing was to survive. And they had survived.

CHAPTER 29

Mechanism Design: Development and Recognition

———

In the 40s and 50s, Leo and others developed and elaborated ideas and techniques around what would come to be known as mechanism design. Important advances made after Leo's classic 1960 article include 1) an increased focus on optimality criteria and 2) what Leo termed "incentive compatibility."

—*Optimality criteria.* If one wants to pick the "best" mechanism(s) from a set of mechanisms, one needs some standard by which to judge which mechanisms are best: an optimality criterion. The 1960 article mentions one such criterion: an outcome (e.g., allocation of resources) may be considered optimal if no one could be made better off without making someone else worse off (Pareto-optimality). In the early 1950s, John Forbes Nash (of *A Beautiful Mind* fame) suggested another: an outcome may be considered optimal if no one would unilaterally change his strategy in order to try to change the outcome, even if he discovers the other player's strategy (Nash equilibrium).

—*Incentive compatibility.* A usual assumption is that economic agents are free to choose whether to participate in the mechanism or not, and whether to tell the truth or not if they do participate: the system works "without shooting people."[1] Leo coined the term "incentive compatibility" for this in 1972.[2] (It is possible to postulate an enforcement agency, at some cost to the mechanism, which may encourage, but cannot ensure, participation or honesty.)

---

1   Leonid Hurwicz to George R. Feiwel in *Arrow and the Ascent of Modern Economic Theory*, Palgrave Macmillan UK, 1987, p. 273.
2   Leonid Hurwicz, "On informationally decentralized systems," in *Decision and Organization: A Volume in Honor of Jacob Marschak*, R. Radner and C.B. McGuire (eds), North-Holland, 1972, pp. 297–336.

Over the next dozen or so years, while teaching at the University of Minnesota, Leo continued to develop his ideas, eventually presenting them in classic papers such as "On the Concept and Possibility of Informational Decentralization" (1969), "On Informationally Decentralized Systems" (1972) and "The Design of Mechanisms for Resource Allocation" (1973).

He never did get his PhD: the only degree he ever earned was the law degree from the University of Warsaw. Nevertheless, on the strength of his abilities and contributions, he became a full professor with tenure at the U of M. He was eventually awarded half a dozen honorary doctorates from other universities.

The year 1968 saw the establishment of the Nobel Memorial Prize in Economic Sciences (officially the Sveriges Riksbank Prize in Economic Sciences in Memory of Alfred Nobel, or even more officially—in Swedish—*Sveriges riksbanks pris i ekonomisk vetenskap till Alfred Nobels minne*) with a donation from Sweden's central bank (*Sveriges Riksbank*) to the Nobel Foundation. While not one of the original Nobel Prizes established in Alfred Nobel's will in 1895, it is awarded by the Nobel Foundation, announced with other Nobel awards, and is often referred to as the Nobel Memorial Prize in Economic Sciences.

It was first awarded in 1969 to Jan Tinbergen and Ragnar Frisch "for having developed and applied dynamic models for the analysis of economic processes."

Paul Samuelson won in 1970 "for the scientific work through which he has developed static and dynamic economic theory and actively contributed to raising the level of analysis in economic science."

Hayek won the award in 1974, Tjalling Koopmans in 1975. Haavelmo won in 1989, John Forbes Nash in 1994.

Leo was often told that he was on the short list to receive the prize, but it seemed the day never came. Perhaps there was someone on the prize committee who was dead set against Leo or mechanism design? It is also true that the usefulness of mechanism design only slowly became apparent as time went on, with important theoretical contributions by Roger Myerson and Eric Maskin starting in the late 70s leading to practical applications in areas such as auction design, environmental policy, aid to developing nations and internet routing policies. However, in the decades over which these advances occurred, it also seemed that awareness of Leo's foundational contributions might have been fading. Articles in economic journals focusing on the latest advances often failed to mention Leo.

Nobel Prizes are awarded only to living people. Leo was getting old. His health was not perfect. It was looking less and less likely that he would receive the award.

After the dissolution of the Soviet Union in the '90s—five decades after he had left Poland—Leo visited Warsaw, giving lectures in economics. The only thing he recognized in his old neighborhood—the only thing left standing—was a single tree in the park where he used to play.

Years passed. By 2007, as he approached his 90th birthday, Leo was receiving dialysis several times a week. His health was declining, and it did not seem at all certain that he would see his 91st birthday.

Then, on Monday, October 15, 2007, well before dawn, the phone rang in Leo and Evelyn's apartment in the Nokomis Square Senior Cooperative in South Minneapolis. The caller identified himself as Adam Smith. He said he was calling from the Nobel Foundation website to congratulate Leo for winning the Nobel Prize in Economics. Hearing the name of the famous eighteenth-century Scottish economist, they quickly determined that it was a "stupid joke" and hung up.

But Adam Smith was persistent. He called back, apologizing for his name, and had a short conversation with Leo, mostly using Evelyn as an intermediary, since Leo at age 90 was hard of hearing. Leo, it seemed, was the oldest ever Laureate in any category in the history of the Prize.[3] Smith tried to get a comment from Leo on this. Evelyn pressed Leo, asking him if he was glad he had lived that long. They both just laughed.

Asked whether there was any particular application of mechanism design that he was most pleased about, Leo cited welfare economics: the branch of economics that aims to achieve overall beneficial social and economic outcomes for all of society.

Just before they hung up, Leo added, "I hope that others who deserve it also got it." (They had. Leonid Hurwicz, Eric S. Maskin and Roger B. Myerson had been awarded the Prize "for having laid the foundations of mechanism design theory.")

By the time the Nobel ceremony approached, Leo's doctor advised against a trip to Sweden. Leo's younger daughter, Ruth, her husband David Markovitz, and their children travelled to Stockholm to represent him at the ceremony which took place on December 10, 2007. Simultaneously, on a chilly Minneapolis morning, a separate award ceremony just for Leo was held in the Ted Mann Theater at the University of Minnesota. When Leo slowly rose from his chair on the stage, slightly hunched over, leaning on his cane, and Jonas Hafström, Swedish Ambassador to the U.S., presented the red leather box containing the gold medal with the embossed profile of Alfred Nobel, those who hadn't

---

3   Superceded in 2018 by Arthur Ashkin (who was 96 when he received the prize), and who was in turn superceded by John B. Goodenough, who was awarded in 2019. https://en.wikipedia.org/wiki/Arthur_Ashkin . Accessed October 13, 2022.

forgotten knew that Leo was harvesting the fruit of a tree he had planted half a century earlier.

The rest of the Nobel ceremony in Stockholm was projected on a screen in the Ted Mann Theater. The family in Minneapolis was excited to see Ruth, David and family on the screen. After the ceremony, the Markovitz family enjoyed a magnificent banquet with other Nobel attendees, while in Minneapolis the extended Hurwicz family proceeded to the Old Country Buffet—Leo's favorite—and had a grand old time.

Epilogue

The genesis of this book dates to 2007, with people asking me why my dad won the Nobel Prize. Assuming I would know! But—strangely—it turned out that my careers as hippie-bum, folksinger, tech writer, occasional fiction attempter, eco-arts-educator, etc. etc. etc., really hadn't prepared me all that well for providing capsule explanations of Nobel-level mathematical economics.

Of course, nobody was really expecting an in-depth answer, and the last thing any of my pals wanted was a function F that preserves privacy over a domain defined as a Cartesian product of sets. They wanted something on the level of a general-interest newspaper or magazine article.

So, with the goal of putting together a 25-words-or-less answer for my curious friends and acquaintances, I went back and re-read some of those general-interest newspaper and magazine articles. Some publications put out by the University of Minnesota, where my father taught for 50 years. Some Wikipedia articles. ("In October 2007, Hurwicz shared the Nobel Memorial Prize in Economic Sciences with Eric Maskin of the Institute for Advanced Study and Roger Myerson of the University of Chicago 'for having laid the foundations of mechanism design theory.'"[1]) I even ended up cracking my dad's book, *Designing Economic Mechanisms*.[2]

My father passed away in June 2008, at the age of 90. A few months after he died, friends, family and colleagues got together to remember his life, his times, his accomplishments.[3] I ended up reviewing some more personal things, including some videos made at a celebration of his 90th birthday,[4] a video in which I interviewed him about his experiences during World War II,[5] my own memories of things he had told me over the years, and things my brother and sisters and other relatives shared with me.

A cousin in Israel, Ari Leon, was creating a family tree. I got involved in that. Ari, and other relatives through him, provided wondrous journals, pictures,

---

1   https://en.wikipedia.org/wiki/Leonid_Hurwicz. Accessed June 14, 2021.
2   Written with his friend and colleague, Stan Reiter: Leonid Hurwicz and Stanley Reiter, *Designing Economic Mechanisms*, Cambridge University Press, 2006.
3   Appendix A—recommended reading.
4   Appendix B—recommended reading.
5   Appendix E. Also https://leonidhurwicz.org/interview/

memoirs and travel documents, complete with Polish, Russian and Hebrew translation services!

I found out that I could request copies of my father's documents—including a trove of correspondence from the World War II era—that had been archived at Duke University.[6]

I created a website[7] to share some of the dramatically unsettling, threatening, even terrifying events that characterized not only my father's early life—up to the age of about 23—but the lives of his family and ancestors for generations.

Ultimately, however, I came to feel that this story could probably best be told in a somewhat extended, continuous narrative—a book.

When I contemplated recounting a saga in which the invention and elaboration of mechanism design, and the history of economics in general, would be important strands, I knew I would need help in weaving those strands. I reached out first to Eric Maskin, co-recipient with my father and Roger Myerson of the 2007 Nobel Memorial Prize in Economic Sciences. He generously agreed to help me and referred me to economic historian Roger Backhouse and author Sylvia Nasar (*A Beautiful Mind*), as mentioned in the Acknowledgements. Roger, in turn, brought in Steve Medema.

A few years down the road, here we are.

I only hope you got half as much satisfaction from reading it as I did from writing it.

---

6   Leonid Hurwicz Papers, David M. Rubenstein Rare Book & Manuscript Library, Duke University. https://archives.lib.duke.edu/catalog/hurwiczleonid
7   https://www.leonidhurwicz.org.

APPENDIX A

Leo's Memorial

———

Transcription of the memorial held at the University of Minnesota Campus Club in Coffman Memorial Union at the University of Minnesota, Friday, October 24, 2008.

The invitation read:

> Leonid Hurwicz, recipient of the 2007 Nobel Memorial Prize in Economic Sciences and University of Minnesota Regents Professor Emeritus, touched many people personally—as a warm and generous colleague and friend, a witty and spirited raconteur, an inspiring and challenging doctoral advisor, and a beloved teacher. He played a transformative role at this University, in the lives of individuals, in his discipline, and in the local, national, and global community.
>
> We would be honored to have you join us on this very special occasion to honor Leo's memory and to celebrate his extraordinary life.
>
> We would appreciate it if you could let us know if you will be attending. Please reply to econdept@econ.umn.edu or let Wendy know as a reply to this message.
>
> Sincerely,
>
> Larry E. Jones,
> Professor and Chair
> Department of Economics

Eric Maskin

Thanks, Larry, and good afternoon to everybody.

Leo Hurwicz quite literally changed my life. I was a math major in college. And I had only a rather vague idea of what economics is all about. And then one term, almost by accident, I wandered into a course on information and uncertainty, taught by Leo's old friend, Kenneth Arrow.

The course was utterly chaotic. But those of you who know Ken will understand that I mean "chaotic" only in the best possible sense. And a major part of the course was devoted to Leo's work on mechanism design.

This was the early 1970s, and mechanism design was still just getting started at that point and not very well-known yet. But it was soon apparent to me that this was great stuff. It had the precision and power and sometimes even the beauty of mathematics, and it could be used to answer some of the big questions in the world: what does decentralization really mean? When does a free market perform better than a planned one? Leo was even able to show in a now a famous theorem that in a two-person economy it is impossible to implement an efficient individually rational allocation in dominant strategies. It doesn't get any better than that.

So, on the basis of Leo's work, I determined I was going to change direction and do mechanism design, too. Well, a couple of years later, I met Leo for the first time in person, at the Stanford summer camp for theorists. And I learned that mechanism design also has a sense of humor.

"Why do most economists prefer french fries to hash browns?" Leo asked me.

"It's because fries are potato optimal."

Well, Andy Postlewaite was also at Stanford that summer, and he had discovered a puzzling phenomenon: it appeared that competitive outcomes on the boundary of the feasible set were not implementable in Nash equilibrium, contrary to what everyone had previously thought. Well, Leo, Andy and I thought about that for a while and soon got to the bottom of it. And we wrote up a short manuscript of eight pages or so, suitable for publication as a note, say, in the *Journal of Economic Theory*.

But did Leo actually want to actually submit the paper for publication?

"Let me put it this way," said Leo, "Wouldn't you first like to know what happens if agents can destroy their endowments?"

Of course we did want to know that. So, about a year later, we had answered that question, and we now had a manuscript of 30 pages, suitable for a regular article in *Econometrica*.

But was Leo now ready to actually send it in?

"Let me put it this way," he said, "Before publishing the paper, it would be very interesting to find out what happens if production can occur."

And it was very interesting to find this out. So, six years later, when we had actually done the finding out, we now had a gargantuan manuscript of 80 pages that was too long for any journal. So we thought we should turn the manuscript into a monograph.

But was Leo prepared yet to actually do this?

"Let me put it this way," Leo said, "No. The proofs still needs some refinement, and so does the exposition."

So over the next 11 years or so, Andy and I would at erratic intervals receive updated versions of the manuscript from Leo, in which the proof of a lemma here, or the definition of a concept there, would be improved. And naturally the paper got only longer.

And I'm sure we would've continued in this way indefinitely if Stan Reiter, who is over there, had not been gracious enough to reach an age where it was appropriate to present him with a Festschrift. And so our paper was finally published in that Festschrift, 20 years after we had started work on it.

But even after that, I would get phone calls or notes from Leo from time to time—actually up till just a couple of years ago.

He said, "We really should think more about the case in which agents can hide their endowments."

And this relentless curiosity never failed to amaze and inspire me.

Well, a few months ago, Leo's daughter, Sarah, sent me a note in which she recalled a summer school in Jerusalem, back in 1993, in which Leo's curiosity and his other personal qualities so enchanted the graduate students there— he was such a beloved figure—that they followed him around like the Pied Piper.

Well, he was my Pied Piper, too. Thank you.

Ket Richter

Leo was the most interesting and complex person I've ever known. It's impossible to capture his essence. So what I'm going to talk about are some personal impressions. These are not really well linked, but they are comments on his style—his style of thinking, his style of seeking. And this comes from a unique opportunity I've had to be a colleague of his for many decades.

I'll try to talk from experience, avoiding hearsay, like rumors about nights of wild dancing . . . energetic dancing at jazz joints. [*Responding to someone in the audience, probably saying "True!"*] Was that Evelyn?

I wasn't supposed to be a colleague of Leo's. Walter Heller brought me here, because Walter Heller thought I would be a public finance person, like he was. Now Walter and Leo were at opposite ends of the economics spectrum: Walter was a policy, applied non-mathematical economist. Leo was a fundamental, abstract, deep—basic, I should say—rather mathematical thinker. But the two of them realized that the growth of the department, the development of the department, depended on mutual respect. Many departments around the country were riven by disputes between mathematical economists—this new field—and traditional, more institutional economics. Walter and Leo—I don't think there was anything explicit, they were too grown-up for that—but they each realized that what was best for the department was best for them.

In any case, Leo was away that year—he was on sabbatical at Stanford, writing a predecessor to his mechanism design—he called them "systems" then. And so, I snuck in. I didn't even know, I must admit, who Leo Hurwicz was, when I came here. He didn't attend my talk, or I might not be here.

The next year, Leo was back from sabbatical. And one morning I was sitting in my office, and Ann Krueger came by, and she said, "Well, aren't you coming?"

And I said, "Where?"

And she said, "To Leo's class."

Well, I wasn't sure who Leo was, but I went. And like Eric, it changed my life—my intellectual life and my real life. I had never seen that kind of mathematics before, but that was minor. It wasn't the traditional East Coast mathematics: analysis, calculus. It was topology and set theory and so forth. But it was the teaching style that really got to me. He had an article that he was going through. Actually, I think it lasted the whole semester, one article. And he went through it line by line, definition by definition, theorem by theorem, proof by proof, until at the end, every student in the class knew exactly what was true and what was not true. It was a different way of searching for truth than I had seen in any classroom before. But Leo felt that if students couldn't read, they couldn't learn. And learning was everything to Leo. It wasn't what you knew, but whether you could learn. And it didn't matter what article he was going through; he could do that with any article, and students would end up smarter and richer. That was one aspect of Leo's search for truth.

Now, Maxim, at the Nobel ceremony, mentioned about Leo being truthful. And he was. He would always remark to me that being truthful was the easiest path: you never had to remember what lie you told which person.

But I'd like to talk about the other side of the coin: Leo's search for truth. And I once got a lecture on truth from Leo. We were waiting outside Walter Heller's office, and I bemoaned the fact that maybe mathematical economics was not really useful. It was a fun game, but did it have any real applications?

And Leo got very serious. He said, "People have argued and fought, killed and died over economic issues. And it's usually been fuzzy arguments and fuzzy notions. And if we don't develop rigorous ways of handling these notions and these analytical proofs, people will continue to argue and fight and die."

I stayed on in mathematical economics.

Truth was more important than speed with Leo. The year he was back from sabbatical he reinstated the departmental bag lunch, which had lapsed the one year he was away, apparently. And when it came my time to present, I delivered a recent discovery of mine—maybe an invention I should call it—of a wonderful index number. It was glorious. It could measure output. It could measure input. It could measure prices. It could measure national income. It could measure productivity. It could measure everything. And it was really much better than the index numbers in use at the time.

Toward the end of my talk, an elder member of the department said, "Could that possibly be the same as Divisia's Index?"

Afterwards I confirmed that Divisia had written a book about it 20-some years before.

But Leo was very encouraging. He said, "If you're only a quarter of a century behind, you're ahead of most economists."

It was not speed that interested him; it was truth, correctness.

Similarly, Leo encouraged all young mathematical economists. Maybe some of you remembered Hugo's comments about how Leo had said mathematical economists were an endangered species, and needed to be protected like whooping cranes. Ever after Hugo and I, when we meet, there are a couple whoops between us.

Truth came to Leo in many forms. I remember sitting in an empty classroom. This is just a personal anecdote, but it had a big impact on me. I was waiting for a chance to talk to Leo: you had to capture Leo, as Stan knows, wherever he was. You had to go out of your way to catch him. And he was going in this empty classroom, where he had escaped from his office, where there were too many people waiting.

He was going through this student's dissertation—line by line, of course. And he was trying to figure out what the heck it was that this student was claiming in this dissertation. And finally, he put it bluntly, "Are you saying that for every 'this' there is a 'that', or are you saying there is a 'that' such that for every 'this', something is true?"

And the student was puzzled, didn't understand at all. Most of us probably didn't. And he shrugged his shoulders and said, "What does it matter?"

This was the central point of the student's dissertation, and he didn't understand really what he was saying. Well, the student got through, went on to a prestigious university—which I shall not name—went on and did some administrative work, too. And the student did very well.

I went on, and I was very struck by Leo's deep understanding of the connection between language and truth and logic. And that was a very significant thing that he understood. Among language, truth and logic, language held a special place for Leo. In our long hours together at a blackboard, we'd veer off in various directions; very often it would be etymological issues that we couldn't resolve. Well, late that night, after we'd gotten home, my wife Sheila and I would get a phone call from Leo and a lengthy etymological discussion, after Leo had consulted his many dictionaries. Now, some of you may remember Leo's dictionaries. I can't reach as far as they reached. I don't know, it was a mile long. If there were twelve languages that Leo was interested in, there'd be what, 144 dictionaries. Not counting things like the Oxford dictionary of English Christian Names. Or its surnames companion volume. And so he was able to educate us quite well.

I remember one dinner at Leo's and Evelyn's. Evelyn's dinners and parties were fantastic. They always had a wonderful guest list. There were Nobel laureates; there were politicians; there were students; there were aunts and nieces and actresses and music teachers, and . . . Some of those may be the same. I remember even one white bunny rabbit. A large one, I think it was about the height of Michael—his son Michael. [*I had a singing telegram company, "Bunnygrams," in which I delivered birthday messages and such dressed as a rabbit—M. H.*]

At one of these dinners, the point is that Sheila and I were down at one end of the table, and we were talking to Arijit Mukherji, a well-known economist in the accounting department here. And Arijit used the word "prequel." Now we all knew the word "sequel," but we challenged him that that was not a real word. And he insisted it was where he came from (Calcutta), and finally he said, "Well, if we had a Hobson-Jobson, we could settle the issue." Leo, down at the other end of the table, heard "Hobson-Jobson," stood up, went to his library, and brought back the Hobson-Jobson glossary of Anglo-English[1] names and places and everything else.

And it wasn't just the usual European languages which interested Leo. I remember after an undergraduate lecture I gave one day, a student came up to

---

1   Should be "Anglo-Indian."

me and said, "Who is that older man sitting in on our Chinese class?" Of course, it turned out to be Leo, preparing to go to China on one of his trips.

Names for Leo were a very important part of language. You could tell a lot of history and a lot of geography by names. At least you could if you were Leo. Students would often say to me, "But I went into his office to talk about my dissertation, and we spent an hour talking about my name, and what it meant and where I came from.

"He knew more about it than I did," they would say.

Those students had often waited hours to talk to Leo.

And they often got impatient. What they didn't realize was that Leo had already taught a class. And, as Stan pointed out, they didn't always end on time, because the students, as Evelyn put it, didn't stop listening. He had already attended the ancient studies group, or perhaps the group on technological development and cultural change. He'd held his regular office hours. He'd engaged in hard-fought debates in the faculty senate. And done half a dozen other things before he was working with that particular student.

What was the ancient studies group? Well, it started out as a collection of linguists and classicists interested in tracing the influx of Indo-European speech into Greece. Leo was interested in that. Leo and a few classicists and a few graduate students were studying that. This was all voluntary and not imposed from above by an administration saying, "Thou shalt work with that department," but just a group of people spontaneously interested in similar topics, interested in learning and interested in talking about them. And under Leo's prodding it expanded to include Leo, an economist, geographers, in addition to linguists and classicists, zoologists, botanists, archaeologists—I don't know what else. That was typical of Leo.

And why waste his time in the faculty senate? If truth was important, academic freedom was important—was essential. And the senate was a place to defend academic freedom. And it wasn't just an idle threat to academic freedom. A colleague of ours, Jacob Schmookler, in the department, at one point was under attack by legislators, in the Minnesota Legislature, for foisting a communist, subversive, radical textbook on the students. And Leo was active in defending this. The radical textbook was "Elements of Economics" by Paul Samuelson. I guess it was "Introductory Economics," it was called.

All those extraneous-seeming activities never stopped Leo's economic research, of course. They merely got pushed to late evening hours. Even his two-year visit when Harvard was wooing him didn't stop his research. I mean, after all, what's the difference between a phone call from Minneapolis to St. Paul versus Cambridge and St. Paul? So it continued.

And the actual research was very simple. As Eric mentioned, he began with small topics, usually from teaching. I believe the article that Eric meant was one that developed originally from his teaching some things about Samuelson's public goods work. Simple beginnings, but very erudite, sophisticated by the end of it.

But it wasn't elegant. He didn't like elegance. Sometimes I'd say, "There's a nice elegant way to do this in two lines, rather than the five pages we have here."

And he would say condescendingly, "Elegance is for tailors."

(A saying attributed variously to his father, Abraham, or sometimes to Einstein or Boltzmann. But perhaps the other two got it from Leo's father.)

All this was very exciting, but it doesn't capture the essence of Leo as a warm friend. For me, he was not only a mentor, a colleague, a co-author, but my very best friend. On occasion, when Sheila and I had personal concerns, he was the most sympathetic and helpful friend one could wish for. We will miss him. Thank you.

Jim Jordan

I had the great privilege to be Leo's colleague here at Minnesota for more than 20 years, and the attendant privilege of working with and learning from the other special people who Leo attracted to come to this wonderful department. Any attempt to describe any significant fraction of the benefit and enjoyment I derived from that experience would far exhaust the time that we have available here. Although one is tempted to follow Leo's example in dealing with this dilemma and simply keep talking until the subject has been adequately covered. And I'm certainly able to keep talking, but I would never pretend to Leo's unique ability to induce all of you to keep listening.

So, instead, I will just describe my first working meeting with Leo, which showed me an aspect of his scholarship of which I was not previously aware.

Leo was on leave at Berkeley the first year I came. But the second year, when he came back, shortly after he arrived, he called me into his office to talk to me about some work that he'd been doing. And Leo's office, of course, was 95% file cabinets and bookcases. So we sat down together in the small clearing next to his desk. And he handed me 20-some Xerox pages of calculations that related to what would later become the Hurwicz-Reiter-Saari theory of differentiable decentralized mechanisms.

And so he said, "Let's discuss this."

And "discussing this" meant working through it line by line by line by line. And this was all handwritten, mostly on airplanes—and it was apparent that some of the flights had encountered turbulence.

It was just calculus, and I knew enough calculus to follow from one line to the next and verify Leo's calculation. But I was sitting there as the young assistant professor with the master, trying to figure out what it was that he expected of me. And I thought he must want me to contribute to this in some meaningful way, and not just check his calculus. He could've gotten that done more cheaply and much better from someone else. But this went on line after line after line, with me having nothing really to say except, "Yes, that's right."

And, like previous speakers, I was beginning to experience a change in life. But in my case it would've been the end of an incipient career.

And just as my intellectual insecurity was verging on panic, the phone rang. And, fortunately for me, it must have been Evelyn, because Leo decided to take the call. And in the respite, as I was desperately trying to think of something to say, I had a flash of pattern recognition and realized that I had seen something like this before.

So I ran back to my office and pulled down my copy of Warner's book on differentiable manifolds, and leafed through until I found the result I was looking for, which stated in a very compact way, and using much more abstract mathematics, exactly what Leo was verifying by brute force using the necessarily more cumbersome calculations of elementary calculus. So I felt very much better about myself then, because although this was hardly a creative observation, at least I would have the pleasure of saving one of the world's great theorists several hours of calculus homework.

So he finally finished the phone call and turned back to me. And I showed him the result, explained to him how this was a much more compact statement that would replace all of his calculations.

And he looked at me and said, "Yes, that's right. Now where were we before the phone rang?"

I guess, in response to what Ket said, I should feel grateful that he had the kindness not to tell me that my comment was purely sartorial. And so we went back, line by line by line by line. And I was by then in a state of complete confusion. Wandered about the halls probably for several days with glazed eyes, wondering what had happened, other than verifying Leo's calculus.

And I think weeks or months later, I finally realized that—although Leo appreciated the power and efficiency of abstract mathematics as much as any of us—he just wasn't intellectually comfortable with any result until he had completely worked through it using the most elementary methods that could be applied to the context in question. And I realized that I had never experienced that level of rigor before.

And it occurred to me that if one added that standard to the standard that I had learned from Stan Reiter in graduate school, that you're not finished with the result until you have an independent example showing the independent necessity of every assumption you've made, and then add that to the standard that I was learning from Ket Richter, that a result should be the clearest possible expression of exactly the economic intuition that's behind it, it occurred to me that being a theorist at Minnesota was going to be rather a lot of work. Enough so that the need to stay indoors during the winter would be completely redundant.

But thankfully all of this was relieved by Leo's remarkable generosity of spirit and what Walter Heller once described as Leo's "relentless sense of humor." So that we were all continually reminded that the enjoyment of doing serious research greatly outweighs any burdens that the work imposes. Thank you.

Stan Reiter

When I was a graduate student at Chicago—it was 1947—I attended a course taught by Jacob Marschak. He introduced me to the Cowles Commission. Koopmans was the director, and I became Koopmans' assistant. Leo was then at Iowa State University. Leo visited the Cowles Commission from time to time to take part in what were called "staff meetings." They were wide-ranging seminars at which new ideas were presented. Koopmans decided I should meet Leo. He introduced us when Leo next came to a Cowles Commission staff meeting.

And Leo and I spent the rest of the day walking in Hyde Park and talking. Leo did most of the talking. It was an exchange of ideas that was stimulating to each of us. That afternoon of walking led to a lifelong collaboration. Leo was the senior partner for a very long time. In fact, Leo supervised my doctoral dissertation, though he was not my official adviser. In fact, he was not a member of the Chicago Economics Department. But Leo's standards allowed my dissertation to be published in a prestigious journal without alteration.

We went to Spain together, with Leo and Evelyn, to see Leo receive an honorary degree in Spain. This was a loving gesture by his Spanish students.

I recall a visit to Leo and Evelyn in Minneapolis. I went with Leo to a class he was teaching. Evelyn, accompanied by Nina, was to pick us up after his class, which was scheduled to end at 5 o'clock. We were to meet at a loading dock of the building we were in. Evelyn had to wait for about half an hour until Leo finally explained something to the class. When we finally appeared, Evelyn asked, "They wouldn't stop listening?"

Leo had many collaborators, and the field that they spanned is huge. He worked with mathematicians, statisticians, archaeologists, political scientists, linguists, agricultural economists, classicists, and others that I don't know about or don't remember. Leo has worked with scientists and scholars from every part of the world—except perhaps for Inuit scholars. (But I could be wrong about that.)

From the time of our initial tour of Hyde Park, we were both deeply interested in mechanism design. That was before it had a name. We worked in this area for a long time, in many locations, and explored a variety of ideas and approaches. We spent part of a summer on Orcas Island. And a substantial part of several summers on a farm in upstate New York, working on material that was later used in our book, "Designing Economic Mechanisms," published by the Cambridge University Press. I know that Leo was pleased with the book. I strongly suspect that he would enjoy the fact that it is to appear in a Chinese translation.

Leo was a lively and interesting person who was fun to be with. He was a mentor to me and a loving friend. His death is a bitter loss to me and to many others. The world is emptier than it was.

Roger Myerson

I am very glad to be able add my words to many others will have in testifying as to how brilliant, how creative and how important Leo Hurwicz was. His place in the history of social science was firmly established long before the Nobel committee added its recognition. To economists of several generations, including mine, he was a mentor and a guide and a link to some of the greatest questions in the history of economics.

He had so much energy and he knew almost everything. I remember once at an academic cocktail party, I made an obscure remark about the divide between the Mississippi and Great Lakes drainage systems—the kind of remark that normally kills the conversation. But not when Leo was there. Then my remark could stimulate a 30-minute discourse on great dams of the Midwest.

What a wonderful scholar and a wonderful colleague he really was. But most important, Leo had a profound vision of something crucial that was missing from the economics that he first learned—a vision of something which by his efforts has now become central to economics. Like the best of visions, it seems to have come from a miracle: when Leo was fleeing the Nazis with virtually no resources but his wits, his path of escape somehow miraculously led him through the classrooms of the leading economists on both sides of the great debate of capitalism versus socialism. He met Friedrich von Hayek in London, then through Ludwig von Mises' classroom in Geneva, and ended up with Oskar Lange in Chicago, before going on to Cambridge with Paul Samuelson. [*MIT is in Cambridge, MA*]

From this extraordinary odyssey, Leo learned that economic theorists in 1940 did not have any analytical framework for making comparative predictions about different economic systems. There was no general theory in which they could compare centralized socialism and decentralized free-market capitalism. So Leo realized that to answer great fundamental questions about different economic systems, economists needed to think about markets and other social institutions at a more fundamental level. And he came to see that all institutions could be considered as mechanisms which collect information from different people, somehow compute appropriate social outcomes, and then coordinate people to achieve these outcomes. He saw that we should understand capitalism and socialism as two such information processing mechanisms for coordinating economic activity, and then we could begin to ask questions about which mechanisms would be best for different criteria. Leo was confident that this new economic theory of institutions could be developed with careful, rigorous mathematics. But it would take time to find the right way to do it. So he worked for decades to develop a framework for analyzing institutions and communication in society.

Around 1972, when he began to ask deep questions about people's incentives to communicate, then he made one of the great breakthroughs in the history of social science. When Leonid Hurwicz introduced the concept of incentive-compatibility, it was as if a pair of blinders had been removed. Suddenly, we could see how to analyze economic incentives without assuming any specific institutional structure, and even how optimal institutions might be characterized.

Then more and more of us recognized that Leo was onto something really important, and we began to follow him in this great project.

We miss him now, but our work will continue to build on his.

Let me say personally, from personal experience: if you get a phone call at 5:30 in the morning to tell you that your name is being put on the same line with the name of Leonid Hurwicz, that is good news, no matter who's calling.

Leo's career had such a long and brilliant trajectory, I'm very grateful for all the times that our paths were linked. But this last one . . . this last one, it was the best. I just want to thank Leo for taking us so far.

Thank you.

Ruth Hurwicz (Markovitz)

In honor of my dad, this talk may be a few minutes longer than what was suggested.

As long as my dad was living, I felt that someone wise and good was watching out for all of us. Dad tracked world events as one who understood that they are happening to us, not "them." He valued an active citizenry, and took his role as guardian to heart, doing his part to help steer the world in good directions.

With his endless curiosity, my dad delved into a broad and eclectic range of areas, and he enjoyed countless interests and enthusiasms. Two constant loves were dark chocolate and sleep. My mom sharply limited his intake of the first, and we kids the latter.

You might have thought him quite the lazy-bones considering the wistful way he spoke of sleep. But I don't think he indulged himself all that often. He did show natural talent early on: as a young man, he could sleep standing up on the streetcar to school, without missing his stop. Insomnia certainly never troubled him. I have fond memories of coming across dad napping in the living room before dinner, while we rambunctious kids raced around the house.

I never wanted the job of waking him up, even for the beautiful dinners my mom made every night. He always looked so happy and content when sleeping, perhaps thanks to having a clear conscience.

Some of my sweetest memories are of curling up with my dad, listening to family bedtime stories, enthralled by his wonderfully expressive voice and funny faces. I savored this delicious time together. Dad could weave in colorful threads from endless experiences and ideas to tell his own fascinating tales.

But he rarely shared stories from his own childhood. Once I was older, I realized that the horrors of pre-World War II Poland did not spare even this innocent child.

No wonder my dad resonated to Alice in Wonderland. He couldn't have landed in any more different life by leaving Europe for America than did Alice when she fell down that rabbit hole.

My dad loved sharing the great classics with us. But one lesser-known book comes to mind as I think back. This was a collection of folk tales from the old country of Georgia, "The Yes and No Stories," which always captured my imagination from their very first magical words: "There was, there was, and yet there was not . . ."

The book begins with the elders of the village gathered around a campfire telling stories. One young boy sits quietly among them, night after night, listening in fascinated silence.

At last, one night, the eldest of the elders turns to the boy and says, "Now it's your turn."

Alarmed and scared, the boy protests, "Oh no I couldn't!"

"Why not?" asked the elder.

"I don't know enough," the boy replies, "and I might not get it right. Please, I prefer just to listen."

The elder responds firmly, "If you want to keep coming to the campfire and listening, then you must take your turn. Don't worry so much. No one gets it all right. If you leave something out, someone else will fix that down the road. But it's vital that we all pass on what we've learned to others."

And so the boy shyly begins, "There was, there was, and yet there was not."

My dad loved that whole process: the learning, sharing, teaching. Yet like that little boy, dad didn't ever believe that he knew the full story. And he was reluctant to declare something the final version. Dad found the process of doing new work far more exciting than publishing something where he already knew how the story turned out.

You may or may not know that my dad actually wrote two complete PhD theses. But he was never satisfied with either one. His adviser was. He wasn't. And he happily went through his career without a PhD.

He was a bit of a perfectionist.

The elders in the story would've approved of how my dad spoke up for his beliefs. It's easy to understand how someone who had escaped the hostile political climate of World War II Europe would feel a strong personal commitment to keeping our democracy vibrant.

Dad arrived in the United States in 1940 thanks to great luck and ingenuity on his part, along with the invaluable assistance of our Chicago relatives, the Kotzins (who are represented by a younger generation today), who generously sponsored him.

Dad loved his adopted homeland. His heart could not and did not rest, though, until his younger brother Henry, who is here with us today, and his parents were released from work camps in Europe to join him safely on American soil.

From the time he and my mom met at the University of Chicago, in 1943, they shared a common passion for politics. Dad served as a delegate to the 1968 Democratic Chicago Convention, and both he and my mom devoted much energy over the years to various liberal issues and candidates. My parents, at age 84 and 90, attended their last Democratic caucus together this year.

Having grown up in a country where Jews were restricted to sitting in the back of the classroom of only certain schools, and were completely barred from various institutions, universities and jobs, dad highly valued America's public education system. And he was very proud of his long association with the University of Minnesota.

Dad loved teaching and cared deeply about his many students, who were in turn devoted to him. He had a great sense of responsibility for his foreign students, who would return to their native countries, where they could influence the economies and institutions of their own countries.

And how lucky was I. I could go to my dad with most any question—well nothing too personal, of course—and miraculously he would probably have already wondered about the same thing. So he had a reserve of knowledge and insights from casual research done sometime over the years, just for fun.

A lot of what I've learned from him has faded, but the love of learning that he sparked in me burns bright. Often we ended up talking about ways to handle various problems and situations, and here is where my dad's wise and sensitive counsel in matters of diplomacy, relationships, strategies and ethics stay indelibly etched on my heart and soul. My dad made it seem as if he had all the time in the world for me. So patient and kind. Now I wonder to myself: how did he do it all? Where did he find the time?

I know he slept: we've established that. He made himself available when family or friends needed help. He was more than happy to spend long hours over the dinner table, relishing conversation with the frequent and varied company made welcome in our home. Late at night he *would* take to his study to work. But still, he made it all look so easy. What was his secret for making time elastic? I asked him so many questions. But I never thought to ask him that.

My guess: it all comes back to his love of learning. He instinctively responded to people seeking his help, because he believed in the primary importance of the cycle of learning and teaching. And that meant that every question, every student, mattered. Dad found something interesting everywhere. You could be frustrated if you tried to rush him along to get a simple answer. But you would never be bored. Traveling alongside dad's mind was exciting. No matter which port you entered, dad—like Marco Polo—would guide you to sights you'd never dreamt of and fill your head with new ideas. Learning was his spice of life.

Now that he has passed away, I hope it's safe to reveal a family secret to the university leadership. Dad confided to us more than once that he loved his job so much, he would've done it for free. That was the truth. For he found tremendous joy and fulfillment in his work.

Dad felt overall very lucky in life. He adored my mom for their 63 years of marriage, and he good-naturedly went along for the wild ride of a very full family life with four kids, a menagerie of pets, and a whirlwind of work, socializing, politics, friends and travel. Dad's subtle sense of humor and light touch made him delightful company. And dad never never risked boredom, as he could always retreat to a unique and wonderful built-in source of stimulation and entertainment: his very own boundless curiosity.

Around the time he turned 75, dad wryly joked that he'd now outlived the risk of dying tragically young. He once explained to me that he had always felt a sense of urgency about getting his ideas recognized: when he was younger and unknown, because he wanted people to listen to him and take his ideas seriously. And then later, when he was older, because he never knew exactly how much time he had left.

The same constant energy fueled dad's efforts to reach out to people and help however he could. He liked imagining his students and his students' students (or his "intellectual grandchildren" as he liked to call them) carrying on this process around the world and across generations.

Now that my dad isn't with us anymore, I feel quite lost at times. For who can I turn to with all my questions? Years ago, when my mother lost her mother, she poignantly confided that when you lose a parent, you feel sometimes—perhaps irrationally—that you have lost a protector standing between you and the cold, cruel world.

In the case of my dad, I think it's true: we have all lost a wise and vigilant guardian. My dad did a tremendous job of watching out for all of us. But now, whether we feel ready or not, it's our turn at the campfire.

My dad was a rather exceptional person. And so, while we can't look to him as a realistic model for everything, still in some basic and important ways he serves as a lovely example of a fine human being.

I deeply regret not having gotten dad's secret for expanding time. But we can emulate him by serving as informed and active citizens, and also not just by finding time, but making time, for those who need our help. Maybe then, like my dad, we, too, will all sleep a bit easier.

Andreu Mas-Colell
(read by Jim Jordan)

Next I'm going to read something from Andreu Mas-Colell, one of Leo's and Ket's students, one of their most successful students that came out of here. He couldn't be here today; he was planning on coming, but he couldn't. So he wrote up a few remarks and asked me to read them, so I'll do that.

He sort of digs me a bit in this, too. Andreu was sort of my advisor, so Leo was kind of my grandfather advisor or something. So he took one small little dig at me. I'll point it out.

Dear Larry,

I'm very sorry not to be able to be to be with all of you honoring Leo. I thought, however, that I could send you some remembrances of my first contacts with Leo. To begin with, Leo is one of the reasons I came to Minnesota, or at least the main reason I came with very high expectations. The U of M was a place that I knew had a good reputation and that was kind enough to offer me a scholarship. But when I looked at the roster of professors, I was immediately taken by Leo's name, because I knew one of his articles, published in a book of the International Economic Association, edited by Bacharach and Malinvaud. I did not understand a thing of the article. But I understood that I wanted to understand it.

And a few months later the occasion was presenting itself. Once I arrived in Minneapolis, it took a few weeks before I managed to see Leo. He passed by me like an exhalation in a corridor. I must've been impressed because I still remember that moment.

Then misfortune struck: it became known that the following academic year Leo was moving—for how long, nobody knew, it turned out to be two years— to Harvard. That meant all these courses I was planning on taking with him in the second year would have to be taken in my first year. The courses were two: in the winter it was the first-year micro course. It consisted of a finite but very large number of Edgeworth boxes, linked in a relentless logical chain. It was fascinating—most likely one of the two or three courses that have had the largest impact on my student life and of course I have ever since drawn Edgeworth boxes the correct way. [Jim Jordan aside: *And Andreu says I don't do them right.*] A number of times in my life as a teacher I've tried to imitate this course—chalk of several colors included—but I have a feeling that I have never approached that model. By the way, Larry, you may been a victim of these, but I hope that at least I taught you to draw them correctly. I do not think I've inspired anyone to try it himself. But it was a great learning experience for me. In summary, Leo's way was simple but inimitable.

The second course was in the spring. It was an advanced topics course. Completely over my head, but then Hurwicz was going away so there wasn't much choice. But it was, I still feel it, a pity, because one year later I would have been much better prepared and more mature to absorb the wealth of ideas that were featured in that one core seminar. There was, on the one hand, informational decentralization. I wrote my first research essay on this line. I think it was called "The Dynamics of the Greed Process." And, on the other hand, there was all that talk around a term I had never heard. But then nobody else had either: incentive-compatibility.

In the successive years, I had great teachers at Minnesota, and through them, in particular Hugo Sonnenschein and Ket Richter, I kept contact with Leo. Through them, he also influenced me and my interest in demand and consumer theory, on which I ended up writing my dissertation with Ket. I think actually that the first acknowledgement footnotes I ever got were in different chapters of the Chipman-Hurwicz-Richter-Sonnenschein book on consumer and demand theory.

And that was it for the PhD years. I could add of course many things that were not specific to me but were shared with all my friends. We were in awe of Leo, of his brilliance, of his European background and the stories that came with it. Well, I should stop. I hope that everybody's having a wonderful day.

Andreu Mas-Colell

Michael Hurwicz

Well, I'm really just going to talk for a few minutes. (*Applause.*) Thank you, thank you.

I just want to share . . . One thing that my sister's talk brought up for me was, when we'd ask my dad what he would want for his birthday, he would inevitably reply, "Twelve hours of uninterrupted sleep." He never got it.

One of my best memories with my family and with my dad . . . My dad was quite a good musician. In fact, when he was a young man, he considered going to the Conservatory as opposed to becoming an economist.[2]

And he would sit and play the piano; he played a lot of Bach in particular. [*Or was it Chopin?—M. H.*] But what I remember is we had an old upright when I was young. And we had the Fireside Book of American Folk Songs. And we would gather around the piano, and we would sing "Oh Susannah" and "The Wraggle Taggle Gypsy." And all these wonderful folksongs . . . "Clementine." And I know that music and folk music became very meaningful to me. And I

---

2   He actually did study piano at the Warsaw Conservatory, now the Fryderyk Chopin University of Music.

wonder how much those experiences of closeness and warmth in my family came from those times.

And I also think to myself, looking back on it now—it didn't occur to me then—but here was a man raised in Poland until he was 19 or 20 years old—I don't think he even spoke English very much at all when he left—and he gathered around with his kids and sang American folk songs. To me that says something very special about adaptability and embracing the place that you are.

Some other good memories that I have are vacations when we went camping. He loved to camp and he loved to hike. He loved nature. And almost every vacation we would go to a national park—Yellowstone or Yosemite or Glacier National Park—and we would pitch tents. The only time we didn't stay in tents, if it just rained torrentially for day after day, we'd go to a motel. But if the weather permitted, we would just sleep in tents and we would get up and make pancakes on our little Coleman gas stove. And at night we would sit around a campfire and talk or sing or talk about things we had seen during the day: he was also very interested in plants and trees and what everything was. And that's another love that I have, for camping and the outdoors. And I'm sure I gained some of that from him, too.

And the last thing I want to share has to do with an argument that I had with my father. I was probably about 19 or 20. This would be in 1968, 1969, so he was in his early 50s I guess. And I was a hippie. And I don't remember what I was espousing. But it was big. And it was a whole new way of thinking, a whole new way of living. It was revolutionary. And my father was discussing this with me, and he didn't completely agree with me. So we talked about this for quite some time. And then I think probably to put an end to it, he said to me, "Well, you know, maybe a few years from now, we'll be on opposite sides of this question."

And that said something very special to me, too: that he was saying, "Well, I don't agree with you. But I think you've got a perfectly valid perspective. And I could see myself taking that perspective." And I think he was also encouraging me to understand that my perspective was coming from where I stood, and that perhaps he had a valid perspective that might someday serve me well. And I think that that same spirit of openness and understanding, I'm starting to sense that that came out in his work, as well, where he didn't necessarily think that there was one way to do things right. That there were systems, and one system worked like this, and another system worked like that, and they could both work, and here were your outcomes, and make your decisions.

So those are just some memories from my father. Thank you.

Evelyn

I think what I really appreciated about Leo was his acceptance of all kinds of people.

I was raised in a family where the generation before me—in fact I think even my generation—didn't have college degrees. I'm the only one of four children in my family who got a college degree. And Leo just—not just accepted everybody—but he had an appreciation for people with almost no education. My family were farmers and factory workers. My mother worked for years in a Chinese laundry. And Leo always found just full explanations for their lives. And he knew that they didn't have opportunities, but that they made an active life in whatever situation they found themselves. And he not just accepted them: he enjoyed them. And he tried to understand people from very very different backgrounds. In my family, farmers and factory workers, and he never looked down on anybody. He sort of looked at their life histories and found a story there that he appreciated. So that's what I really appreciated about him. Thank you.

Carla Rosenlicht

I've known Evelyn since before she met Leo—even before all of us worked for the meteorology project at the University of Chicago during the war. When she announced she had become engaged to Leo, I was thrilled. Both she and I were not yet 20. I think she was 18 and I was 17. And Leo was 27. So I said to Leo, "Isn't it wonderful, that Evelyn—with such a difficult youth—marrying an older settled man." May I say that he was disgusting enough, when I was a child of 27, he reminded me of that remark. The other thing that today's remarks have brought up in me is how angry Leo was when it became more efficient to fly rather than take the train. Because how was he going to prepare the speeches that he was to give at the end of the journey? Thank you very much.

Herb Mohring

I'm Herb Mohring, a colleague of Leo's for, oh what, 40 years. Before I came to Minnesota, I was at Northwestern University. There, lunches with faculty members often involved criticism, tales of various kinds about the inadequacies of colleagues who weren't at the lunch. Coming to Minnesota, the environment changed. A frequent topic of conversation here was whether any of us could tell a funnier story than Leo about the stupid thing they did yesterday. Leo was a raconteur of stupid stories, tales about the stupid stories that he did yesterday. He set the personality for the department: kind, generous, helpful, friendly, a wonderful place to be.

Second talk about Leo: during my last year as director of graduate studies, during the mid 1980's, the acceptance on my aid offers to incoming graduate students went from about a third to a half. Bankruptcy threatened the department. Fortunately, Ed Foster and I had managed to entrepreneur a grant from the Sloan Foundation to deal with . . . well, to deal with something. My word went out to members of the department, if anyone wanted a research assistant, please get in touch. Leo was asked for a student, a very able Israeli whose name I've forgotten. His sole duty was to become intimately acquainted with a working paper that Leo had written two or three years earlier. He wanted to be absolutely certain that nothing was wrong with it. Now, if God has to be absolutely certain that something he has written about has absolutely no errors, who were we mortals to dash quick articles to be sent to inferior journals? This department was never one for publishing lots of secondary stuff. And that's Leo's responsibility.

Harlan Smith

My first experience of Leo was the University of Chicago in the late '30s or early '40s, I don't remember exactly. We were both students in a course with Oskar Lange in advanced economic theory. And one of the assignments that Lange gave us, he assigned each of us an article in one of the professional economic journals to report on to the class. And the class would be free to discuss it, and he would.

I remember he gave me an article that I enjoyed very much. I learned a great deal from it. I don't now remember the name of the article or who wrote it. But I know that it impressed me a great deal. So when I went in, I gave a very enthusiastic report of this article, how much I'd learned by it. And then the class was supposed to react, and only one or two people said anything.

And then Leo started out talking. I didn't know Leo at all at that point, except I knew he was in the class. But so were a lot of other people, probably a couple of dozen people, as far as I remember. And Leo started in his nice slow way, "Well," he says, "if I were going to think about this, I would come about it a little bit different way. And he started in in a general way, and just slowly demolished the article. By the time he got through, I knew it wasn't worth anything, and that I had been impressed by and learned something from an article that I should have been critical of. And then Leo slowly demolished my report, and I didn't have a leg to stand on by the end of the day. But he did it so nicely, that I realized that he was just smarter than I, and that I was learning something that I needed to learn. So I didn't resent it in the very least. And I learned that that's the way to deal with other people when you disagree with them.

I didn't know at that time that Leo and I would both appear at the University of Minnesota a few years later—well, many years later, actually. I came in 1950, and Leo came in 1951. And I wondered when he came, how we would get along, and indeed how he would get along with the rest of the department, because I had on that one occasion learned how much smarter Leo was. I realized at the time that he could probably have taught the course as well as Oskar Lange could have, and that he was teaching me at that time. So I wondered how he would get along with others, and I worried just a little bit about that.

I told Leo this one day, and he says, "Well, how did I do?"

I said, "Leo, I shouldn't have had the least bit of worry about you. I didn't know that you were such a wonderful guy at the time."

And we were by then very good friends. And Leo always supported me in everything I wanted to do in the department. I think it was his way of handling other people. And I have learned since, of course, that he handles everybody so beautifully. I've been in many public meetings with him, with a group of other professional economists, and they had all given their reports, and there would be a lot of talking in the room while other were reporting, and finally somebody would say, "Leo, why didn't you say anything?" And Leo would say in his nice, calm way, "Well, if I were to think about this," he says, "I believe I'd go about it in a little different way." And the minute he would start to talk, complete silence would fall upon that room. Everybody would stop and listen to just what Leo would have to say. Because we all knew that he was smarter than all the rest of us.

And indeed when Leo and Evelyn held New Year's Eve parties at their home, as they did for the department, no matter what the discussion was, Leo knew more about what was going on than anybody else there did. He always knew more about anything than anybody else did. He was the only real genius I've ever known, that was also one of the best and finest people I ever knew, in the way he treated other people. So we all miss Leo very very much, and we all honor his work.

I couldn't do a thing with his work; I couldn't even read anything he wrote, because I didn't have that much training in mathematics and statistics. But I was a social scientist with a quite different background, and he was quite happy to support anything I did, as well as the type of work that he did.

So that's my story about Leo. Thank you very much for the opportunity to tell others what a fine person Leo was in every possible way.

Mahmood Zaidi

Leo, all the people who have paid tribute to you today, and tribute people paid to you on your 90th birthday, or your Nobel Prize ceremony, I couldn't agree more, because I have been here since '66, when I came and joined as the assistant professor, in the Carlson School, with the open arm and generosity you received me, and remained my mentor throughout my career here.

I especially remember two very important parts. One has to do with our battle in the Senate for our tenure and the faculty welfare issue, when I had the honor of chairing the Faculty Affairs and the Consultative Committee. Secondly, I also remember when you were president of the Econometric Society, and the meetings in Chicago, I also remember your way, how well you handled Walter Heller and you. So, as far as long I live, I learn not only economics from you, but I learn about music, art, geography, languages, everything which people have talked about. You were the wholesome person. And as long as I live, I'll remember and cherish those moments very much. Good luck to all the family members.

Nina Reiter

I just wanted to say that Leo was my friend, and I miss him. The thing about Leo was, he not only didn't make a distinction between people who were well educated and people who weren't, people who were of his race or his religion—he didn't care if you were a man or a woman. And that was a very refreshing and wonderful thing. Not every male academic has the facility or the desire to be friends with the wives of his colleagues, and Leo did. And he was a good friend—a very good friend, indeed. He would be with us on the farm for weeks at a time, and I thoroughly enjoyed his company.

I suppose one of the triumphs was that, on one of our morning walks, we had an argument about a tree, which I identified—I don't even remember what—but whatever the identification was, Leo was sure I was wrong. And I was right! It was an amazing triumph, one not duplicated very often. Because Leo knew a great deal about trees and plants and flowers, as well as about economics.

It was a pleasure to be with him. It was a pleasure to talk to him about many different things, personal and otherwise. He was a lovely man, and I miss him. That's it.

A Celebration of Leo's 90th Birthday, Held at the Holiday Inn Metrodome, 1500 Washington Avenue South, in Minneapolis on April 14, 2007

———————

(This event was written up in *Minnesota Economics*, Fall, 2007: https://leonidhurwicz.org/wp-content/uploads/2018/10/minnesota_economics_fall_2007.pdf)

Ket Richter

There were so many people who wanted to make remarks that we cannot accommodate them all. So what we've done is to sample a few different friends of Leo's from a few different walks of life. Their associations with Leo all fall somewhere in the timeline that you have here.

[Appendix F is a slightly expanded version of this timeline—M. H.]

And they're continuing. That timeline does not do justice to the richness of Leo's 90 years so far. And therefore as a prelude to what the other people will be saying, I'd like to read a little between the lines that may not be apparent and I think that some of you may not be aware of.

You should beware: this is my own interpretation; Leo and family are not responsible for this, for the fallacies and inaccuracies.

1917: Leo was born in Moscow. His family had fled from the Kaiser's armies invading Poland, and Leo was born in 1917 in Moscow. We could not put the exact date, because that would have involved deciding whether to use the Julian calendar, which was still in effect, or the Gregorian calendar, the current calendar—and we did not want footnotes in this document. So a reasonable compromise would be to say that he was born between the Kerensky revolution in the Spring of 1917 in the Lenin Bolshevik Revolution in the Fall. And I think that's our first perspective on Leo: he was born before the Communist revolution, outlasted it and is still going strong.

(*applause*)

While getting his law degree, Leo had taken a couple economics courses. In '38 he had got his *Magister* law degree from the University of Warsaw in both, I believe, civil law and canon law. He had taken some economics courses and enjoyed them, so in 1938 after he got his degree he was off to study at the London School of Economics. And there the plot thickens. His Polish passport eventually expired, so he couldn't stay in London. He appealed to the British officials for an extension of his visa on condition, on the promise of his getting a renewal of his passport from Poland. The British replied, "We are not in the habit of doing that." That was a simple answer. So what was Leo to do? War was in the air in Europe in 1939, and his instincts told him not to go back to Poland to get a renewal of his passport. So he planned a traipsing around European capitals to Polish consulates to see if he could get a renewal.

When he was in Paris, right after his 22nd birthday, the Molotov-Ribbentrop pact, the Nazi-Soviet nonaggression pact, was announced in the newspapers. And he realized that something serious was about to happen, and he thought the best course would be to go to a neutral country. He headed for Switzerland.

The day after he arrived, he read in the morning's newspaper that Hitler's blitzkrieg, and the bombing of the Polish cities, had started the day before, on September 1st. In fact, his home in Warsaw—the family home—was bracketed by bombs. So with World War II having started, once again his mother and father, and now Leo's young brother, headed eastward. His father was arrested by the Russians and send to the Gulag. The charge was that he was "capable of intellectual leadership." Those of us who had the privilege of knowing him know that he was seriously guilty of charge—and it seems to have been a hereditary condition.

His mother and brother, incidentally, were sent to a different slave camp in Siberia.[1]

1940 it says "came to United States." Simple to say, but it almost did not happen. Leo was in Geneva. Relatives in Chicago sent money for his ticket to the US. But the US would not give him a visa unless he has certificates of good conduct over the last five years—from all the countries in which he had visited in the last five years.

The French obliged very willingly. The British response was, "we are not in the habit of issuing good conduct certificates." Mere mortals would've despaired. But Leo, the consummate Polish logician, suggested to the Geneva police that they wire Scotland Yard saying that Leo was under suspicion, and did Scotland Yard have any dirt on Leo. Scotland Yard of course replied no, they didn't. That satisfied the US officials, who apparently were still working with Aristotelian two-valued logic, and he got his visa.

There was no possibility of air travel to the US from Geneva, but he learned that he could get a ticket on an Italian ship from Lisbon. So he traveled again, Geneva to Barcelona to Lisbon. But by the time he arrived in Lisbon, Italy had entered the war on the German side. So Italian ships could not come to the US. And he had spent all his money on the ticket. Leo asked, of course, for his money back, and they laughed at him and said he could have it back after the war. A little more Polish logic that I won't go into—this time it was applied to the chief of the Harbor police—got him his money back, another ticket and escape on a Greek ship to Hoboken, New Jersey.

1941 we find 23-year-old Leo as research assistant to 25-year-old Paul Samuelson, at the very beginning of MIT's economic Renaissance. To commemorate tonight's event, Leo, Paul has written the following letter. And this is an extended thing that I'll say as quickly as I can.[2]

---

1   Technically it was not a "slave camp" but a "village of compulsory residence"—not as harsh or deadly as a gulag, for example. In addition, it was not Siberia, but "Northern Russian swamps." Hurwicz to "Dear Mr. Lash" [Joseph P. Lash], Leonid Hurwicz Papers, David M. Rubenstein Rare Book & Manuscript Library, Duke University, Box 23, File: Academic records, 1930s–1940s.
    Specifically, the family was deported initially to Nyandoma in the Archangel Oblast (province)—"not Siberia, but something just as good," Nina Shepherd, "The Wisdom of an Economist's Economist," *University of Minnesota Update*, October 1987, Volume 14, Number 9.

2   Used by permission of the Paul Samuelson estate. This is archived as P.A. Samuelson, Undated, "The Hurwicz 1940–41 year when MIT launched its graduate degree rocket," Paul A. Samuelson papers, David M. Rubenstein Rare Book and Manuscript Library, Duke University, box 39. Although the document is undated, one can surmise that it was written not too long before this celebration took place on April 14, 2007.

MIT's Rupert MacLaurin asked new arrival Paul Samuelson, "Who's the world's greatest economist?"

[Ket added, "Rupert MacLaurin was chair of the Economics Department."]

"Ragnar Frisch," I suggested.

[*Frisch was awarded the first Nobel Memorial Prize in Economic Sciences in 1969—M. H.*]

"Okay. Let's get him here at MIT."

"No, we can't do that. He's a Norwegian patriot, sequestered right now in a Nazi concentration camp, where he's reduced to studying Darwinian bee genetics."[3]

So to speak, therefore, I had to palm off on go-getter MacLaurin 23-year-old Leo Hurwicz, instead of Frisch or Tinbergen or for that matter Keynes.

[*Jan Tinbergen was co-recipient with Frisch of the first Nobel Memorial Prize in Economic Sciences in 1969—M. H.*]

[*Ket did not read this part below, up to "frenetic." The author got it from the Samuelson archives at Duke University—M. H.*]

There's a story behind this story. Whilst Harvard was keeping in its court the ball that was put there by an October 1940 MIT invite to 25-year-old Paul to levitate three miles down the Charles River, frenetic MacLaurin phoned me nightly. One warm evening, he dangled before me what follows: "If you come to MIT, for your research you will have at your disposal the Roger Babson grant to study how Newton's Second [*sic, but should be third—M. H.*] Law of Action and Reaction applies to macroeconomics."

Babson, who personally owned only two New England colleges, won Andy Warhol celebrity fame for—now listen to my words—correctly predicting in advance the Great Wall Street Crash of October 1929. Never mind that Babson made that prediction in 1925, when the Dow Jones Index was about one-tenth of its 1929 peak. (Maybe Newton had told him, "What goes up must fall down.")

The rest is history: I quit my late September Harvard lecturing on Econ 1 abruptly at the mid-hour. Arriving by Massachusetts Avenue streetcar, what I found awaiting me at MIT were both half a secretary and my own telephone. (Ten years later, Schumpeter at Harvard still hadn't attained that affluence.)

While I couldn't fetch Frisch for MacLaurin, I still could deliver to him some new star. But who? Oskar Lange—then at Chicago or Berkeley [*It was Chicago. Berkeley came later—M. H.*]—narrowed down the field for me. He suggested two names: Hungarian Tibor de Scitovsky or a young Pole, Leonid Hurwicz,

---

3 "Frisch's most important hobby was bee-keeping, for which Frisch performed genetic studies." Wikipedia, https://en.wikipedia.org/wiki/Ragnar_Frisch.

late of Warsaw, Geneva, Barcelona and Lisbon—always one step ahead of Hitler's mobile tanks.

Tibor's work at the LSE I knew and admired. But applying Lange's needs test, Hurwicz was the one in more desperate financial need.

Think of it this way: suppose Niels Bohr could choose between say, Heisenberg or Pauli. My die was cast, and MIT was the beneficiary.

Historians of stochastic intertemporal U.S. time series, and Isaac Newton in his dissenting Anglican Valhalla, must know how we did early spectral analysis of Frickey's aggregate U.S. output for the timeslot 1865 to 1935.

[*Edwin Frickey was a former professor of Samuelson's at Harvard, who had compiled data on which the "galley-slaves" could perform mathematical searches for regularly recurring patterns—M. H.*]

When I say "we" I do not refer to Leo and Paul only. Instead I can still see in my mind's eye Leo, whip in one hand, slide rule in the other, marshaling his crew of mostly young female National Youth Administration galley-slave computers. *Parallel* computer computation thus merits a marble marker at the northwest corner of Massachusetts Avenue and Memorial Drive. Leo began that there.

Even more melodramatic was the new Hurwicz-Samuelson grading system for my first regular statistics course. MIT engineers have always been notorious whiners. They are grade chasers beyond Philadelphia barracks lawyers anywhere.

One of us—I will point no finger—said: let's add a hard extra-credit exam question, with a proviso that it can only *raise, but not lower,* your grade.

[Ket added, "Think a minute about that."]

All hell broke loose when undergraduate commerce course nerds learned that their exam mark of 115 put them below the median of the class grades. It did not help when Leo explained that this was the famous Chicago grading system. Leo had little to lose. The Babson pittance was already spent. It was my tenure and future lifetime career that dangled on the razor's edge.

[Ket added, "I'm told that Samuelson told Leo, you have ten minutes to explain to them: figure out an answer."]

[*The written version in the Rubenstein Library includes the following statement by Samuelson:* "Fortunately, Japan at Pearl Harbor saved my bacon and as well that of Hitler-hating Franklin Roosevelt"—*M. H.*]

Best of all, the Leo MIT year was a fun year. You know you're a has-been when you hear yourself saying, "I gave Goethe his first job." Well, damn it, I did give Leo his.

[*Thus ends the contribution from Samuelson, read by Ket. It was followed by laughter and applause from guests at the birthday celebration. Ket's comments continue below—M. H.*]

The years 1941 on, on your timeline, show Leo at the University of Chicago, first as a research assistant to Oskar Lange in economics and then as a research associate in meteorology.

In 1943, I think it must've been, Leo was visiting in Washington DC investigating statistical systems for long-range weather forecast (long-range in those days meant three days), when he received some upsetting news. His assistant in meteorology back in Chicago had quit. On the phone he was advised a young economics undergraduate named Evelyn Jensen had applied for the job, and that she seemed very bright. So Leo hired her sight unseen. What he didn't know was that his previous assistant had told Evelyn that it was really great job; the only problem with it is the man you have to work for. Evelyn solved the problem within a year by marrying him.

Just looking at all the places on your timeline they have lived, it is obvious that Evelyn is more than merely bright: she's adventurous as well. Later, asked whether she would be taking a job after her children were in school, she replied, "Why should I work for a stupid man, when I can give orders to a brilliant man?"

Did you really say that, Evelyn?

[*She apparently nods—M. H.*]

My sources . . . Evelyn confirms it.

And that's the backdrop for the rest of the line: it's obviously been a very productive partnership.

And now, to bring us back to economics, I'd like to call on Hugo Sonnenschein for a few further remarks.

Hugo Sonnenschein

Bravo, Leo! Toast to Leo! Another toast to Leo!

So each have our own stories. Forty-three years ago tomorrow—I know it's tomorrow because it was tax day—I visited the University of Minnesota to be considered for a position, and after I gave my talk everybody took off to do their taxes, actually. The position existed because of Leo, who had written it into his NSF proposal. And so I came to Minnesota as an assistant professor with no teaching responsibilities in my first year.

As a student of Stan Reiter, Leo was my academic grandfather, which reaffirms the importance of the social networks that Ken Arrow was speaking about earlier in the day. I joined Leo, John Chipman and Ket Richter and many other wonderful people, so many who it's wonderful to see looking particularly well, people I wrote first papers with—Ed Foster—Ann right here. It was very special.

Leo had successfully argued that the department required a critical mass of mathematical economists—it's another part of the Polish logic—that we were like whooping cranes and could disappear if the flock was not kept at adequate size.

Of course Leo was the intellectual leader and also the values leader of the department, and because of this, it really was the best of times. We were led to believe—not told—that the number of papers we wrote was far less important than quality, originality and depth of ideas. Leo had little patience for matters of evaluation and tenure. We were simply colleagues to work together, to do our best. Exams and CVs would circle the world in that worn, stuffed black briefcase that he carried—all unread and deadlines passed.

But he always had time for ideas, and he had and has the very best taste. He knows. He's wise, and uncommonly generous. Time would expand for a hapless undergraduate who had wandered near his office with a calculus book in hand. An hour-long appointment to explain your work with a junior faculty member or a student would become two hours, or would become three hours. Graduate students and faculty learned what it meant to understand, just as Walter Heller learned to understand (in that case Keynes via Hanson), and this enabled Walter to successfully teach macroeconomics to John Kennedy. But it was by way of Leo, I assure you. And we all knew that in the department.

Leo's leadership and Leo's values—scientific and human—bring out the best in us. I really do believe this has been a department of overachievers. Such a privilege to be a part of it. He's really been responsible for our successes.

So again a toast: master scholar, master teacher, intellectual giant, and exemplary human being. (Getting harder and harder to live with, huh?) It is magnificent for us who you influenced greatly to come together on your birthday.

Congratulations!

John Chipman

I first came across Leo during my postdoc in Chicago with the Cowles Commission.

But my relationship with Leo really started when I arrived at Minnesota way back in 1955, I think it was. In those days there was no economics department. We were all in the business school. And the business school was divided into areas. And the area in which I was supposed to belong to was called Economic Theory and Statistics. And I was supposed to be there for statistics. Leo was in that group, Oz Brownlee in that group, in that area. Walter Heller was in the

Finance area. Lloyd Ulman in the Industrial Relations area. And of course we found it rather frustrating to work in this environment, especially since . . . Well, for instance, one of the areas in the business school was Typing and Shorthand. And when we were on committees to make hiring recommendations, the dean made sure we had representation from all these areas. So we had to have professors of typing and shorthand and marketing and so on, on all the committees to hire economists. And this situation was rather uncomfortable. So there was turmoil as soon as I arrive in the department because of a feeling that economists really wanted to be together. And so for two years there were arduous meetings to try and create an economics department within the business school—which was greatly resented by the other members of the business school. One of whom proposed at one of these meetings that if that's what you want, why don't you apply to join the department of the school mortuary science?

Well, we finally managed to persuade the university administration to create an economics department. Of course, Leo and Walter were the two leading figures in this. And the remarkable thing is that they were opposite in their economic research and in their economic points of view. And this was a trait that I saw many more times later in Leo: he respected quality. And so did Walter. And so the two trusted each other and joined forces and were successful in persuading university administration first to put pressure on the dean to create an economics department within the business school. Of course this wasn't terribly successful because of the frictions with the other members of the business school.

We were reluctant at that time to join the liberal arts college, because they thought that economists shouldn't be paid any more than professors of Greek. But when a new dean of the liberal arts college was appointed and invited us to join them, we did that.

So those were the first struggling years of the economics department. The cooperation between Leo and Walter really was a tremendous force. And Leo was—and still is—a tremendous intellectual force.

I remember him saying emphatically when people complained about the use of mathematics in economics, "You can't quarrel with logic." That was his legal background coming to the fore, of course.

Also I remember some of his wonderful phrases. Once there was a lecture by somebody—I won't mention whom—who presented a theorem and instead of providing details of proof, said "Well, isn't it obvious?" when he was questioned about the proof. And so Leo coined the phrase "proof by intimidation." And this is only one of the many wonderful phrases that Leo came up with.

During those early years Leo would organize bag lunch seminars. We would hold these in what came to be called "Buttrick" [Hall] on the east bank of the

Mississippi. And these informal meetings to discuss each other's ideas were just a tremendous stimulus I think to everybody in the department and set the tone for the department. And so as an intellectual leader, Leo has been incomparable. And he I think more than anybody else, almost single-handedly, was the one responsible for the department of economics, starting from nothing, ending up ranked fifth in the country by the National Research Council. That was because he realized before the rest of the profession how important it was to have exact thinking in economics. And before Leo was around, I think mathematical economics was looked down upon by most departments: Harvard, Princeton, Yale, all those departments. Leo made this a respectable part of economics, an indispensable part of economics. So he actually had a tremendous influence on all of economics in the United States.

So, finally, I have been asked to present to Leo a small token of appreciation by the department. And I would like to ask his daughter Ruth to come up and collect it for him.

There were remarks made earlier about Leo's punctuality. So this clock is an appreciation.

Congressman Don Fraser

Ket:
I would just like to mention that he was in the Minnesota state Senate for eight years, the US House of Representatives for 16 years, and served as Mayor of Minneapolis for 13 years, which is the longest tenure in history.

Congressman Fraser:
I'm not really that old: I just walk that way because I had a tennis game an hour ago.

Arvonne and I are both delighted to have a chance to participate tonight in this event. Leo and I are both getting old, but we are both still around. So I'd like to indulge in a few memories.

Leo and Evelyn and a lot of university faculty started me on my political career. I ran for the state Senate in 1954 because the incumbent Senator was attacking the university. Margaret Harding, head of the University Press, became my campaign chairperson. Mrs. Harding commandeered everyone she could into the campaign, including a young couple she and I both admired: Leo and Evelyn Hurwicz. That was, if my arithmetic part of my brain still functions, 53 years ago. And if my memory still serves me right, they were active members of the

Second Ward DFL club. Leo has always had cogent, down-to-earth comments on politics, both on issues and strategy. And I was delighted when he was named a Regents Professor. And that proves what an active political life can do for you.

I have noticed in looking at the record of Leo's work the fact that in 1968 he was at the Chicago Democratic National Convention. Not everybody in the room will remember that, but it was quite an experience. That was the convention at which there was rioting in the streets. It was one of the critical points, politically speaking, with reference to our continued involvement in the Viet Nam war. Leo was, as is indicated here, on the platform committee to help draft . . . at that point, I think, help draft a provision in the platform that the candidates could live with.

I have been struck tonight by the international character of the people who've come to help honor and recognize Leo on his 90th birthday. It suggests to me that the involvement of people who work in our universities and who provide scholarship . . . how badly that is needed in helping to manage particularly the international affairs of this nation. I've thought over the last few weeks of a sentiment that others have shared, that this period of time in American history may represent the end of the role that we've played over the last 50 or 60 years, since World War II and all that ensued afterwards. My own perspective—and this is one reason why I counted Leo as a supporter—has been the importance of building an international system based on the rule of law, and building the international institutions that can make that a reality. And we've come to a time now when the United States' attitude and responsiveness to international concerns leaves a large gap and much to be desired. And with the changing nature of the international economic scene, I'm thinking that we need to begin to adjust to a new world. It's going to demand the kind of collaborative, cooperative leadership that can come from the relationships we build across national borders.

I cast some very controversial votes early in my Congressional career. Leo never threw me out the door. He was always tolerant and willing to give me another chance home. One of the initiatives we took: we started the first international . . . the first parliamentary exchange with the European Union, which we hoped would lead to more effective dialogue. I don't think that's really happened, although there've been exchanges back and forth since. But it suggests to me that that's the direction in which we need to be moving.

Well, this is not a night to be serious. It's just that Leo's support of my work, my admiration for Leo and Evelyn and their role in politics has always made a very strong impression on me, and how people deeply engaged in research and scholarship can also take the time to be a part of our active civic and political community. So Arvonne and I are delighted to be here to congratulate Leo and Evelyn and hope for many more years to come.

Thank you.

Stan Reiter

Ket:
And now Stan Reiter has a few remarks to make.
[*Ket bent the gooseneck microphone upwards—M. H.*]

Ket:
Stan is tall.

Stan:
Did you mean that "few" remarks?

It's a pleasure to be at this event in Leo's life. I met Leo through the Cowles Commission, that's been mentioned a number of times today, a very influential and important organization. I was a graduate student, and Jacob Marschak stopped me one day after class and he invited me to come to the Cowles Commission. I had no idea what it was. It turned out it was located behind a door opposite the door to the Economics Department, and all this stuff was going on behind that door and invisible to me as a graduate student.

I became Koopmans' assistant, and I started bothering him with some ideas that I had. They were not fully formed. Koopmans was a very precise thinker, very smart. Couldn't figure out what I was talking about. There was a reason for that. But his solution to the problem was to tell me, after a couple of attempts to understand what I was trying to say, and when I was trying to understand what I was trying to say, he said, "You should talk to Leo Hurwicz." And I had no idea who Leo Hurwicz was. And he said, "He'll be coming in to attend a Cowles Commission staff meeting." A very fine-sounding, serious-sounding title, but it was that everybody got together in a room with blackboards, and they spent the whole day talking at each other—about interesting things. So he said, "When he comes, I'll introduce you, and you can talk with him." And this way he got rid of me.

So Leo did show up. And he was then coming from Ames, Iowa. And they had trains in those days, and that's how he got to Chicago. Well, I was summoned to

Koopmans' office. Leo was there. We were introduced, and Leo said, "Let's go for a walk."

So we went out, and we spent the entire . . . the rest of the day walking around in Hyde Park and discovering that the ideas that I was groping toward, and trying to make straight, were similar to the ideas that Leo had about what we now call mechanism design. And that was the beginning of a long relationship, as we know—and an intermittent one because Leo was busy with a lot of stuff, I had a career to make. But it was from my point of view a wonderful journey.

(*looking to the side, toward Ket*)

I have a deadline.

So I'm going to close with one reminiscence about Leo. He rashly told me once that when he was a child, somebody gave him a set of dominos. And while he was playing with the dominos—he didn't say this, but what he explained to me was that he discovered a formula that Gauss had invented many, many years ago. Discovered it by . . . It's the formula for counting. He arrayed the dominos one, two, three, four, five and so on. And then he had other dominos and he arrayed them in reverse order, so starting from the other end. And when you do that, you can see that the sum of the domino numbers is constant. And from that you can figure out a neat way to add up . . . to get that sum.

Now I don't know how old Gauss was when he discovered this. But I do know how old Leo was. He was very young. Probably couldn't read yet. It's amazing that he could count. And I tell this story because I think it is a clue, if you weren't already convinced, about Leo's mind. It was a clue that his mind was present when he was four years old, or whatever that episode . . . how old he was when that episode happened.

I recently taught my grandson this formula in just that way—not with dominos. And he was very excited about it, too.

Thank you.

Ket:

Thank you Stan. That's a very interesting piece of information. I think Gauss was actually older: he was in school when that happened. The probably apocryphal story is that the teacher had set a task to keep the students busy while he wrote personal letters, of adding up all the numbers from 1 to 100, and Gauss immediately got the answer, in three seconds. And everybody else was adding up the numbers from 1 to 100. The teacher was furious. So, Leo, congratulations, you were a lot younger than Gauss on that.

[*Wikipedia says, "A contested story relates that, when he was eight, he figured out how to add up all the numbers from 1 to 100"—M. H.*]

Ket:

I'd like to call now on Sophie—on Sarah Kogut, who . . . Can you hear? Oh okay. Leo has a footnote comment. Will it fit on one page?

Leo:

Yeah. Fine. It's really very brief. Can you hear me?

Ket:

Yes, we can.

Leo:

Okay. I have one comment that occurred to me while I was listening to various words of unlimited praise. And that's something that I heard from Executive Secretary of the department . . . Institute of Meteorology. He said, "There was a group of us once and we were talking about the weather yesterday. And it was a very stormy kind of summer afternoon weather. And there was hail. And one of the meteorologists present said, 'You know, I saw some pieces of hail that were one inch in diameter.' And then the man sitting next to him, he said, 'Well, I saw something that was the size of a baseball.' And the third one said, 'Well I saw something that looked more like a football.' And there was one man left, and he only made this comment: 'The first liar hasn't got a chance.'"

Ken Arrow

I find there's an omission made in all the discussion of Leo's accomplishments. We've heard—of course, and as an academic I can't help regarding the research on mechanism design and of course his teaching, as the most important matters—but the world does consider political activity also as important. We've heard from our congressman friend here about the importance of some of Leo's roles. But one of the most important, the most successful political step he's done was not mentioned. I refer to Andreas Papandreou, who should be mentioned here. Leo, of course, was friendly with Andreas when he was a colleague here at Minnesota. I subsequently came to know him when he was chairman of the department in Berkeley and in Greece.

In 1967, as many of you will remember, Andreas was arrested by . . . there was a coup by the Colonels, not the—the Generals were somehow not involved in this—it was the Colonels who took over the Greek government and drove out the politicians, including Andreas' father, and arrested Andreas. And of course we had every reason to believe that his life was in very grave danger, as I think indeed it was. So this is not a joke; this is serious matter.

Immediately, Leo got on the phone. He must have been on the phone 24 hours a day, as far as I can make out. I would hear from him once or twice every day. He was calling about 50 other people at the same time. And we were starting to . . . we had a telephone campaign to get officials at every level in Washington involved. I remember some poor assistant secretary for Middle Eastern affairs, or whatever exactly his scope was—Luke Battle,[4] if I remember his name correctly. Am I right, Leo?

[Leo: I think so, I am not sure . . .]

Some name like that, who indicated rather clearly he had been getting lots and lots of calls, all driven by Leo, who was the center of this academic network pushing for Andreas' . . . well for his life, for his safety and life.

In the end, he finally managed to reach the highest levels. This was I think via Ken Galbraith, who—although he was already a critic of the war, and not friendly with Lyndon Johnson at this point—nevertheless knew plenty of people, including Joseph Califano, the President's—some of you may remember the name—President Johnson's aide, and later Secretary of . . . whatever it was . . . I forgot now . . . he was in a cabinet position later.

[*"Special Assistant to President Lyndon B. Johnson . . . In this position, Califano served as LBJ's top domestic aide, developing the President's legislative program as well as helping coordinate economic policies and handling domestic crises." Later Secretary of Health, Education and Welfare. Wikipedia*]

And Johnson was in Germany attending Adenauer's funeral. Came back and immediately went to a diplomatic reception. Califano caught him on the floor of the reception and told him the great concern that Leo Hurwicz and the whole academic contingent were zealous, worried about Andreas Papandreou's life. To which President Johnson—some of you may have heard this—replied, "Okay, you tell those bastards to lay off that sonofabitch, whatever his name is." That was Leo's greatest triumph in the political sphere.

---

4   Lucius D. Battle, https://en.wikipedia.org/wiki/Lucius_D._Battle.

APPENDIX C

The Theory of Economic Behavior,[1] by Leonid Hurwicz[2]

———

Reprinted by permission of *The American Economic Review*: The Theory of Economic Behavior Author(s): Leonid Hurwicz. Source: *The American Economic Review*, Vol. 35, No. 5 (Dec., 1945), pp. 909–925 Published by: American Economic Association

Had it merely called to our attention the existence and exact nature of certain fundamental gaps in economic theory, the *Theory of Games and Economic Behavior* by von Neumann and Morgenstern would have been a book of outstanding importance. But it does more than that. It is essentially constructive: where existing theory is considered to be inadequate, the authors put in its place a highly novel analytical apparatus designed to cope with the problem.

It would be doing the authors an injustice to say that theirs is a contribution to economics only. The scope of the book is much broader. The techniques applied by the authors in tackling economic problems are of sufficient generality to be valid in political science, sociology, or even military strategy. The applicability to games proper (chess and poker) is obvious from the title. Moreover, the book is of considerable interest from a purely mathematical point of view. This review,

———

[1] John von Neumann and Oskar Morgenstern, *Theory of Games and Economic Behavior*, Princeton University Press, 1944, pp. xviii, 625.

[2] Cowles Commission Papers, New Series, No. 13A.
The author, on leave from Iowa State College where he is associate professor, is now on a Guggenheim Memorial Fellowship, working with the Cowles Commission for Research in Economics, of which he is a research associate. The tables and figures used in this article were drawn by Mrs. D. Friedlander of the University of Chicago.

however, is in the main confined to the purely economic aspects of the *Theory of Games and Economic Behavior*.

To a considerable extent this review is of an expository[3] nature. This seems justified by the importance of the book, its use of new and unfamiliar concepts and its very length which some may find a serious obstacle.

The existence of the gap which the book attempts to fill has been known to the economic theorists at least since Cournot's work on duopoly, although even now many do not seem to realize its seriousness. There is no adequate solution of the problem of defining "rational economic behavior" on the part of an individual when the very rationality of his actions depends on the probable behavior of other individuals: in the case of oligopoly, other sellers. Cournot and many after him have attempted to sidetrack the difficulty by assuming that every individual has a definite idea as to what others will do under given conditions. Depending on the nature of this expected behavior of other individuals, we have the special, well-known solutions of Bertrand and Cournot, as well as the more general Bowley concept of the "conjectural variation."[4] Thus the individual's "rational behavior" is determinate if the pattern of behavior of "others" can be assumed *a priori* known. But the behavior of "others" cannot be known *a priori* if the "others," too, are to behave rationally! Thus a logical *impasse* is reached.

The way, or at least a way,[5] out of this difficulty had been pointed out by one of the authors[6] over a decade ago. It lies in the rejection of a narrowly interpreted maximization principle as synonymous with rational behavior. Not that maximization (of utility[7] or profits) would not be desirable if it were feasible, but there can be no true maximization when only one of the several factors which

---

3   The exposition is mostly carried out by means of comparatively simple numerical examples. This involves loss of generality and rigor, but it may be hoped that it will make the presentation more accessible.

4   More recent investigations have led to the idea of a kinked demand curve. This, however, is a special—though very interesting—case of the conjectural variation.

5   *Cf.* reference to von Stackelberg in footnote 18 and some of the work quoted by von Stackelberg, *op. cit.*

6   J. von Neumann, "Zur Theorie der Gesellschaftsspiele," *Math. Annalen* 1928.

7   A side-issue of considerable interest discussed in the *Theory of Games* is that of measurability of the utility function. The authors need measurability in order to be able to set up tables of the type to be presented later in the case where utility rather than profit is being maximized. The proof of measurability is not given; however, an article giving the proof is promised for the near future and it seems advisable to postpone comment until the proof appears. But it should be emphasized that the validity of the core of the *Theory of Games* is by no means dependent on measurability or transferability of the utilities and those who feel strongly on the subject would perhaps do best to substitute "profits" for "utility" in most of the book in order to avoid judging the achievements of the *Theory of Games* from the point of view of an unessential assumption.

decide the outcome (of, say, oligopolistic competition) is controlled by the given individual.

Consider, for instance, a duopolistic situation[8] where each one of the duopolists A and B is *trying* to maximize his profits. A's profits will depend not only on his behavior ("strategy") but on B's strategy as well. Thus, if A could control (directly or indirectly) the strategy to be adopted by B, he would select a strategy for himself and one for B so as to maximize his own profits. But he cannot select B's strategy. Therefore, he can in no way make sure that by a proper choice of his own strategy his profits will actually be unconditionally maximized.

It might seem that in such a situation there is no possibility of defining rational behavior on the part of the two duopolists. But it is here that the novel solution proposed by the authors comes in. An example will illustrate this.

Suppose each of the duopolists has three possible strategies at his disposal.[9] Denote the strategies open to duopolist A by A_1, A_2, and A_3, and those open to duopolist B by B_1, B_2, and B_3. The profit made by A, to be denoted by a, obviously is determined by the choices of strategy made by the two duopolists. This dependence will be indicated by subscripts attached to a, with the first subscript referring to A's strategy and the second subscript to that of B; thus, *e.g.*, a_{13} is the profit which will be made by A if he chooses strategy A_1 while B chooses the strategy B_3. Similarly, b_{13} would denote the profits by B under the same circumstances. The possible outcomes of the "duopolistic competition" may be represented in the following two tables:

A's Profits

B's choice of strategies / A's choice of strategies	B_1	B_2	B_3
A_1	a_{11}	a_{12}	a_{13}
A_2	a_{21}	a_{22}	a_{23}
A_3	a_{31}	a_{32}	a_{33}

Table 1a

B's Profits

B's choice of strategies / A's choice of strategies	B_1	B_2	B_3
A_1	b_{11}	b_{12}	b_{13}
A_2	b_{21}	b_{22}	b_{23}
A_3	b_{31}	b_{32}	b_{33}

Table 1b

8   It is assumed that the buyers' behavior may be regarded as known.
9   Actually the number of strategies could be very high, perhaps infinite.

Table la shows the profits A will make depending on his own and B's choice of strategies. The first row corresponds to the choice of A_1, etc.; columns correspond to B's strategies. Table 1b gives analogous information regarding B's profits.

In order to show how A and B will make decisions concerning strategies, we shall avail ourselves of a numerical example given in Tables 2a and 2b.

A's Profits

B's choice of strategies / A's choice of strategies	B_1	B_2	B_3
A_1	2	8	1
A_2	4	3	9
A_3	5	6	7

Table 2a

B's Profits

B's choice of strategies / A's choice of strategies	B_1	B_2	B_3
A_1	11	2	20
A_2	9	15	3
A_3	8	7	6

Table 2b

Now let us watch A's thinking processes as he considers his choice of strategy. First of all, he will notice that by choosing strategy A_3 he will be sure that his profits cannot go down below 5, while either of the remaining alternatives would expose him to the danger of going down to 3 or even to 1.

But there is another reason for his choosing A_3. Suppose there is a danger of a "leak": B might learn what A's decision is before he makes his own. Had A chosen, say, A_1, B—if he knew about this—would obviously choose B_3 so as to maximize his own profits; this would leave A with a profit of only 1. Had A chosen A_2, B would respond by selecting B_2, which again would leave A with a profit below 5 which he could be sure of getting if he chose A_3.

One might perhaps argue whether A's choice of A_3 under such circumstances is the only way of defining rational behavior, but it certainly is *a* way of accomplishing this and, as will be seen later, a very fruitful one. The reader will verify without difficulty that similar reasoning on B's part will make him choose B_1 as the optimal strategy. Thus, the outcome of the duopolistic competition is determinate and can be described as follows: A will choose A_3, B will choose B_1, A's profit will be 5, B's 8.

An interesting property of this solution is that neither duopolist would be inclined to alter his decision, even if he were able to do so, after he found out what the other man's strategy was.

To see this, suppose B has found out that A's decision was in favor of strategy A_3. Looking at the third row of Table 2b, he will immediately see that in no case could he do better than by choosing B_1, which gives him the highest profit consistent with A's choice of A_3. The solution arrived at is of a very stable nature, independent of finding out the other man's strategy.

But the above example is artificial in several important respects. For one thing, it ignores the possibility of a "collusion" or, to use a more neutral term, coalition between A and B. In our solution, yielding the strategy combination (A_3, B_1), the joint profits of the two duopolists amount to 13; they could do better than that by acting together. By agreeing to choose the strategies A_1 and B_3 respectively, they would bring their joint profits up to 21; this sum could then be so divided that both would be better off than under the previous solution.

A's Profits

B's choice of strategies / A's choice of strategies	B_1	B_2	B_3
A_1	2	8	1
A_2	4	3	9
A_3	5	6	7

Table 3a

B's Profits

B's choice of strategies / A's choice of strategies	B_1	B_2	B_3
A_1	8	2	9
A_2	6	7	1
A_3	5	4	3

Table 3b

A major achievement of the *Theory of Games* is the analysis of the conditions and nature of coalition formation. How that is done will be shown below. But, for the moment, let us eliminate the problem of coalitions by considering a case which is somewhat special but nevertheless of great theoretical interest: the case of *constant sum* profits. An example of such a case is given in Tables 3a and 3b.

Table 3a is identical with Table 2a. But figures in Table 3b have been selected in such a manner that the joint profits of the two duopolists always amount to the same (10), no matter what strategies have been chosen. In such a case, A's gain is B's loss and *vice versa*. Hence, it is intuitively obvious (although the authors take great pains to show it rigorously) that no coalition will be formed.

The solution can again be obtained by reasoning used in the previous case and it will again turn out to be (A_3, B_1) with the respective profits 5 and 5 adding up to 10. What was said above about stability of solution and absence of advantage in finding the opponent[10] out still applies.

There is, however, an element of artificiality in the example chosen that is responsible for the determinateness of the solution. To see this it will suffice to interchange 5 and 6 in Table 3a. The changed situation is portrayed in Table 4 which gives A's profits for different choices of strategies.[11]

A's Profits

B's choice of strategies / A's choice of strategies	B_1	B_2	B_3
A_1	2	8	1
A_2	4	3	9
A_3	6	5	7

Table 4

There is no solution now which would possess the kind of stability found in the earlier example. For suppose A again chooses A_3; then if B should find that out, he would obviously "play" B_2 which gives him the highest possible profit consistent with A_3. But then A_3 would no longer be A's optimum strategy: he could do much better by choosing A_1; but if he does so, B's optimum strategy is B_3, not

---

10 In this case the interests of the two duopolists are diametrically opposed and the term "opponents" is fully justified; in the previous example it would not have been.

11 The table for B's profits is omitted because of the constant sum assumption. Clearly, in the constant sum case, B may be regarded as minimizing A's profits since this implies maximization of his own.

B_2, etc. There is no solution which would not give at least one of the opponents an incentive to change his decision if he found the other man out! There is no stability.[12]

What is it in the construction of the table that insured determinateness in the case of Table 3 and made it impossible in Table 4? The answer is that Table 3 has a *saddle point* ("minimax") while Table 4 does not.

The saddle point has the following two properties: it is the highest of all the row minima and at the same time is lowest of the column maxima. Thus, in Table 3a the row minima are respectively 1, 3, and 5, the last one being highest among them (*Maximum Minimorum*); on the other hand, the column maxima are respectively 5, 8, and 9 with 5 as the lowest (*Minimum Maximorum*). Hence the combination (A_3, B_1) yields both the highest row minimum and the lowest column maximum, and, therefore, constitutes a saddle point. It is easy to see that Table 4 does not possess a saddle point. Here 5 is still the *Maximum Minimorum*, but the *Minimum Maximorum* is given by 6; the two do not coincide, and it is the absence of the saddle point that makes for indeterminateness in Table 4.

Why is the existence of a unique saddle point necessary (as well as sufficient) to insure the determinateness of the solution? The answer is inherent in the reasoning used in connection with the earlier examples: if A chooses his strategy so as to be protected in case of any leakage of information concerning his decision, he will choose the strategy whose row in the table has the highest minimum value, i.e., the row corresponding to the *Maximum Minimorum*—A_3 in case of Table 4—for then he is sure he will not get less than 5, even if B should learn of this decision. B, following the same principle, will choose the column (i.e., strategy) corresponding to the *Minimum Maximorum*—B_1 in Table 4—thus making sure he will get at least 4, even if the information does leak out.

In this fashion both duopolists are sure of a certain minimum of profit—5 and 4, respectively. But this adds up to only 9. The residual—1—is still to be allocated and this allocation depends on outguessing the opponent. It is this residual that provides an explanation, as well as a measure, of the extent of indeterminacy. Its presence will not surprise economists familiar with this type of phenomenon from the theory of bilateral monopoly. But there are cases when this residual does equal zero, that is, when the *Minimum Maximorum* equals the *Maximum Minimorum*, which (by definition) implies the existence of the saddle point and complete determinacy.

---

12 There is, however, a certain amount of determinateness, at least in the negative sense, since certain strategy combinations are excluded: e.g. (A_2, B_1); A would never choose A_3 if he knew B had chosen B_1, and vice versa.

At this stage the authors of the *Theory of Games* had to make a choice. They could have accepted the fact that saddle points do not always exist so that a certain amount of indeterminacy would, in general, be present. They preferred, however, to get rid of the indeterminacy by a highly ingenious modification of the process which leads to the choice of appropriate strategy.

So far our picture of the duopolist making a decision on strategy was that of a man reasoning out which of the several possible courses of action is most favorable (*"pure strategy"*). We now change this picture and put in his hands a set of dice which he will throw to determine the strategy to be chosen. Thus, an element of chance is introduced into decision making (*"mixed strategy"*)[13] But not everything is left to chance. The duopolist A must in advance formulate a rule as to what results of the throw—assume that just one die is thrown—would make him choose a given strategy. In order to illustrate this we shall use a table that is somewhat simpler, even if less interesting than those used previously. In this new table (Table 5)[14] each duopolist has only two strategies at his disposal.

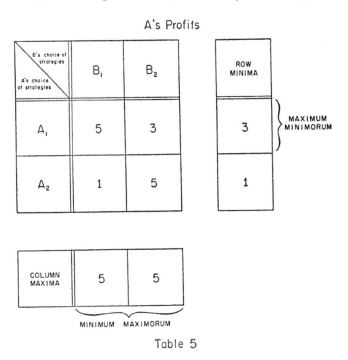

A's Profits

Table 5

---

13   The authors' justification for introducing "mixed strategies" is that leaving one's decision to chance is an effective way of preventing "leakage" of information since the individual making the decision does not himself know which strategy he will choose.
14   In Table 5 there is no saddle point.

An example of a rule A might adopt would be:

If the result of the throw is 1 or 2, choose A_1;
if the result of the throw is 3, 4, 5, or 6, choose A_2.

If this rule were followed, the probability that A will choose A_1 is 1/3, that of his choosing A_2 is 2/3. If a different rule had been decided upon (say, one of choosing A_1 whenever the result of the throw is 1, 2, or 3), the probability of choosing A_1 would have been 1/2. Let us call the fraction giving the probability of choosing A_1 A's *chance coefficient*; in the two examples, A's chance coefficients were 1/3 and 1/2 respectively.[15]

As a special case the value of the chance coefficient might be zero (meaning, that is, definitely choosing strategy A_2) or one (meaning that A is definitely choosing strategy A_1); thus in a sense "pure strategies" may be regarded as a special case of mixed strategies. However, this last statement is subject to rather important qualifications which are of a complex nature and will not be given here.

Mathematical Expectations : of A's Profits

A's chance coefficients \ B's chance coefficients	0	$\frac{1}{3}$	$\frac{2}{3}$	1	ROW MINIMA	
0	5	$3\frac{2}{3}$	$2\frac{1}{3}$	1	1	
$\frac{1}{3}$	$4\frac{1}{3}$	$3\frac{2}{3}$	3	$2\frac{1}{3}$	$2\frac{1}{3}$	
$\frac{2}{3}$	$3\frac{2}{3}$	$3\frac{2}{3}$	$3\frac{2}{3}$	$3\frac{2}{3}$	$3\frac{2}{3}$	MAXIMUM MINIMORUM
1	3	$3\frac{2}{3}$	$4\frac{1}{3}$	5	3	
COLUMN MAXIMA	5	$3\frac{2}{3}$	$4\frac{1}{3}$	5		

MINIMUM MAXIMORUM

Table 6

15   Since the probability of choosing A_2 is always equal to one minus that of choosing A_1, specification of the probability of choosing A_1 is sufficient to describe a given rule. However, when the number of available strategies exceeds two, there are several such chance coefficients to be specified.

Now instead of choosing one of the available strategies the duopolist A must choose the optimal (in a sense not yet defined) chance coefficient. How is the choice of the chance coefficient made? The answer lies in constructing a table which differs in two important respects from those used earlier. Table 6 provides an example. Each row in the table now corresponds to a possible value of A's chance coefficient; similarly, columns correspond to possible values of B's chance coefficient. Since the chance coefficient may assume any value between zero and one (including the latter two values), the table is to be regarded merely as a "sample." This is indicated by spaces between rows and between columns.

COMPUTATION OF THE MATHE-
MATICAL EXPECTATION FOR THE
2ND ROW, 3RD COLUMN IN TABLE 6

B's choice of strategies		B_1	B_2
A's choice of strategies	B's chance coefficients / A's chance coefficients	$\frac{2}{3}$	$\frac{1}{3}$
A_1	$\frac{1}{3}$	5	3
A_2	$\frac{2}{3}$	1	5

$$\tfrac{1}{3} \times \tfrac{2}{3} \times 5 + \tfrac{1}{3} \times \tfrac{1}{3} \times 3$$
$$+ \tfrac{2}{3} \times \tfrac{2}{3} \times 1 + \tfrac{2}{3} \times \tfrac{1}{3} \times 5$$
$$= 27/9 = 3$$

The numbers entered in the table are the average values (mathematical expectations) corresponding to the choice of chance coefficients indicated by the row and column.[16] (One should mention that Table 6 is only an expository

---

16 To see this we shall show how, e.g., we have obtained the value in the second row and third column of Table 6 (viz., 3).
     We construct an auxiliary table (valid only for this particular combination of chance coefficients (A's 1/3, B's 2/3).
     This table differs from Table 5 only by the omission of row maxima and column minima and by the insertion of the probabilities of choosing the available strategies corresponding to the second row third column of Table 6. The computation of the mathematical expectation is indicated in Table 6.

device: the actual procedures used in the book are algebraic and much simpler computationally.)

If we now assume with the authors that each duopolist is trying to maximize the mathematical expectation of his profits (Table 6) rather than the profits themselves (Table 5), it might seem that the original source of difficulty remains if a saddle point does not happen to exist. But the mixed strategies were not introduced in vain! It is shown (the theorem was originally proved by von Neumann in 1928) that in the table of mathematical expectations (like Table 6) a saddle point *must* exist; the problem is always determinate.[17]

The reader who may have viewed the introduction of dice into the decision-making process with a certain amount of suspicion will probably agree that this is a rather spectacular result. Contrary to the initial impression, it is possible to render the problem determinate. But there is a price to be paid: acceptance of mixed strategies, assumption that only the mathematical expectation of profit (not its variance, for instance) matters, seem to be necessary. Many an economist will consider the price too high. Moreover, one might question the need for introducing determinateness into a problem of this nature. Perhaps we should consider as the "solution" the interval of indeterminacy given by the two critical points: the *Minimum Maximorum* and *Maximum Minimorum*.

As indicated earlier in this review, one should not ignore, in general, the possibility of a collusion. This is especially evident when more complex economic situations are considered.

We might, for instance, have a situation where there are two sellers facing two buyers. Here a "coalition" of buyers, as well as one of sellers, may be formed. But it is also conceivable that a buyer would bribe a seller into some sort of cooperation against the other two participants. Several other combinations of this type can easily be found.

When only *two* persons enter the picture, as in the case of duopoly (where the role of buyers was ignored), it was seen that a coalition would not be formed if the sum of the two persons' profits remained constant. But when the number of participants is *three* or more, subcoalitions can profitably be formed even if the sum of all participants' profits is constant; in the above four-person example it might pay the sellers to combine against the buyers even if (or, perhaps, especially if) the profits of all four always add to the same amount.

Hence, the formation of coalitions may be adequately treated without abandoning the highly convenient constant-sum assumption. In fact, when the sum

---

17 In Table 6 the saddle point is in third row second column; it is to be stressed that Table 5 has no saddle point.

is known to be non-constant, it is possible to introduce (conceptually) an additional fictitious participant who, by definition, loses what all the real participants gain and *vice versa*. In this fashion a non-constant sum situation involving, say, three persons may be considered as a special case of a constant-sum four-person situation. This is an additional justification for confining most of the discussion (both in the book and in the review) to the constant-sum case despite the fact that economic problems are as a rule of the non-constant sum variety.

We shall now proceed to study the simplest constant-sum case which admits coalition formation, that involving three participants. The technique of analysis presented earlier in the two-person case is no longer adequate. The number of possibilities increases rapidly. Each of the participants may be acting independently; or else, one of the three possible two-person coalitions (A and B vs. C, A and C vs. B, B and C vs. A) may be formed. Were it not for the constant-sum restriction, there would be the additional possibility of the coalition comprising all three participants.

Here again we realize the novel character of the authors' approach to the problem. In most[18] of traditional economic theory the formation—or absence—of specific coalitions is *postulated*. Thus, for instance, we discuss the economics of a cartel without rigorously investigating the necessary and sufficient conditions for its formation. Moreover, we tend to exclude *a priori* such phenomena as collusion between buyers and sellers even if these phenomena are known to occur in practice. The *Theory of Games*, though seemingly more abstract than economic theory known to us, approaches reality much more closely on points of this nature. A complete solution to the problems of economic theory requires an answer to the question of coalition formation, bribery, collusion, etc. This answer is now provided, even though it is of a somewhat formal nature in the more complex cases; and even though it does not always give sufficient insight into the actual workings of the market.

Let us now return to the case of three participants. Suppose two of them are sellers, one a buyer. Traditional theory would tell us the quantity sold by each seller and the price. But we know that in the process of bargaining one of the sellers might bribe the other one into staying out of the competition. Hence the seller who refrained from market operations would make a profit;

---

18 In his *Grundlagen einer reinen Kostentheorie* (Vienna, 1932) H. von Stackelberg does point out (p. 89) that "the competitors, [duopolists] must somehow unite; they must supplement the economic mechanics, which in this case is inadequate, by economic politics." But no rigorous theory is developed for such situations (although an outline of possible developments is given). This is where the *Theory of Games* has made real progress.

on the other hand, the nominal profit made by the man who did make the sale would exceed (by the amount of bribe) the actual gain made.

It is convenient, therefore, to introduce the concept of *gain*: the bribed man's gain is the amount of the bribe, the seller's gain is the profit made on a sale minus the bribe, etc. A given distribution of gains among the participants is called an *imputation*. The imputation is not a number: it is a set of numbers. For instance, if the gains of the participants in a given situation were g_A, g_B, g_C, it is the set of these three g's that is called the imputation. The imputation summarizes the outcome of the economic process. In any given situation there are a great many possible imputations. Therefore, one of the chief objectives of economic theory is that of finding those among all the possible imputations which will actually be observed under rational behavior.

In a situation such as that described (three participants, constant-sum) each man will start by asking himself how much he could get acting independently, even if the worst should happen and the other two formed a coalition against him. He can determine this by treating the situation as a two-person case (the opposing coalition regarded as one person) and finding the relevant *Maximum Minimorum*, or the saddle point, if that point does exist; the saddle point would, of course, exist if "mixed strategies" are used. Next, the participant will consider the possibility of forming a coalition with one of the other two men. Now comes the crucial question: under what conditions might such a coalition be formed?

Before discussing this in detail, let us summarize, in Table 8, all the relevant information.

TABLE 8

I. If A acts alone, he can get	5
If B acts alone, he can get	7
If C acts alone, he can get	10.
II. If A and B form a coalition, they can get	15
If A and C form a coalition, they can get	18
If B and C form a coalition, they can get	20.
III. If A, B, and C act together, they can get	25.

Among the many possible imputations, let us now consider the three given Table 9.

TABLE 9

	A	B	C
#1	6.5	8.3	10.2
#2	5.0	9.5	10.5
#3	4.0	10.0	11.0

It will be noted that under imputation #1, B and C are each better off than if they had been acting individually: they get respectively 8.3 and 10.2 instead of 7 and 10. Hence, there is an incentive for B and C to form a coalition since without such a coalition imputation #1 would not be possible. But once the coalition is formed, they can do better than under #1; viz., under #2, where each gets more (9.5 and 10.5 instead of 8.3 and 10.2, respectively). In such a case we say that imputation #2 *dominates* imputation #1. It might seem that #3, in turn, dominates #2 since it promises still more to both B and C. But it promises too much: the sum of B's and C's gains under #3 is 21, which is more than their coalition could get (*cf.* Table 8)! Thus #3 is ruled out as unrealistic and cannot be said to dominate any other imputation.

Domination is an exceptionally interesting type of relation. For one thing, it is not transitive: we may have an imputation i_1 dominating the imputation i_2 and i_2 dominating i_3, without thereby implying that i_1 dominates i_3; in fact, i_1 might be dominated by i_3.[19] Moreover, it is easy to construct examples of, say, two imputations, neither of which dominates the other one.[20]

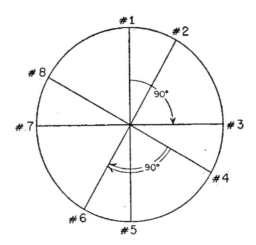

FIGURE 1

---

19   I.e., domination may be a cyclic relation. For instance, consider the following three imputations in the above problem: #1 and #2 as in Table 9, and #4, where

	A	B	C
#4	6.0	7.0	12.0.

Here #2 (as shown before) dominates #1 (for the coalition B, C), #4 dominates #2 (for coalition A, C), but at the same time #1 dominates #4 (for the coalition A, B): the cycle is completed.

20   For instance, #2 and #3 in Table 9.

To get a geometric picture of this somewhat unusual situation one may turn to Figure 1, where points on the circle represent different possible imputations. (The reader must be cautioned that this is merely a geometrical analogy, though a helpful one.) Let us now say that point #1 dominates point #2 if #2 is less than 90° (clockwise) from #1. It is easy to see in Figure 1 that #1 dominates #2 and #2 dominates #3, but in spite of that, #1 does not dominate #3.

This geometrical picture will help define the very fundamental concept of a *solution*.

Consider the points (imputations) #1, 3, 5, and 7 in Figure 1. None of them dominates any other since any two are either *exactly* or more than 90° apart. But any other point on the circle #2 is dominated by at least (in this case: exactly) one of them: all points between #1 and #3 are dominated by #1, etc. There is no point on the circle which is not dominated by one of the above four points. Now we *define* a solution as a set of points (imputations) with two properties: (1) no element of the set dominates any other element of the set, and (2) any point outside the set must be dominated by at least one element within the set.

We have seen that the points #1, 3, 5, 7 do have both of these properties; hence, the four points together form a solution. It is important to see that none of the individual points by itself can be regarded as a solution. In fact, if we tried to leave out any one of the four points of the set, the remaining three would no longer form a solution; for instance, if #1 were left out, the points between #1 and #3 are not dominated by any of the points #3, 5, 7. This violates the second property required of a solution and the three points by themselves are not a solution. On the other hand, if a fifth point were added to #1, 3, 5, 7, the resulting five element set would not form a solution either; suppose #2 is the fifth point chosen; we note that #2 is dominated by #1 and it also dominates #3. Thus, the first property of a solution is absent.

Contrary to what would be one's intuitive guess, an element of the solution may be dominated by points outside the solution: #1 is dominated by #8, etc. There can easily be more than one solution. The reader should have no trouble verifying the fact that #2, 4, 6, 8 also form a solution, and it is clear that infinitely many other solutions exist.

Does there always exist at least one solution? So far this question remains unanswered. Among the cases examined by the authors none has been found without at least one solution. But it has not yet been proved that there must always be a solution. To see the theoretical possibility of a case without a solution we shall redefine slightly our concept of domination (*cf.* Figure 2): #1 dominates #2 if the angle between them (measured clockwise) does not exceed 180°.

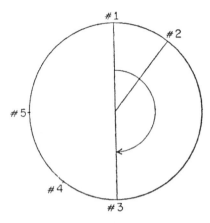

FIGURE 2

Hence, in Figure 2 point #1 dominates #3, but not #4, etc. It can now be shown that in this case *no* solution exists. For suppose there is one; then we may, without loss of generality, choose #1 as one of its points. Clearly, #1 by itself does not constitute a solution, for there are points on the circle (*e.g.*, #4) not dominated by #1; thus the solution must have at least two points. But any other point on the circle either is dominated by #1 (*e.g.*, #2), or it dominates #1 (*e.g.*, #4), or both (#3), which contradicts the first requirement for the elements of a solution. Hence there is no solution consisting of two points either. *A fortiori*, there are no solutions containing more than two points. Hence we have been able to construct an example without a solution. But whether this type of situation could arise in economics (or games, for that matter) is still an open question.

Now for the economic interpretation of the concept of solution. Within the solution there is no reason for switching from one imputation to another since they do not dominate each other. Moreover, there is never a good reason for going outside a given solution: any imputation outside the solution can be "discredited" by an imputation within the solution which dominates the outside. But, as we have seen, the reverse is also usually true: imputations within the solution may be dominated by those outside. If we are to assume that the latter consideration is ignored, the given solution acquires an institutional, if not accidental, character. According to the authors, a solution may be equivalent to what one would call the "standards of behavior" which are accepted by a given community.

The multiplicity of solutions can then be considered as corresponding to alternative institutional setups; for a given institutional framework only one solution would be relevant. But even then a large number of possibilities remains since, in general, a solution contains more than one imputation. More indeterminacy yet would be present if we had refrained from introducing mixed strategies.

It would be surprising, therefore, if in their applications von Neumann and Morgenstern should get no more than the classical results without discovering imputations hitherto neglected or ignored. And there are some rather interesting "unorthodox" results pointed out, especially in the last chapter of book.

In one case, at least, the authors' claim to generality exceeding that of economic theory is not altogether justified in view of the more recent literature. That is the case of what essentially corresponds to bilateral monopoly (p. 564, proposition 61:C). The authors obtain (by using their newly developed methods) a certain interval of indeterminacy for the price; this interval is wider than that indicated by Böhm-Bawerk, because (as the authors themselves point out) of the dropping of Böhm-Bawerk's assumption of a unique price. But this assumption has been abandoned, to give only one example, in the theories of consumer's surplus, with analogous extension of the price interval.

It will stand repeating, however, that the *Theory of Games* does offer a greater generality of approach than could be attained otherwise. The existence of "discriminatory" solutions, discovered by purely analytical methods, is an instance of this. Also, the possibility of accounting for various types of deals and collusions mentioned earlier in connection with the three-person and four-person cases go far beyond results usually obtained by customarily used methods and techniques of economic theory.

The potentialities of von Neumann's and Morgenstern's new approach seem tremendous and may, one hopes, lead to revamping, and enriching in realism, a good deal of economic theory. But to a large extent they are only potentialities: results are still largely a matter of future developments.

The difficulties encountered in handling, even by the more powerful mathematical methods, the situations involving more than three persons are quite formidable. Even the problems of monopoly and monopsony are beyond reach at the present stage of investigation. The same is true of perfect competition, though it may turn out that the latter is not a "legitimate" solution since it excludes the formation of coalitions which may dominate the competitive imputations. A good deal of light has been thrown on the problem of oligopoly, but there again the results are far from the degree of concreteness desired by the economic theorist.

The reviewer therefore regards as somewhat regrettable some of the statements made in the initial chapter of the book attacking (rather indiscriminately) the analytical techniques at present used by the economic theorists. True enough, the deficiencies of economic theory pointed out in the *Theory of Games* are very

real; nothing would be more welcome than a model giving the general properties of a system with, say, m sellers and n buyers, so that monopoly, duopoly, or
perfect competition could simply be treated as special cases of the general analysis. Unfortunately, however, such a model is not yet in sight. In its absence less
satisfactory, but still highly useful, models have been and no doubt will continue
to be used by economic theorists. One can hardly afford to ignore the social
need for the results of economic theory even if the best is rather crude. The fact
that the theory of economic fluctuations has been studied as much as it has is
not a proof of "how much the attendant difficulties have been underestimated"
(p. 5). Rather it shows that economics cannot afford the luxury of developing in
the theoretically most "logical" manner when the need for the results is as strong
as it happens to be in the case of the ups and downs of the employment level!

Nor is it quite certain, though of course conceivable, that, when a rigorous
theory developed along the lines suggested by von Neumann and Morgenstern
is available, the results obtained in the important problems will be sufficiently
remote from those obtained with the help of the current (admittedly imperfect) tools to justify some of the harsher accusations to be found in the opening
chapter of the book. It must not be forgotten, for instance, that, while theoretical derivation of coalitions to be formed is of great value, we do have empirical
knowledge which can be used as a substitute (again imperfect) for theory. For
example, cartel formation may be so clearly "in the cards" in a given situation
that the economic theorist will simply include it as one of his assumptions while
von Neumann and Morgenstern would (at least in principle) be able to prove
the formation of the cartel without making it an additional (and logically unnec-
essary) assumption.

The authors criticize applications of the mathematical methods to economics in a way which might almost, in spite of protests to the contrary, mislead
some readers into thinking that von Neumann and Morgenstern are not aware
of the amount of recent progress in many fields of economic theory due largely
to the use of mathematical tools. They also seem to ignore the fact that economics developed in literary form is, implicitly, based on the mathematical techniques which the authors criticize. (Thus it is not the methods of mathematical
economics they are really questioning, but rather those elements of economic
theory which literary and mathematical economics have in common.) While it
is true that even mathematical treatment is not always sufficiently rigorous, it is
as a rule more so than the corresponding literary form, even though the latter is
not infrequently more realistic in important respects.

There is little doubt in the reviewer's mind that nothing could have been further from the authors' intentions than to give aid and comfort to the opponents

of rigorous thinking in economics or to increase their complacency. Yet such may be the effect of some of the vague criticisms contained in the first chapter; they hardly seem worthy of the constructive achievements of the rest of the book.

Economists will probably be surprised to find so few references to more recent economic writings. One might almost form the impression that economics is synonymous with Böhm-Bawerk plus Pareto. Neither the nineteenth-century pioneers (such as Cournot) nor the writers of the last few decades (Chamberlin, Joan Robinson, Frisch, Stackelberg) are even alluded to. But, perhaps, the authors are entitled to claim exemption from the task of relating their work to that of their predecessors by virtue of the tremendous amount of constructive effort they put into their opus. One cannot but admire the audacity of vision, the perseverance in details, and the depth of thought displayed on almost every page of the book.

The exposition is remarkably lucid and fascinating, no matter how involved the argument happens to be. The authors made an effort to avoid the assumption that the reader is familiar with any but the more elementary parts of mathematics; more refined tools are forged "on the spot" whenever needed.

One should also mention, though this transcends the scope of the review, that in the realm of strategic games proper (chess, poker) the results obtained are more specific than some of the economic applications. Those interested in the nature of determinacy of chess, in the theory of "bluffing" in poker, or in the proper strategy for Sherlock Holmes in his famous encounter with Professor Moriarty, will enjoy reading the sections of the book which have no direct bearing on economics. The reader's views on optimum military or diplomatic strategies are also likely to be affected.

Thus, the reading of the book is a treat as well as a stage in one's intellectual development. The great majority of economists should be able to go through the book even if the going is slow at times; it is well worth the effort. The appearance of a book of the caliber of the *Theory of Games* is indeed a rare event.

APPENDIX D

The Hurwicz Criterion

———

The Hurwicz Criterion, presented in a paper[1] in 1951, is probably the earliest novel contribution to the field of economics for which Leo has been recognized. It provides a formula for balancing pessimism and optimism in decision-making under uncertainty—that is, when future conditions are to some extent unknown. A defining feature of the Hurwicz Criterion is that it allows the decision-maker to simultaneously take into account both the best and the worst possible outcomes. To do this, the decision-maker chooses a "coefficient of pessimism," called alpha (α), which is a decimal number between 0 and 1. This number determines the emphasis on the worst possible outcome. Then the number ($1-\alpha$) determines the emphasis to be placed on the best outcome. So, if the coefficient of pessimism is .4, then the emphasis on the best outcome will be .6.

(If alpha determines the emphasis to be placed on the best outcome, it may be called a "coefficient of optimism." Either a "coefficient of pessimism" or a "coefficient of optimism" may also be called a "coefficient of realism.")

This contrasts with other approaches, such as:

- **Maximin** (pessimistic), which looks only at the worst possible result in each scenario, and chooses the "best of the worst."
- **Maximax** (optimistic), which looks only at the best possible result in each scenario, and chooses the "best of the best"

The Hurwicz Criterion is sometimes confused with **Minimax Regret**, which compares what I *actually* did with what I *would have done* if I could have predicted

———

1   The paper in which the Hurwicz Criterion was originally stated is: "The Generalised Bayes Minimax Principle: A Criterion for Decision Making Under Uncertainty," Cowles Commission Discussion Paper 355, February 8, 1951, p. 7.

the future. Another way of putting this is that Minimax Regret looks at the maximum possible regret: the maximum difference, for each scenario, between what I actually did and what I "coulda-shoulda-woulda" done. It then takes the path that minimizes potential regret.

The table below shows assumed "pay-offs" (economic results expressed in monetary units such as dollars) for building either no reservoir, a small reservoir or a large reservoir under three scenarios: low, medium and high climate-change impacts.[2] For the hypothetical example discussed below, it is assumed that the pay-offs are known. What isn't known is the degree to which climate change will impact the activities, such as agriculture, that would be supported by the reservoir. The numbers in **bold** represent the result that should be chosen under each approach.

("Optimistic" in this context means "maximizing return on investment." It does not mean a belief that "all will be well." For instance, a large investment in insurance may give the best return in case of a catastrophe. This is, in fact, the thinking represented in the example below.)

Taking the different approaches one at a time, from right to left in the table:

- Using **Maximin**, the option that has the largest minimum is a small reservoir, with a minimum pay-off of 600 (which will occur under low impacts).
- Under the **Hurwicz Criterion**, with a coefficient of pessimism of .4 (slightly optimistic), the large reservoir is built, based on a minimum pay-off of 400, a maximum pay-off of 800, and a Hurwicz Criterion pay-off of 640 (which "beats" −20 and 630).
- Under the **Hurwicz Criterion**, with a coefficient of pessimism of .5 (neutral), the small reservoir is built, based on a minimum pay-off of 600, a maximum pay-off of 650, and a Hurwicz Criterion pay-off of 625 (which "beats" −25 and 600).
- Under the **Hurwicz Criterion**, with a coefficient of pessimism of .6 (slightly pessimistic), the small reservoir is built, again based on a minimum

2   The author got the idea for this example from M. Green and E.K. Weatherhead, "Coping with climate change uncertainty for adaptation planning," Climate Risk Management, Volume 1, 2014, pp. 63–75. https://www.sciencedirect.com/science/article/pii/S2212096313000028. However, the present example is hypothetical, is the author's alone, and does not make use of their data or the novel strategy that they propose.

pay-off of 600 and a maximum pay-off of 650, but this time with a Hurwicz Criterion pay-off of 620 (which "beats" −30 and 560).

- Under **Maximax**, the large reservoir is built, because it has the highest possible pay-off of any option in the table, namely 800. This pay-off occurs under high climate change impacts, so this choice reflects "optimism" only in the sense of maximizing potential return on investment in the limited context of building (or not building) a reservoir.

- Under **Minimax Regret**, the small reservoir is built, because the largest disparity between actual and "coulda-shoulda-woulda" for the small reservoir is 150 (occurring under high impacts, where the small reservoir pay-off is 650 and the large reservoir pay-off would have been 800). Potential regrets for other scenarios are bigger. For example, if we don't build a reservoir, then under the high impacts scenario, the potential regret is a whopping 850 (the difference between −50 and 800). The large reservoir has less potential for regret, but still more than 150: The largest "spread" there is 200, occurring in the low impacts scenario.

	Low Impacts	Medium Impacts	High Impacts	Maximin	Hurwicz (alpha = 0.4)	Hurwicz (alpha = 0.5)	Hurwicz (alpha = 0.6)	Maximax	Minimax Regret
No Reservoir	0	−10	−50	−50	$(.4*{-50})$ $+ (.6*0)$ $= -20$	$(.5*{-50})$ $+ (.5*0)$ $= -25$	$(.6*{-50})$ $+ (.4*0)$ $= -30$	0	850
Small Reservoir	600	620	650	**600**	$(.4*600)$ $+ (.6*650)$ $= 630$	$(.5*600)$ $+ (.5*650)$ $= 625$	$(.6*600)$ $+ (.4*650)$ $= 620$	650	**150**
Large Reservoir	400	640	800	400	$(.4*400)$ $+ (.6*800)$ $= 640$	$(.5*400)$ $+ (.5*800)$ $= 600$	$(.6*400)$ $+ (.4*800)$ $= 560$	**800**	200

Table of pay-offs for building a reservoir under differing climate scenarios with Hurwicz Criterion alpha = coefficient of pessimism

Edited Transcript of 2007 Interview with Leo, Conducted by the Author

———————

(Video at: https://leonidhurwicz.org/interview/)

(Q: Your family . . .)

My narrow family—Adek, Zina and Leo (not Henry, Henry wasn't born yet—Henry was born in 1922, that's already after the Bolshevik war; but I was born before). The two stories why the others didn't return was: one was that it was too dangerous to travel with girls, because there were marauding Bolsheviks and soldiers of various kinds, you know, they were likely to attack a family with girls. The other story or comment that I heard, you know, but very much third hand, is that they felt, especially Max, that the Poles were so antisemitic, that he really preferred to stay in Russia. I don't know, there were probably some elements of each.

The problem was how to travel from Moscow to Warsaw. You had to hire your own wagon and a horse—or two horses—to pull it. At that time there were no trains going in the direction from Moscow to Poland, which would be westward. And you couldn't get a good horse, because the armies were confiscating them. So they had some lame horse. When they came to the frontier between Russia and Poland, the width of the tracks changed. Russia has wider track than western Europe. So you had to physically change trains. So when they got to Vilnius, Lithuania, they took a train. That was probably in February or so of 1919. I have seen the house where my father was born or at least lived as a small baby, in Warsaw.

The family spoke with the same ease Russian, Polish, and my grandparents—Max and Sara and that generation—I think also spoke Lithuanian. We have a more remote relative on the Frydland side, Abichke Ragoler. Michael Kotzin visited in that area in the 80's with some congressman. Abichke was the owner of a *karczma*, an inn.

At that time my father had a degree from the Sorbonne in law. I think he had also gone through a process of what I think is called "nostrification" for practicing law in Russia. But then he came to Poland, and that required another kind of validation. The process was really internship, two years of clerkship to a judge, and three years of internship or assistantship to an attorney. After each internship there were examinations, certainly oral but I think partly written. During this period he couldn't support himself as a lawyer, so he was teaching history at a Jewish school, conducted in Polish, called "chinuch."[1] When we visited in Israel in 1966 on the way back from India, which is the first time that I was in Israel, I met some people who were my father's students from chinuch. He was always interested in history, as I think is our family interest. [*Adek is listed as teaching Hebrew in 1926—M. H.*][2]

(Q: Where would his brothers Stefan and Monjo have been at that time?)

I think Stefan was in Warsaw, also returning approximately at the same time as my father. I don't know where from. But when I remember Stefan from the earliest times, he lived in Warsaw in a part of the city not far from our part. But during World War I he may have retreated also eastward into Russia proper. And Monjo (Solomon) was living with the rest of the sisters, probably, in Moscow. He was the youngest of the children. He visited Warsaw, I don't know exactly when, as part of a peace delegation. But you can see that Monjo was no longer living when this picture was taken.[3]

Max died I believe in 1927, when I was ten years old. He knew me, but I didn't know him, I was under one and a half years old. After that, he was in Moscow and I was in Warsaw. When we were both in Moscow, when I was one year old, he was perhaps 51 years old, according to the story I was told, he looked at me when I was one year old and said "a chochem" (a wise man), so I consider him a good judge of character. But I have no memory of him, except indirect.

When Max was approaching college age, in the nineteenth century, he was hoping to go to college, the first person in the family. The tsar at that time I think was named Alexander, of the Romanov dynasty.[4]

---

1   Hebrew חינוך
2   https://www.leonidhurwicz.org/chinuch/
3   Picture at: https://leonidhurwicz.org/first-hurwicz-family/
4   Alexander II was assassinated in 1881.

It must have been possible for a Jew to enter the University. But this Alexander, if I am right about the name, was assassinated by an anarchist. This resulted in a big move to the right politically, and one of the "reforms" so-called was that Jews could not attend the university. But all the six of Max's surviving children were university graduates; but that was already under the Communist regime.

(Q: You told me a story when you were nine or ten years old, there was an uprising, and you were off picking flowers by the Vistula, and your mother was worried about you?)

There was a coup d'état, under a man who was regarded I think somewhat unfairly as a great military hero, since he never really conducted war I don't think, but had a military title from the German/Austrian side of World War I. Piłsudski. His coup d'état could be regarded as a left-wing coalition kind of thing, because it was indirectly a result of the assassination of the previous president, I think the first president of Poland after World War I. Piłsudski was before World War I a socialist, but not a Marxist, but a socialist of a generalized kind. I think the Jews regarded him as something of a friend, actually.

In 1927 [Max] died, and that was the year of the coup d'état.[5] [*Actually, the coup occurred in May 12, 1926—M. H.*] I was maybe nine and half or something like that. We had little kind of fields. The idea was for children to learn agriculture and so on. There was shooting. Piłsudski was a leader of the army. It happened to be that these gardens that we were cultivating were close to Stefan's apartment. I was nine years old, we didn't have a car, and I walked the city without any fear. And I knew where Stefan lived there, so I went there.

I don't know if they had a telephone or not. My mother didn't know where I was. She got as far as the taxi driver was willing to go. Ultimately she also went to Stefan's apartment and found me I think. I don't have a clear memory of this.

I remember we were taping the windows with something or another, because they were shot out or whatever. And I wasn't allowed to look out.

Sara Lea died I think about 1935.

My father and Stefan and Monjo were all Max's children.

---

5   Editor's note: on May 12, 1926, Józef Piłsudski, leaning on 15 army units loyal to him, staged a *coup d'etat*, taking the capital Warsaw in street fighting. http://www.zum.de/whkmla/region/eceurope/poland19191939.html (Accessed October 11, 2022.) Also see the https://en.wikipedia.org/ article on Piłsudski. Leo would have been almost nine at this time.

This picture . . . I can only infer from the fact that Max was still alive, so it was probably before 1927. My father is not in the picture because he was in Warsaw. This whole group never got out of Moscow.

One of them has a fox fur kind of scarf. I think that's to show that they were not some peasants or something, to emphasize their status. Two even, all those who had it.

I never met any except Helenka.

So, you see, where the confusion is, Aunt Helen, who in later life was in Chicago, was the sister of Sara Lea, one of four Frydland sisters. That was Aunt Helen. But Helenka was one of the daughters of Sara Lea, and she could not get out of Russia until there was improvement in relations under Richard Nixon's presidency. She came to the U.S. shortly thereafter, in 1973.

(Evelyn thinks Helenka is the one on the right in the picture.)

Probably standing in the back, because she was the youngest.

(Q: So Stefan and Adek were in Warsaw in 1927.)

There were other sisters of Sara Lea. There were four sisters with maiden name Frydland: Sara Lea, Salcia (who married a Frydland, also. That was the coal seller, in Warsaw, Adolf Frydland), Gitla (who was Maniek's mother), and Aunt Helen.

The Frydlands probably didn't leave Warsaw during world War I.

There was a quarrel between the Moscow branch and the Chicago branch. The reason (with different versions depending on who you were talking to) is because Moritz Kotzin tried to emigrate to Canada, maybe very early after World War I was over. He went to Canada, but somehow wasn't able to make a job, was not successful. And Max somehow helped him financially to make this trip to Canada.

Moritz got money—I don't know if it was called a loan or a gift—from Max to try to get settled in Canada, but was unsuccessful and came back to Poland. And then he decided to try again, and he asked Max for more money. And Max said, "I don't have any more money." Moritz was very angry at this and they stopped talking to each other. Now, not talking to each other was a very favorite form of punishment in the Hurwicz family. You have to take into account that they were not talking with one another while one side was in Moscow and the other was in Chicago, so it was very easy not to talk with each other.

However, the two sisters, Aunt Helen and Sara Lea, secretly corresponded with each other, and broke the boycott, but didn't tell the others.

I didn't know this whole story, but I knew there was some bad blood. But I didn't even know whether I should try to contact them. I was in Geneva.[6]

The first few days of WW II, I was in Berne, which is the capital of Switzerland. On the second (or third, but I think the second) day of the war, the 2nd of September 1939, I got a telegram from father, from my father, from Adek. It said something like "We are OK." (Actually it was a lie, because there was bombing all over Warsaw, the Nazis were attacking.)

But then what it gave was the address of the Kotzins in Chicago: 3605 Dickens Avenue.

A few days later, I moved to Geneva from Berne. And I spent the first year of war actually there, academic year '39–'40. That's where I lost my money in the post office.

The academic year '39–'40 I spent there in Switzerland.

I started out in the fall quarter of 1938 at the London School of Economics, and the war broke out a year later, roughly. When the academic year 1938-'39 was ending (so, roughly speaking, May or June) I asked the British to extend my visa, which was only for one academic year. But they said they couldn't do it, because my passport was only valid up to the end [of the academic year]. They said I had to extend the passport, and then they could extend the visa. Well, the Poles were making difficulties with extending the passport. So I tried to get the British to permit me to stay a little longer. But they said that that was not their custom. By that time I knew enough about the British, is when they say it's not their custom, if you stand on your head, they won't do it. So then, what I did is, I pretended essentially to be trying to go back to Poland without actually going there. So, I got transit visas through several countries, one of which was Switzerland. The first thing I did was to go to Paris. And I stayed in Paris for a couple of weeks, maybe a month, of the year 1939. And one day in August, close to my birthday, there was the big news, the Ribbentrop-Molotov pact, the agreement between Stalin and Hitler to divide up Poland. I was at that point in Paris. Well, when I saw what was happening with this Ribbentrop-Molotov pact, I took the first train to Berne. That was very good, because otherwise I would have been caught in France under the Nazis. I really, as usual, paid attention to the headlines. When I traveled from Paris to Berne, I remember the blue lights inside the train; they didn't have any real light that you could read in, because there was conviction that the war would break out without much delay.

---

6   For a different perspective on the story of Moritz's emigration, see Chapter 16, "A Lifeline," and https://leonidhurwicz.org/sol-kotzin.

The reason that I didn't stay in Berne was that the Swiss have a Swiss-German dialect. Actually, many dialects. People who live in neighboring valleys have different a dialect, and may well not be able to understand each other. I thought, I don't want to start learning a Swiss dialect. The Swiss insisted on Swiss dialect to show that they were anti-Nazi. They weren't using the literary so-called "High German." So then I took the first train that I could from Berne to Geneva. Geneva speaks classical French.

I spent the academic year '39–'40 in Berne [*sic, but clearly means Geneva—M. H.*] until I got the U.S. visa to emigrate. The U.S. Consulate in Switzerland, which was in Zurich in Switzerland, said that they must have certificates of good conduct from authorities in each of the countries I had lived in the previous five years, which was Poland (which was occupied by the Nazis) and England and France. When I wrote the French, the French didn't have any difficulty, the certificate was routine. The British was a different story. They said they were not in the custom of issuing certificates of good conduct. And the U.S. Consulate in Zurich insisted on that.

At first I didn't know what to do. Then I went to the office of the chief of police in Geneva, and I said if I don't get something like that from the British, I will not be able to emigrate to the U.S., and I'll be a burden on the Swiss taxpayer.

He said, "How do you expect me to do anything about it?"

I said, and I think it was a good idea, "Write to the police office of London, as if one policeman to another wants to know if a suspect has a bad record."

He said, "All right, I'll try it."

And he wrote to the police in London, and they said they had nothing against me. He got it very quickly, because it was a collegial relationship between the police in western European countries.

At some point the Kotzins sent me some money, after I lost my wallet in this post office. And I bought passage on an Italian boat. I already had the visa. This was early June. And just at that time, Italy joined Germany as partner in the war. So, of course, they couldn't operate ships between Europe and the United States. So I was stuck again without money. I couldn't ask Kotzins a second time.

So I essentially used a similar technique. I went to the harbor police. I was in Lisbon already by that time. I got that far. First I went to the Italian shipping lines and I asked for my money back. They just laughed at me. They said, "Yes, you are an enemy, and come back after the war." That was not a good solution. Then I went to the harbor police, and essentially I used a variant of my trick in Geneva. I explained to him, that if I cannot go to America, I cannot work in Lisbon, I'll be a public burden. So he said, "What do you expect me to do?" Well, I knew that Portugal was a dictatorship. The dictator was an economist. I knew that the police could do anything they wanted. So I said, "Just tell them you'll take away their license." And within two days I got my money back.

But how I got these inspirations, I mean, I really acted as if I was an experienced person. I never had . . . It was really desperation. But finally then I bought a ticket on a Greek boat. I was 23. The world was totally changed. The rules of the game were changed. But I somehow found if you sort of think through logically from the point of view of the other person . . . And everybody wanted to get rid of the refugees.

One thing that also was funny. How did I get to Lisbon from Geneva? I had to get a transit visa. I showed each of them my U.S. visa, which was good. Because I was flying. They just opened an airline—for a few months I think it operated— from Switzerland to Barcelona. So I had to get a Spanish visa, and then of course a Portuguese visa, and then I had to cross the ocean. In peacetime, since I had the U.S. visa, you see, they didn't hesitate. But all these consulates were corrupt. But I think it was the Spanish or Portuguese consulate, they said he had to consult with his head office and he has to do it by telegram, and I had to pay him supposedly for a telegram. When I came back a week later, they said they hadn't heard anything and needed money for another telegram. So I said, "Well, are you sure you'll get an answer?" He said, "Yes I'll have an answer this afternoon." So it was made obvious that all these telegrams were a fiction.

So then I traveled from Geneva to . . . I forget what that city was called, but a city at the other end of Switzerland, to take off.[7] Switzerland is kind of in the shape of a croissant. At the westmost end of that croissant was Geneva. At the other end was this other city. We got into the airplane. It got dark. They circled somehow or other trying to take off from that airport. I wasn't really worried. But that was the first time in my life I had been in an airplane. Then they gave up. They said it was too dark and so on. And they put us up in a hotel. The next morning, they put us back on the plane. Then I looked out the window, I really got frightened. Because this was just a small flat area with huge mountains all around. How an airplane would expect to gather enough speed to take off. But we did take off that following morning. And the airline or somebody put us up. The only time in my life I stayed in a Ritz hotel.

---

7   The city was Locarno.
   "But at the end of May I obtained an American visa, flew from Locarno to Spain . . ."
   Letter from Leonid Hurwicz, 3605 Dickens Ave., Chicago, Ill., to "Miss Ryder," i.e. Miss
   E. M. Ryder, Assistant Registrar at LSE, Aug. 22, 1940, in "The Postgraduate File of Leonid
   Hurwicz at the London School of Economics 1938–1939: A Summary," p. 8, by Jim Thomas,
   Research Associate, STICERD, London School of Economics, dated May 26, 2009, emailed
   to the author on January 4, 2019.

There was a little bus after we landed in Barcelona. I was chatting with some Portuguese businessman who was sitting next to me. The bus taking us to the ticket office or whatever. I looked out the window and I saw planes with swastikas. So I said something to my neighbor about that I didn't know that there were Nazi planes in Barcelona. He said to me very emphatically, "Here, we don't notice these things."

Then I took a train, and a day later or so from Barcelona, by way of Madrid to Lisbon. When I got to Lisbon, you know, I had some money, but not really very much. And I found that there was a place in a suburb called Estoril, that was sort of like a Monte Carlo, you know, a gambling place. And I found that there were many French families there in this casino who had escaped the Nazi invasion. They were very worried because it was just when their kids were supposed to take these final examinations to graduate from high school. So I got to talking to these people, I told them I could keep them in good shape in things like mathematics and so on. So that's how I earned small change.

APPENDIX F

A Timeline of the Life of Leo Hurwicz

———

[*This timeline was mostly taken from a handout distributed at "Perspectives on Leo Hurwicz, A Celebration of 90 Years," held at the Holiday Inn Metrodome, 1500 Washington Avenue South, Minneapolis, MN, April 14, 2007. The author lightly edited it and added a few items, including two items at the end—M. H.*]

Year	Event
1917	Born in Moscow, Russia, where his parents had fled when Germany invaded Poland. In 1919, they returned to Poland, where Leo had his early education.
1938	*Magister Utriusque Iuris* (LL.M.) University of Warsaw
1938	Student, London School of Economics
1939	Student, *Institut des Hautes Etudes Internationales*, Geneva, Switzerland
1940	Came to United States
1941	Research Assistant to Paul Samuelson at MIT
1941	Research Assistant to Oskar Lange at University of Chicago
1942	Research Associate at University of Chicago in Meteorology
1944	Married Evelyn Jensen
1944	Research Associate, Cowles Commission for Economic Research, Chicago
1945	Guggenheim Fellowship
1945	Review of "Theory of Games and Economic Behavior"
1946	Associate Professor, Iowa State College, Ames
1946	First child born, daughter Sarah
1947	Walk in Hyde Park with Stanley Reiter
1947	Father, mother and brother join him in the United States
1948	United Nations Economic Commission for Europe, Geneva, Switzerland
1949	Second child born, son Michael
1949	Professor of Economics and Mathematical Statistics, University of Illinois
1949	Fellow, Econometric Society

Year	Event
1951	Professor of Economics and Mathematics, University of Minnesota
1951	Third child born, daughter Ruth
1953	Fourth child born, son Maxim
1954	Member, National Research Council of the National Academy of Sciences
1955	Visiting Professor and Fellow, Center for Advanced Study in the Behavioral Sciences, Stanford University
1958	Visiting Professor, Stanford University
1959	Stanford Symposium where Leo's paper "Optimality and Informational Efficiency in Resource Allocation Processes" is first presented, introducing concepts of mechanism design and incentive-compatibility
1960	"Optimality and Informational Efficiency in Resource Allocation Processes" published by Stanford University Press
1961	Chairman, Statistics Department, University of Minnesota
1964	Member, NSF Commission on Weather Modification
1965	Visiting Lecturer, Bangalore University, India
1965	Member, American Society of Arts and Sciences
1968	Minnesota delegate to the National Democratic Party Convention, and member of the National Democratic Party Platform Committee, Chicago
1969	President, Econometric Society
1969	Regents Professor of Economics, University of Minnesota
1969	Visiting Research Professor and Professor of Economics, Harvard University
1972	Ely Lecture, AEA, a contribution to mechanism design
1974	Member, National Academy of Sciences
1976	Visiting Professor of Economics, University of California, Berkeley
1977	Distinguished Fellow, American Economic Association
1979	American Academy of Independent Scholars
1980	Doctor of Sciences (honorary), Northwestern University
1982	Visiting Professor of Economics, Tokyo University
1982	Council Member, Econometric Society
1984	Honorary Professor of Central China University of Science and Technology, Wuhan
1984	Distinguished Scholar, California Institute of Technology
1986	Lecturer, People's University, Beijing
1987	Information, Incentives, and Economic Mechanisms: Essays in Honor of Leonid Hurwicz, edited by T. Groves, R. Radner, S. Reiter, University of Minnesota Press
1988	Visiting Professor, Northwestern University
1988	Visiting Scholar in Decentralization Theory, University of Indonesia, Jakarta
1989	Visiting Professor, Northwestern University
1989	*Doctor Honoris Causa*, Universitat Autònoma de Barcelona

Year	Event
1989	Curtis L. Carlson Professor of Economics, University of Minnesota
1990	*Preferences, Uncertainty, and Optimality: Essays in Honor of Leonid Hurwicz*, edited by John Chipman, Daniel McFadden, Marcel Richter, Westview Press
1990	National Medal of Sciences from President George H. W. Bush
1992	Inaugural Leo Hurwicz Lecture, Midwest Economics Association
1993	Doctor of Economics, *honoris causa*, Keio University, Tokyo
1993	Doctor of Laws (honorary), University of Chicago
1994	Doctor, *honoris causa*, Warsaw School of Economics
1998	Visiting Professor, University of California, Santa Barbara
1999	Visiting Professor, California Institute of Technology
2001	Visiting Distinguished Professor, University of Illinois
2002	Visiting Professor, University of Michigan
2004	*Doctor rer. pol.* (*doctor rerum politicarum*) *honoris causa*, University of Bielefeld
2006	Publication of *Designing Economic Mechanisms*, with Stanley Reiter, Cambridge University Press
2007	Nobel Memorial Prize in Economic Sciences (with Eric Maskin and Roger Myerson) for work on mechanism design
2008	Died at age 90

What Is Mechanism Design?

Leo won the Nobel Memorial Prize in Economic Sciences (along with Eric Maskin and Roger Myerson) in 2007 for laying laid the foundations of mechanism design theory. So, what is mechanism design?

Basically, mechanism design is about designing a new economic system, one that works the way you want it to. It could be a big system, like a country or even the whole world. It could be a smaller system, like a household or a company. The point is, you decide what you value, like fairness, a minimum standard of living—whatever—and then you design a system (or systems) to produce those results.

This may sound like the most natural thing in the world. But previously, though there were *normative* descriptions of ideal economic policies or systems, they were seldom mathematical. For example, people promoted socialism because it encouraged equality and community, or they promoted capitalism because it encouraged freedom and personal self-realization. On the other hand, mathematical economists typically did research that was either:

* *exploratory* (suggesting basic economic patterns or hypotheses that seemed worth investigating),
* *descriptive* (describing the workings of economic systems as they exist) and *analytical* (analyzing and explaining causal relationships within economic systems) and/or
* *predictive* (forecasting when, where and why certain economic phenomena might be likely to manifest in the future). Alternative policies could be considered, but some overall structure had to be assumed: how else could you predict outcomes?

All three of the above mathematical approaches take some economic framework as given and attempt to identify, describe, optimize or predict outcomes.

Mechanism design turns that on its head: it takes the *outcomes* as given and uses systematic, mathematical techniques to generate models of economic institutions that produce those outcomes. Mechanism design is sometimes referred to as the engineering side of economics, since it attempts to produce implementable designs for economic institutions, given detailed design specs. Importantly, in order to be practical, mechanisms must be efficient (not too costly to operate) and "incentive compatible" i.e. workable when economic agents (individuals, companies, countries, etc.) try to maximize their own benefit.

There are of course many instances, even going back to ancient times, of creating mechanisms to achieve desired goals. For example, John Moore[1] illustrates mechanism design using the Bible story in which King Solomon has to determine which of two women is the real mother of a baby, when one is claiming that the other stole the child from her. Solomon suggests cutting the baby in two and giving each woman half. Only the real mother objects to this solution, revealing that the one who doesn't protest is not the real mother. (And *is* a psychopath who can accept the idea of a baby being cut in half.) This has all the classic characteristics of a mechanism: something valuable at stake (the baby), "agents" (the women) who have private information unknown to the mechanism designer (King Solomon), a set of "environments" or states of reality in which the mechanism must work (either the real mom is woman A, or else it's woman B), and a goal (identifying the real mother). Moore uses modern mathematical methods which were (like DNA testing) unavailable to Solomon, to analyze the efficacy and weaknesses of Solomon's mechanism. This example suggests one of the reasons for mechanism design's importance: its potential applicability to areas beyond what we typically think of as economics.[2]

---

1   John Moore, "Implementation, contracts, and renegotiation in environments with complete information," in J. Laffont (ed.), *Advances in Economic Theory: Sixth World Congress* (Econometric Society Monographs), Cambridge University Press, 1993, pp. 182–282, DOI:10.1017/CCOL0521416663.007.

2   "And I often think how imperceptibly foundational it was, not only for me but for all the social sciences here at Minnesota, to have only a few steps away dedicated mathematical theorists working away at the foundations of what will someday be the general theory of human behavior, asking questions that had never been asked before, inventing methods to answer them."
    Professor Guillermina "Willie" Jasso, Department of Sociology, New York University, in an email, Monday, October 15, 2007. subject: "Warmest congratulations!!!"
    Leonid Hurwicz Papers, David M. Rubenstein Rare Book & Manuscript Library, Duke University, Box 24, File: Messages from Friends and Colleagues.

Along more typically economic lines, Moore describes a method used in ancient Greek city-states to determine who would pay for certain public rituals or other civic needs: "Someone nominated the man who was reputed to be the richest. Let us call him Spyros. Spyros would then have to pay up, or claim 'I am not the richest, old Timon over there is richer than me.' Then Timon was faced with a choice. Either he could pay, or he could insist that Spyros exchange all his wealth with him, after which Spyros would have to pay."[3] Here, the goal is to exact payment from a man who is believed to be the richest, and who agrees with that assessment. The mechanism motivates that man to honestly reveal his agreement, or lack thereof.

Arijit Sen and Anand V. Swamy provide another example from nineteenth-century India, which they term "taxation by auction."[4] Used by guilds to raise funds, this mechanism required all guild members but one to close their shops on a designated day. The right to remain open was then auctioned off, with the funds from the winning bid going to the guild. The design goal in this case is to ensure that the cost to each member is proportional to the member's profitability. This could presumably be accomplished through some sort of income tax. However, the authors provide pages of mathematical analysis, showing how and why taxation by auction might be better than standard revenue-based taxation in terms of equity, efficiency and potential appeal to guild members. In particular, revenue-based taxation would be more costly to operate and more susceptible to cheating, since it would require the guild to check the revenue of each shop. With taxation by auction, the shop with the highest revenue will generally make the highest bid, since they stand to gain the most by remaining open. The mechanism incentivizes the participants to honestly reveal their revenues via their bids. The ancient Greek mechanism has similar truth-inducing qualities.

Since we have no evidence that these ancient Greek or nineteenth-century Indian mechanisms were created using any systematic, mathematical procedure, they are instances of "mechanism design" only in a broad, generic sense. Leo is credited with creating the foundations of mechanism design in a narrower, more

3   John Moore, *op. cit.*, p. 192.
     A similar ancient Greek mechanism is described by Samuel Bowles in "Nicolò Machiavelli and the Origins of Mechanism Design," *Journal of Economic Issues*, Vol. XLVIII No. 2 June 2014, DOI 10.2753/JEI0021-36244804, http://sites.santafe.edu/~bowles/Nicolo%20Machiavelli.pdf. Accessed October 11, 2022.
4   Arijit Sen and Anand V. Swamy, "Taxation by Auction: Fund-Raising by 19th Century Indian Guilds," November 2000, https://www.semanticscholar.org/paper/Taxation-by-auction%3A-fund-raising-by-19th-century-Sen-Swamy/1947c5eb3787b9a3a02cb36cc775e4faa75f49f1?p2df. Accessed October 13, 2022. Also *Journal of Development Economics*, 2004, vol. 74, issue 2, 411–428.

technical sense: by defining certain elements and procedures in a rigorous mathematical form, he opened the way for mechanism design to become the basic
tool of modern economics that it is today.

The foundational idea of mechanism design—taking desired outcomes as
the starting point, and treating appropriate mechanisms as the unknown of the
problem—was first presented by Leo in published form (without using the
term "mechanism design") in 1960: "In a broader perspective, these findings
suggest the possibility of a more systematic study of resource allocation mechanisms. In such a study, unlike in the more traditional approach, the mechanism
becomes the unknown of the problem, rather than a datum."[5] Leo expanded on
these ideas in 1972,[6] while focusing less on resource allocation (flows of money,
goods, capital and labor) and more on communication (information transfer
and processing). This view of the economy as message transfer, innovative at the
time, now has many adherents.[7]

---

5   Leonid Hurwicz, "Optimality and Informational Efficiency in Resource Allocation
Processes," *Mathematical Methods in the Social Sciences*, edited by Arrow, Karlin and Suppes,
Stanford University Press, 1980, p. 28. See Chapter 27, "Just a Closer Walk with Stan" for
more on the history of this article.

6   "On Informationally Decentralized Systems," in *Decision and Organization*, edited by C.B.
McGuire and R. Radner, North Holland, 1972, pp. 297–336. Roger Myerson said of this
article, "Around 1972, when he began to ask deep questions about people's incentives to
communicate, then he made one of the great breakthroughs in the history of social science.
When Leonid Hurwicz introduced the concept of incentive-compatibility, it was as if a pair
of blinders had been removed. Suddenly, we could see how to analyze economic incentives
without assuming any specific institutional structure, and even how optimal institutions
might be characterized." (In Appendix A of this book).

7   When friend and colleague Ken Arrow congratulated Leo on winning the Nobel Prize, he
cited understanding the economy as information transfer, and didn't mention mechanism
design as such: "Your entire transformation of the way we understand the economy as
information transfer has changed much economic thinking, even to practical consequences
in many areas. Your concentration and depth of thought have been necessary to opening
this field, which now has so many followers." Kenneth Arrow in an email, subject "Wow!"
Monday, October 15, 2007. Leonid Hurwicz Papers, David M. Rubenstein Rare Book &
Manuscript Library, Duke University, Box 24, File: Messages from Friends and Colleagues.

Index

Printed in the USA
CPSIA information can be obtained
at www.ICGtesting.com
JSHW012220080724
66058JS00006B/72